The Essence of Globalization

The Essence of Globalization

Edited by Gabriel Lucas

CLANRYE
INTERNATIONAL
www.clanryeinternational.com

Clanrye International,
750 Third Avenue, 9th Floor,
New York, NY 10017, USA

ISBN: 978-1-63240-736-8

Cataloging-in-Publication Data

The essence of globalization / edited by Gabriel Lucas.
    p. cm.
Includes bibliographical references and index.
ISBN 978-1-63240-736-8
1. Globalization. 2. Globalization--Social aspects. 3. Globalization--Political aspects.
4. Anti-globalization movement. I. Lucas, Gabriel.
JZ1318 .E87 2018
303.482--dc23

For information on all Clanrye International publications
visit our website at www.clanryeinternational.com

Contents

Permissions

Index

Preface

Globalization has been a catalyst in making trade flow freely in the worldwide market. It has played a major role in enabling companies to spread their roots in many under-developed and developing countries. Globalization has facilitated the exchange of goods, services, knowledge, capital, services, and technology in this world. Thus, it is a very pivotal part of world economy today. Global trade policies effect the day-to-day working of many global, multinational and national companies. This book elucidates the concepts and innovative models around prospective developments with respect to globalization. It includes topics which deal with globalization and its effects on world trade. This textbook aims to serve as a resource guide for students and experts alike and contribute to the growth of the discipline.

To facilitate a deeper understanding of the contents of this book a short introduction of every chapter is written below:

Chapter 1- Globalization is the integration of markets of the world. There are four aspects of globalization: trade and transactions, migration and movement of people, capital and investment movements and dissemination of knowledge. Archaic globalization, proto-globalization, democratic globalization, environmental globalization, global regionalization and globality are some of the topics discussed in regard with globalization. This is an introductory chapter which will introduce briefly all the significant aspects of globalization.

Chapter 2- Modernization theory discusses the pattern of social evolution and argues for a relatively similar development of urbanization and industrialization. Postmodernism, globalism and global citizenship are other themes discussed here. The topics elaborated in this chapter will help in gaining a better perspective about the theories related to globalization.

Chapter 3- Cultural globalization is the spreading of ideas and values globally. Cultural imperialism, cultural appropriation, Cross-cultural communication, multiculturalism and multiculturalism are some significant and important topics related to cultural globalization. The following chapter unfolds its crucial aspects in a critical yet systematic manner.

Chapter 4- Political globalization studies the worldwide political system in correspondence with new agents of political change. Political globalization along with economic globalization and cultural globalization forms the basics of globalization. Global politics, global civics, global commons and transnationalism are topics that have been explained in this section.

Chapter 5- This chapter studies the challenges and issues that globalization faces. Critics cite political, environmental, social, cultural and psychological factors to curb globalization. The topics discussed in the chapter are of great importance to broaden the existing knowledge on issues and challenges of globalization.

I would like to share the credit of this book with my editorial team who worked tirelessly on this book. I owe the completion of this book to the never-ending support of my family, who supported me throughout the project.

Editor

An Introduction to Globalization

Globalization is the integration of markets of the world. There are four aspects of globalization: trade and transactions, migration and movement of people, capital and investment movements and dissemination of knowledge. Archaic globalization, proto-globalization, democratic globalization, environmental globalization, global regionalization and globality are some of the topics discussed in regard with globalization. This is an introductory chapter which will introduce briefly all the significant aspects of globalization.

Globalization

Globalization refers to the free movement of goods, capital, services, people, technology and information. It is the action or procedure of international integration of countries arising from the convergence of world views, products, ideas, and other aspects of culture. Advances in the means of transport (such as the steam locomotive, steamship, jet engine, and container ships) and in telecommunications infrastructure (including the rise of the telegraph and its modern offspring, the Internet and mobile phones) have been major factors in globalization, generating further interdependence of economic and cultural activities. Though many scholars place the origins of globalization in modern times, others trace its history long before the European Age of Discovery and voyages to the New World, some even to the third millennium BC. Large-scale globalization began in the 1820s. In the late 19th century and early 20th century, the connectivity of the world's economies and cultures grew very quickly. The term *globalization* is recent, only establishing its current meaning in the 1970s. In 2000, the International Monetary Fund (IMF) identified four basic aspects of globalization: trade and transactions, capital and investment movements, migration and movement of people, and the dissemination of knowledge. Further, environmental challenges such as global warming, cross-boundary water and air pollution, and overfishing of the ocean are linked with globalization. Globalizing processes affect and are affected by business and work organization, economics, socio-cultural resources, and the natural environment. Academic literature commonly subdivides globalization into three major areas: economic globalization, cultural globalization, and political globalization.

Etymology and Usage

The term *globalization* is derived from the word *globalize*, which refers to the emergence of an international network of economic systems. One of the earliest known usages of the term as a noun was in a 1930 publication entitled *Towards New Education*, where it denoted a holistic view of human experience in education. A related term, *corporate giants*, was coined by Charles Taze Russell (of the Watch Tower Bible and Tract Society) in 1897 to refer to the largely national trusts and other large enterprises of the time. By the 1960s, both terms began to be used as synonyms by economists and other social scientists. Economist Theodore Levitt is widely credited with coining the term in an article entitled "Globalization of Markets", which appeared in the May–June 1983 issue of *Harvard Business Review*. However, the term 'globalization' was in use well before this (at least as early as 1944) and had been used by other scholars as early as 1981. Levitt can be credited with popularizing the term and bringing it into the mainstream business audience in the later half of the 1980s. Since its inception, the concept of globalization has inspired competing definitions and interpretations, with antecedents dating back to the great movements of trade and empire across Asia and the Indian Ocean from the 15th century onwards. Due to the complexity of the concept, research projects, articles, and discussions often remain focused on a single aspect of globalization.

Sociologists Martin Albrow and Elizabeth King define globalization as "all those processes by which the people of the world are incorporated into a single world society." In *The Consequences of Modernity*, Anthony Giddens writes: "Globalization can thus be defined as the intensification of worldwide social relations which link distant localities in such a way that local happenings are shaped by events occurring many miles away and vice versa." In 1992, Roland Robertson, professor of sociology at the University of Aberdeen, an early writer in the field, defined globalization as "the compression of the world and the intensification of the consciousness of the world as a whole."

In *Global Transformations*, David Held and his co-writers state:

Although in its simplistic sense globalization refers to the widening, deepening and speeding up of global interconnection, such a definition begs further elaboration. Globalization can be located on a continuum with the local, national and regional. At one end of the continuum lie social and economic relations and networks which are organized on a local and/or national basis; at the other end lie social and economic relations and networks which crystallize on the wider scale of regional and global interactions. Globalization can refer to those spatial-temporal processes of change which underpin a transformation in the organization of human affairs by linking together and expanding human activity across regions and continents. Without reference to such expansive spatial connections, there can be no clear or coherent formulation of this term. A satisfactory definition of globalization must capture each of these elements: extensity (stretching), intensity, velocity and impact.

Held and his co-writers' definition of globalization in that same book as "transformation in the spatial organization of social relations and transactions—assessed in terms of their extensity, intensity, velocity and impact—generating transcontinental or interregional flows" was called "probably the most widely-cited definition" in the 2014 DHL Global Connectiveness Index.

Swedish journalist Thomas Larsson, in his book *The Race to the Top: The Real Story of Globalization*, states that globalization:

is the process of world shrinkage, of distances getting shorter, things moving closer. It pertains to the increasing ease with which somebody on one side of the world can interact, to mutual benefit, with somebody on the other side of the world.

Paul James defines globalization with a more direct and historically contextualized emphasis:

Globalization is the extension of social relations across world-space, defining that world-space in terms of the historically variable ways that it has been practiced and socially understood through changing world-time.

Manfred Steger, professor of global studies and research leader in the Global Cities Institute at RMIT University, identifies four main empirical dimensions of globalization: economic, political, cultural, and ecological, with a fifth dimension—the ideological—cutting across the other four. The ideological dimension, according to Steger, is filled with a range of norms, claims, beliefs, and narratives about the phenomenon itself.

James and Steger assert that the concept of globalization "emerged from the intersection of four interrelated sets of 'communities of practice' (Wenger, 1998): academics, journalists, publishers/editors, and librarians." They note the term was used "in education to describe the global life of the mind"; in international relations to describe the extension of the European Common Market; and in journalism to describe how the "American Negro and his problem are taking on a global significance". They have also argued that four different forms of globalization can be distinguished that complement and cut across the solely empirical dimensions. According to James, the oldest dominant form of globalization is embodied globalization, the movement of people. A second form is agency-extended globalization, the circulation of agents of different institutions, organizations, and polities, including imperial agents. Object-extended globalization, a third form, is the movement of commodities and other objects of exchange. He calls the transmission of ideas, images, knowledge, and information across world-space disembodied globalization, maintaining that it is currently the dominant form of globalization. James holds that this series of distinctions allows for an understanding of how, today, the most embodied forms of globalization such as the movement of refugees and migrants are increasingly restricted, while the most disembodied forms such as the circulation of financial instruments and codes are the most deregulated.

The journalist Thomas L. Friedman popularized the term "flat world", arguing that globalized trade, outsourcing, supply-chaining, and political forces had permanently changed the world, for better and worse. He asserted that the pace of globalization was quickening and that its impact on business organization and practice would continue to grow.

Economist Takis Fotopoulos defined "economic globalization" as the opening and deregulation of commodity, capital, and labor markets that led toward present neoliberal globalization. He used "political globalization" to refer to the emergence of a transnational elite and a phasing out of the nation-state. Meanwhile, he used "cultural globalization" to reference the worldwide homogenization of culture. Other of his usages included "ideological globalization", "technological globalization", and "social globalization".

Lechner and Boli (2012) define globalization as more people across large distances becoming connected in more and different ways.

Globophobia has been used to refer to the fear of globalization, though it can also mean the fear of balloons.

History

There are both distal and proximate causes which can be traced in the historical factors affecting globalization. Large-scale globalization began in the 19th century.

Archaic

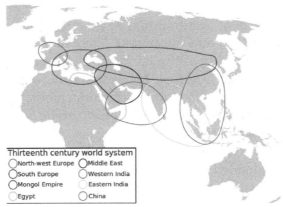

The 13th century world-system, as described by Janet Abu-Lughod.

Archaic globalization conventionally refers to a phase in the history of globalization including globalizing events and developments from the time of the earliest civilizations until roughly the 1600s. This term is used to describe the relationships between communities and states and how they were created by the geographical spread of ideas and social norms at both local and regional levels.

In this schema, three main prerequisites are posited for globalization to occur. The first is the idea of Eastern Origins, which shows how Western states have adapted and implemented learned principles from the East. Without the traditional ideas from the East, Western globalization would not have emerged the way it did. The second is distance. The interactions amongst states were not on a global scale and most often were confined to Asia, North Africa, the Middle East, and certain parts of Europe. With early globalization, it was difficult for states to interact with others that were not within close proximity. Eventually, technological advances allowed states to learn of others' existence and another phase of globalization was able to occur. The third has to do with interdependency, stability, and regularity. If a state is not dependent on another, then there is no way for either state to be mutually affected by the other. This is one of the driving forces behind global connections and trade; without either, globalization would not have emerged the way it did and states would still be dependent on their own production and resources to function. This is one of the arguments surrounding the idea of early globalization. It is argued that archaic globalization did not function in a similar manner to modern globalization because states were not as interdependent on others as they are today.

Also posited is a "multi-polar" nature to archaic globalization, which involved the active participation of non-Europeans. Because it predated the Great Divergence of the nineteenth century, in which Western Europe pulled ahead of the rest of the world in terms of industrial production and economic output, archaic globalization was a phenomenon that was driven not only by Europe but also by other economically developed Old World centers such as Gujarat, Bengal, coastal China, and Japan.

Portuguese carrack in Nagasaki, 17th-century Japanese Nanban art.

The German historical economist and sociologist Andre Gunder Frank argues that a form of globalization began with the rise of trade links between Sumer and the Indus Valley Civilization in the third millennium B.C.E. This archaic globalization existed during the Hellenistic Age, when commercialized urban centers enveloped the axis of Greek culture that reached from India to Spain, including Alexandria and the other Alexandrine cities. Early on, the geographic position of Greece and the necessity of importing wheat forced the Greeks to engage in maritime trade. Trade in ancient Greece was largely unrestricted: the state controlled only the supply of grain.

Trade on the Silk Road was a significant factor in the development of the civilizations of China, the Indian subcontinent, Persia, Europe, and Arabia, opening long-distance political and economic interactions between the civilizations. Though silk was certainly the major trade item from China, many other goods were traded, and religions, syncretic philosophies, and various technologies, as well as diseases, also traveled along the Silk Routes. In addition to economic trade, the Silk Road served as a means of carrying out cultural trade among the civilizations along its network. The movement of people, such as refugees, artists, craftsmen, missionaries, robbers, and envoys, resulted in the exchange of religions, art, languages, and new technologies.

Native New World crops exchanged globally: Maize, tomato, potato, vanilla, rubber, cacao, tobacco.

Early Modern

"Early modern-" or "proto-globalization" covers a period of the history of globalization roughly spanning the years between 1600 and 1800. The concept of "proto-globalization" was first introduced by historians A. G. Hopkins and Christopher Bayly. The term describes the phase of increasing trade links and cultural exchange that characterized the period immediately preceding the advent of high "modern globalization" in the late 19th century. This phase of globalization was characterized by the rise of maritime European empires, in the 16th and 17th centuries, first the Portuguese and Spanish Empires, and later the Dutch and British Empires. In the 17th century, world trade developed further when chartered companies like the British East India Company (founded in 1600) and the Dutch East India Company (founded in 1602, often described as the first multinational corporation in which stock was offered) were established.

During the early 19th century the United Kingdom was a global superpower.

Early modern globalization is distinguished from modern globalization on the basis of expansionism, the method of managing global trade, and the level of information exchange. The period is marked by such trade arrangements as the East India Company, the shift of hegemony to Western Europe, the rise of larger-scale conflicts between powerful nations such as the Thirty Years' War, and a rise of new commodities—most particularly slave trade. The Triangular Trade made it possible for Europe to take advantage of resources within the Western Hemisphere. The transfer of animal stocks, plant crops, and epidemic diseases associated with Alfred W. Crosby's concept of the Columbian Exchange also played a central role in this process. Early modern trade and communications involved a vast group including European, Muslim, Indian, Southeast Asian, and Chinese merchants, particularly in the Indian Ocean region.

Modern

During the 19th century, globalization approached its form as a direct result of the Industrial Revolution. Industrialization allowed standardized production of household items using economies of scale while rapid population growth created sustained demand for commodities. In the 19th century, steamships reduced the cost of international transport significantly and railroads made inland transport cheaper. The transport revolution occurred some time between 1820 and 1850. More nations embraced international trade. Globalization in this period was decisively shaped by nineteenth-century imperialism such as in Africa and Asia. The invention of shipping containers in 1956 helped advance the globalization of commerce.

After World War II, work by politicians led to the agreements of the Bretton Woods Conference, in which major governments laid down the framework for international monetary policy, commerce, and finance, and the founding of several international institutions intended to facilitate economic growth by lowering trade barriers. Initially, the General Agreement on Tariffs and Trade (GATT) led to a series of agreements to remove trade restrictions. GATT's successor was the World Trade Organization (WTO), which provided a framework for negotiating and formalizing trade agreements and a dispute resolution process. Exports nearly doubled from 8.5% of total gross world product in 1970 to 16.2% in 2001. The approach of using global agreements to advance trade stumbled with the failure of the Doha Development Round of trade negotiation. Many countries then shifted to bilateral or smaller multilateral agreements, such as the 2011 South Korea–United States Free Trade Agreement.

Since the 1970s, aviation has become increasingly affordable to middle classes in developed countries. Open skies policies and low-cost carriers have helped to bring competition to the market. In the 1990s, the growth of low-cost communication networks cut the cost of communicating between different countries. More work can be performed using a computer without regard to location. This included accounting, software development, and engineering design.

Student exchange programs became popular after World War II, and are intended to increase the participants' understanding and tolerance of other cultures, as well as improving their language skills and broadening their social horizons. Between 1963 and 2006 the number of students studying in a foreign country increased 9 times.

In the late 19th and early 20th century, the connectedness of the world's economies and cultures grew very quickly. This slowed down from the 1910s onward due to the World Wars and the Cold War, but picked up again in the 1980s and 1990s. The revolutions of 1989 and subsequent liberalization in many parts of the world resulted in a significant expansion of global interconnectedness. The migration and movement of people can also be highlighted as a prominent feature of the globalization process. In the period between 1965 and 1990, the proportion of the labor force migrating approximately doubled. Most migration occurred between the developing countries and least developed countries (LDCs). As economic integration intensified workers moved to areas with higher wages and most of the developing world oriented toward the international market economy. The collapse of the Soviet Union not only ended the Cold War's division of the world- it also left the United States its sole policeman and an unfettered advocate of free market. It also resulted in the growing prominence of attention focused on the movement of diseases, the proliferation of popular culture and consumer values, the growing prominence of international institutions like the UN, and concerted international action on such issues as the environment and human rights. Other developments as dramatic were the Internet has become influential in connecting people across the world. As of June 2012, more than 2.4 billion people—over a third of the world's human population—have used the services of the Internet. Growth of globalization has never been smooth. One influential event was the late 2000s recession, which was associated with lower growth (in areas such as cross-border phone calls and Skype usage) or even temporarily negative growth (in areas such as trade) of global interconnectedness. The DHL Global Connectedness Index studies four main types of cross-border flow: trade (in both goods and services), information, people (including tourists, students, and migrants), and capital. It shows that the depth of global integration fell by about one-tenth after 2008, but by 2013 had recovered well above its pre-crash peak. The report also found a shift of economic activity to emerging economies.

Globalized society offers a complex web of forces and factors that bring people, cultures, markets, beliefs, and practices into increasingly greater proximity to one another.

Movement of People

An essential aspect of globalization is movement of people. As transportation technology improved, travel time and costs decreased dramatically between the 18th and early 20th century. For example, travel across the Atlantic ocean used to take up to 5 weeks in the 18th century, but around the time of the 20th century it took a mere 8 days. Today, modern aviation has made long-distance transportation quick and affordable.

Tourism is travel for pleasure. The developments in technology and transport infrastructure, such as jumbo jets, low-cost airlines, and more accessible airports have made many types of tourism more affordable. International tourist arrivals surpassed the milestone of 1 billion tourists globally for the first time in 2012. A visa is a conditional authorization granted by a country to a foreigner, allowing them to enter and temporarily remain within, or to leave that country. Some countries – such as those in the Schengen Area – have agreements with other countries allowing each other's citizens to travel between them without visas. The World Tourism Organization announced that the number of tourists who require a visa before traveling was at its lowest level ever in 2015.

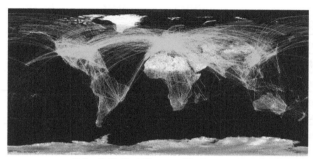
Scheduled airline traffic in 2009

Immigration is the international movement of people into a destination country of which they are not natives or where they do not possess citizenship in order to settle or reside there, especially as permanent residents or naturalized citizens, or to take-up employment as a migrant worker or temporarily as a foreign worker. According to the International Labour Organization, as of 2014 there were an estimated 232 million international migrants in the world (defined as persons outside their country of origin for 12 months or more) and approximately half of them were estimated to be economically active (i.e. being employed or seeking employment). International movement of labor is often seen important to economic development. For example, freedom of movement for workers in the European Union means that people can move freely between member states to live, work, study or retire in another country.

Globalization is associated with a dramatic rise in international education. More and more students are seeking higher education in foreign countries and many international students now consider overseas study a stepping-stone to permanent residency within a country. The contributions that foreign students make to host nation economies, both culturally and financially has encouraged major players to implement further initiatives to facilitate the arrival and integration of overseas students, including substantial amendments to immigration and visa policies and procedures.

A transnational marriage is a marriage between two people from different countries. A variety of special issues arise in marriages between people from different countries, including those related to citizenship and culture, which add complexity and challenges to these kinds of relationships. In an age of increasing globalization, where a growing number of people have ties to networks of people and places across the globe, rather than to a current geographic location, people are increasingly marrying across national boundaries. Transnational marriage is a by-product of the movement and migration of people.

Movement of Information

Internet users by region			
	2005	**2010**	**2016**[a]
Africa	2%	10%	25%
Americas	36%	49%	65%
Arab States	8%	26%	42%
Asia and Pacific	9%	23%	42%
Commonwealth of Independent States	10%	34%	67%
Europe	46%	67%	79%
[a] Estimate. Source: International Telecommunication Union.			

Before electronic communications, long-distance communications relied on mail. Speed of global communications was limited by the maximum speed of courier services (especially horses and ships) until the mid-19th century. The electric telegraph was the first method of instant long-distance communication. For example, before the first transatlantic cable, communications between Europe and the Americas took weeks because ships had to carry mail across the ocean. The first transatlantic cable reduced communication time considerably, allowing a message and a response in the same day. Lasting transatlantic telegraph connections were achieved in the 1865-1866. The first wireless telegraphy transmitters were developed in 1895.

The Internet has been instrumental in connecting people across geographical boundaries. For example, Facebook is a social networking service which has more than 1.65 billion monthly active users as of March 31, 2016.

Globalization can be spread by Global journalism which provide massive information and rely on internet to interact, "makes it into an everyday routine to investigate how people and their actions, practices, problems, life conditions etc. in different parts of the world are interrelated. possible to assume that global threats such as climate change precipitate the further establishment of global journalism."

Movement of Goods and Services

Number of countries having a banking crisis in each year since 1800. This is based on *This Time is Different: Eight Centuries of Financial Folly* which covers only 70 countries. The general upward trend might be attributed to many factors. One of these is a gradual increase in the percent of people who receive money for their labor. The dramatic feature of this graph is the virtual absence of banking crises during the period of the Bretton Woods agreement, 1945 to 1971. This analysis is similar to Figure in Reinhart and Rogoff (2009).

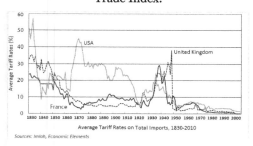

Singapore is the top country in the Enabling Trade Index.

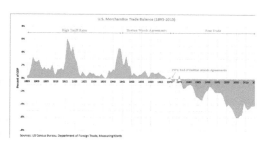

U.S. Trade Balance (1895–2015)

Average Tariff Rates (France, UK, US)

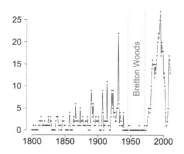

Economic globalization is the increasing economic interdependence of national economies across the world through a rapid increase in cross-border movement of goods, services, technology, and capital. Whereas the globalization of business is centered around the diminution of international trade regulations as well as tariffs, taxes, and other impediments that suppresses global trade, economic globalization is the process of increasing economic integration between countries, leading to the emergence of a global marketplace or a single world market. Depending on the paradigm, economic globalization can be viewed as either a positive or a negative phenomenon. Economic globalization comprises the globalization of production, markets, competition, technology, and corporations and industries. Current globalization trends can be largely accounted for by developed economies integrating with less developed economies by means of foreign direct investment, the reduction of trade barriers as well as other economic reforms, and, in many cases, immigration.

International standards have made trade in goods and services more efficient. An example of such standard is the intermodal container. Containerization dramatically reduced transport of its costs, supported the post-war boom in international trade, and was a major element in globalization. International Organization for Standardization is an international standard-setting body composed of representatives from various national standards organizations.

A multinational corporation or worldwide enterprise is an organization that owns or controls production of goods or services in one or more countries other than their home country. It can also be referred as an international corporation, a transnational corporation, or a stateless corporation.

A free-trade area is the region encompassing a trade bloc whose member countries have signed a free-trade agreement (FTA). Such agreements involve cooperation between at least two countries to reduce trade barriers – import quotas and tariffs – and to increase trade of goods and services with each other. If people are also free to move between the countries, in addition to a free-trade agreement, it would also be considered an open border. Arguably the most significant free-trade area in the world is the European Union, a politico-economic union of 28 member states that are located primarily in Europe. The EU has developed European Single Market through a standardised system of laws that apply in all member states. EU policies aim to ensure the free movement of people, goods, services, and capital within the internal market,

Trade facilitation looks at how procedures and controls governing the movement of goods across national borders can be improved to reduce associated cost burdens and maximise efficiency while safeguarding legitimate regulatory objectives.

Global trade in services is also significant. For example, in India, business process outsourcing has been described as the "primary engine of the country's development over the next few decades, contributing broadly to GDP growth, employment growth, and poverty alleviation".

William I. Robinson's theoretical approach to globalization is a critique of Wallerstein's World Systems Theory. He believes that the global capital experienced today is due to a new and distinct form of globalization which began in the 1980s. Robinson argues not only are economic activities expanded across national boundaries but also there is a transnational fragmentation of these activities. One important aspect of Robinson's globalization theory is that production of goods are increasingly global. This means that one pair of shoes can be produced by six different countries, each contributing to a part of the production process.

Cultural Globalization

Cultural globalization refers to the transmission of ideas, meanings, and values around the world in such a way as to extend and intensify social relations. This process is marked by the common consumption of cultures that have been diffused by the Internet, popular culture media, and international travel. This has added to processes of commodity exchange and colonization which have a longer history of carrying cultural meaning around the globe. The circulation of cultures enables individuals to partake in extended social relations that cross national and regional borders. The creation and expansion of such social relations is not merely observed on a material level. Cultural globalization involves the formation of shared norms and knowledge with which people associate their individual and collective cultural identities. It brings increasing inter-connectedness among different populations and cultures.

Shakira, a Colombian multilingual singer-songwriter, playing outside her home country.

Cross-cultural communication is a field of study that looks at how people from differing cultural backgrounds communicate, in similar and different ways among themselves, and how they endeavour to communicate across cultures. Intercultural communication is a related field of study.

Cultural diffusion is the spread of cultural items—such as ideas, styles, religions, tech-nologies, languages etc. Cultural globalization has increased cross-cultural contacts, but may be accompanied by a decrease in the uniqueness of once-isolated commu-nities. For example, sushi is available in Germany as well as Japan, but Euro-Disney outdraws the city of Paris, potentially reducing demand for "authentic" French pastry. Globalization's contribution to the alienation of individuals from their traditions may be modest compared to the impact of modernity itself, as alleged by existentialists such as Jean-Paul Sartre and Albert Camus. Globalization has expanded recreational oppor-tunities by spreading pop culture, particularly via the Internet and satellite television.

Religions were among the earliest cultural elements to globalize, being spread by force, migration, evangelists, imperialists, and traders. Christianity, Islam, Buddhism, and more recently sects such as Mormonism are among those religions which have taken root and influenced endemic cultures in places far from their origins.

Globalization has strongly influenced sports. For example, the modern Olympic Games has athletes from more than 200 nations participating in a variety of competitions.

The FIFA World Cup is the most widely viewed and followed sporting event in the world, exceeding even the Olympic Games; a ninth of the entire population of the planet watched the 2006 FIFA World Cup Final.

The term globalization implies transformation. Cultural practices including traditional music can be lost or turned into a fusion of traditions. Globalization can trigger a state of emergency for the preservation of musical heritage. Archivists may attempt to collect, record, or transcribe repertoires before melodies are assimilated or modified, while local musicians may struggle for authenticity and to preserve local musical traditions. Globalization can lead performers to discard traditional instruments. Fusion genres can become interesting fields of analysis.

Music has an important role in economic and cultural development during globalization. Music genres such as jazz and reggae began locally and later became international phenomena. Globalization gave support to the world music phenomenon by allowing music from developing countries to reach broader audiences. Though the term "World Music" was originally intended for ethnic-specific music, globalization is now expanding its scope such that the term often includes hybrid subgenres such as "world fusion", "global fusion", "ethnic fusion", and worldbeat.

Use of chilli pepper has spread from the Americas to cuisines around the world, including India, Thailand, Korea, Mexico, China, and Italy.

Bourdieu claimed that the perception of consumption can be seen as self-identification and the formation of identity. Musically, this translates into each individual having their own musical identity based on likes and tastes. These likes and tastes are greatly influenced by culture, as this is the most basic cause for a person's wants and behavior. The concept of one's own culture is now in a period of change due to globalization. Also, globalization has increased the interdependency of political, personal, cultural, and economic factors.

A 2005 UNESCO report showed that cultural exchange is becoming more frequent from Eastern Asia, but that Western countries are still the main exporters of cultural goods.

In 2002, China was the third largest exporter of cultural goods, after the UK and US. Between 1994 and 2002, both North America's and the European Union's shares of cultural exports declined while Asia's cultural exports grew to surpass North America. Related factors are the fact that Asia's population and area are several times that of North America. Americanization is related to a period of high political American clout and of significant growth of America's shops, markets and objects being brought into other countries.

Some critics of globalization argue that it harms the diversity of cultures. As a dominating country's culture is introduced into a receiving country through globalization, it can become a threat to the diversity of local culture. Some argue that globalization may ultimately lead to Westernization or Americanization of culture, where the dominating cultural concepts of economically and politically powerful Western countries spread and cause harm to local cultures.

Globalization is a diverse phenomenon which relates to a multilateral political world and to the increase of cultural objects and markets between countries. The Indian experience particularly reveals the plurality of the impact of cultural globalization.

Transculturalism is defined as "seeing oneself in the other". Transcultural is in turn described as "extending through all human cultures" or "involving, encompassing, or combining elements of more than one culture".

Political Globalization

The United Nations Headquarters in New York City.

In general, globalization may ultimately reduce the importance of nation states. Supranational institutions such as the European Union, the WTO, the G8 or the International Criminal Court replace or extend national functions to facilitate international agreement.

Intergovernmentalism is a term in political science with two meanings. The first refers to a theory of regional integration originally proposed by Stanley Hoffmann; the second treats states and the national government as the primary factors for integration. Multi-level governance is an approach in political science and public administration theory that originated from studies on European integration. Multi-level governance gives expression to the idea that there are many interacting authority structures at work in the emergent global political economy. It illuminates the intimate entanglement between the domestic and international levels of authority.

Some people are citizens of multiple nation-states. Multiple citizenship, also called dual citizenship or multiple nationality or dual nationality, is a person's citizenship status, in which a person is concurrently regarded as a citizen of more than one state under the laws of those states.

Increasingly, non-governmental organizations influence public policy across national boundaries, including humanitarian aid and developmental efforts. Philanthropic organizations with global missions are also coming to the forefront of humanitarian efforts; charities such as the Bill and Melinda Gates Foundation, Accion International, the Acumen Fund (now Acumen) and the Echoing Green have combined the business model with philanthropy, giving rise to business organizations such as the Global Philanthropy Group and new associations of philanthropists such as the Global Philanthropy Forum. The Bill and Melinda Gates Foundation projects include a current multibillion-dollar commitment to funding immunizations in some of the world's more impoverished but rapidly growing countries. and hundreds of millions of dollars in the next few years to programs aimed at encouraging saving by the world's poor. The Hudson Institute estimates total private philanthropic flows to developing countries at US$59 billion in 2010.

As a response to globalization, some countries have embraced isolationist policies. For example, the North Korean government makes it very difficult for foreigners to enter the country and strictly monitors their activities when they do. Aid workers are subject to considerable scrutiny and excluded from places and regions the government does not wish them to enter. Citizens cannot freely leave the country.

Other Dimensions

Scholars also occasionally discuss other, less common dimensions of globalization, such as environmental globalization (the internationally coordinated practices and regulations, often in the form of international treaties, regarding environmental protection) or military globalization (growth in global extent and scope of security relationships). Those dimensions, however, receive much less attention the three described above, as academic literature commonly subdivides globalization into three major areas: economic globalization, cultural globalization and political globalization.

Globalization of the World's Food Supply

Since 1961, human diets across the world have become more diverse in the consumption of major commodity staple crops, with a corollary decline in consumption of local or regionally important crops, and thus have become more homogeneous globally. The differences between the foods eaten in different countries were reduced by 68% between 1961 and 2009. The modern "global standard" diet contains an increasingly large percentage of a relatively small number of major staple commodity crops, which have increased substantially in the share of the total food energy (calories), protein, fat, and food weight that they provide to the world's human population, including wheat, rice, sugar, maize, soybean (by +284%), palm oil (by +173%), and sunflower (by +246%). Whereas nations used to consume greater proportions of locally or regionally important crops, wheat has become a staple in over 97% of countries, with the other global staples showing similar dominance worldwide. Other crops have declined sharply over the same period, including rye, yam, sweet potato (by −45%), cassava (by −38%), coconut, sorghum (by −52%) and millets (by −45%). Such globalization of food supplies is associated with mixed effects on food security, improving under-nutrition in some regions but contributing to the diet-related diseases caused by over-consumption of macronutrients.

Measurement

One index of globalization is the *KOF Index of Globalization*, which measures three important dimensions of globalization: economic, social, and political. Another is the A.T. Kearney / Foreign Policy Magazine Globalization Index.

2014 KOF Index of Globalization		2006 A.T. Kearney / Foreign Policy Magazine Globalization Index	
Rank	**Country**	**Rank**	**Country**
1	Ireland	1	Singapore
2	Belgium	2	Switzerland
3	Netherlands	3	United States
4	Austria	4	Ireland
5	Singapore	5	Denmark
6	Denmark	6	Canada
7	Sweden	7	Netherlands
8	Portugal	8	Australia
9	Hungary	9	Austria
10	Finland	10	Sweden

Measurements of economic globalization typically focus on variables such as trade,

Foreign Direct Investment (FDI), Gross Domestic Product (GDP), portfolio investment, and income. However, newer indices attempt to measure globalization in more general terms, including variables related to political, social, cultural, and even environmental aspects of globalization.

Support and Criticism

Reactions to processes contributing to globalization have varied widely with a history as long as extraterritorial contact and trade. Philosophical differences regarding the costs and benefits of such processes give rise to a broad-range of ideologies and social movements. Proponents of economic growth, expansion and development, in general, view globalizing processes as desirable or necessary to the well-being of human society.

Antagonists view one or more globalizing processes as detrimental to social well-being on a global or local scale; this includes those who question either the social or natural sustainability of long-term and continuous economic expansion, the social structural inequality caused by these processes, and the colonial, imperialistic, or hegemonic ethnocentrism, cultural assimilation and cultural appropriation that underlie such processes.

Globalization tends to bring people into contact with foreign people and cultures. Xenophobia is the fear of that which is perceived to be foreign or strange. Xenophobia can manifest itself in many ways involving the relations and perceptions of an ingroup towards an outgroup, including a fear of losing identity, suspicion of its activities, aggression, and desire to eliminate its presence to secure a presumed purity.

Critiques of globalization generally stem from discussions surrounding the impact of such processes on the planet as well as the human costs. They challenge directly traditional metrics, such as GDP, and look to other measures, such as the Gini coefficient or the Happy Planet Index, and point to a "multitude of interconnected fatal consequences–social disintegration, a breakdown of democracy, more rapid and extensive deterioration of the environment, the spread of new diseases, increasing poverty and alienation" which they claim are the unintended consequences of globalization. Others point out that, while the forces of globalization have led to the spread of western-style democracy, this has been accompanied by an increase in inter-ethnic tension and violence as free market economic policies combine with democratic processes of universal suffrage as well as an escalation in militarization to impose democratic principles and as a means to conflict resolution .

Public Opinion on Globalization

A 2005 study by Peer Fiss and Paul Hirsch found a large increase in articles negative towards globalization in the years prior. In 1998, negative articles outpaced positive articles by two to one. In 2008 Greg Ip claimed this rise in opposition to globalization can be explained, at least in part, by economic self-interest. The number of newspaper articles showing negative framing rose from about 10% of the total in 1991 to 55% of the total in 1999. This increase occurred during a period when the total number of articles concerning globalization nearly doubled.

A number of international polls have shown that residents of Africa and Asia tend to view globalization more favorably than residents of Europe or North America. In Africa, a Gallup poll found that 70% of the population views globalization favorably. The BBC found that 50% of people believed that economic globalization was proceeding too rapidly, while 35% believed it was proceeding too slowly.

In 2004, Philip Gordon stated that "a clear majority of Europeans believe that globalization can enrich their lives, while believing the European Union can help them take advantage of globalization's benefits while shielding them from its negative effects." The main opposition consisted of socialists, environmental groups, and nationalists. Residents of the EU did not appear to feel threatened by globalization in 2004. The EU job market was more stable and workers were less likely to accept wage/benefit cuts. Social spending was much higher than in the US. In a Danish poll in 2007, 76% responded that globalization is a good thing.

Fiss, *et al.*, surveyed US opinion in 1993. Their survey showed that, in 1993, more than 40% of respondents were unfamiliar with the concept of globalization. When the survey was repeated in 1998, 89% of the respondents had a polarized view of globalization as being either good or bad. At the same time, discourse on globalization, which began in the financial community before shifting to a heated debate between proponents and disenchanted students and workers. Polarization increased dramatically after the establishment of the WTO in 1995; this event and subsequent protests led to a large-scale anti-globalization movement. Initially, college educated workers were likely to support globalization. Less educated workers, who were more likely to compete with immigrants and workers in developing countries, tended to be opponents. The situation changed after the financial crisis of 2007. According to a 1997 poll 58% of college graduates said globalization had been good for the US. By 2008 only 33% thought it was good. Respondents with high school education also became more opposed.

According to Takenaka Heizo and Chida Ryokichi, as of 1998 there was a perception in Japan that the economy was "Small and Frail". However, Japan was resource-poor and used exports to pay for its raw materials. Anxiety over their position caused terms such as *internationalization* and *globalization* to enter everyday language. However, Japanese tradition was to be as self-sufficient as possible, particularly in agriculture.

Many in developing countries see globalization as a positive force that lifts them out of poverty. Those opposing globalization typically combine environmental concerns with nationalism. Opponents consider governments as agents of neo-colonialism that are subservient to multinational corporations. Much of this criticism comes from the middle class; the Brookings Institution suggested this was because the middle class perceived upwardly mobile low-income groups as threatening to their economic security.

Economics

The literature analysing the economics of free trade is extremely rich with extensive work having been done on the theoretical and empirical effects. Though it creates winners and losers, the broad consensus among economists is that free trade is a large and unambiguous net gain for society. In a 2006 survey of American economists (83 responders), "87.5% agree that the U.S. should eliminate remaining tariffs and other barriers to trade" and "90.1% disagree with the suggestion that the U.S. should restrict employers from outsourcing work to foreign countries."

Quoting Harvard economics professor N. Gregory Mankiw, "Few propositions command as much consensus among professional economists as that open world trade increases economic growth and raises living standards." In a survey of leading economists, none disagreed with the notion that "freer trade improves productive efficiency and offers consumers better choices, and in the long run these gains are much larger than any effects on employment." Most economists would agree that although increasing returns to scale might mean that certain industry could settle in a geographical area without any strong economic reason derived from comparative advantage, this is not a reason to argue against free trade because the absolute level of output enjoyed by both "winner" and "loser" will increase with the "winner" gaining more than the "loser" but both gaining more than before in an absolute level.

In the book *The End of Poverty*, Jeffrey Sachs discusses how many factors can affect a country's ability to enter the world market, including government corruption; legal and social disparities based on gender, ethnicity, or caste; diseases such as AIDS and malaria; lack of infrastructure (including transportation, communications, health, and trade); unstable political landscapes; protectionism; and geographic barriers. Jagdish Bhagwati, a former adviser to the U.N. on globalization, holds that, although there are obvious problems with overly rapid development, globalization is a very positive force that lifts countries out of poverty by causing a virtuous economic cycle associated with faster economic growth. However, economic growth does not necessarily mean a reduction in poverty; in fact, the two can coexist. Economic growth is conventionally measured using indicators such as GDP and GNI that do not accurately reflect the growing disparities in wealth. Additionally, Oxfam International argues that poor people are often excluded from globalization-induced opportunities "by a lack of productive assets, weak infrastructure, poor education and ill-health;" effectively leaving these marginalized groups in a poverty trap. Economist Paul Krugman is another staunch supporter of globalization and free trade with a record of disagreeing with many critics of globalization. He argues that many of them lack a basic understanding of comparative advantage and its importance in today's world.

The flow of migrants to advanced economic countries has been claimed to provide a means through which global wages converge. An IMF study noted a potential for skills to be transferred back to developing countries as wages in those a countries rise. Lastly, the dissemination of knowledge has been an integral aspect of globalization. Technological innovations (or technological transfer) is conjectured to benefit most the developing and least developing countries (LDCs), as for example in the adoption of mobile phones.

There has been a rapid economic growth in Asia after embracing market orientation-based economic policies that encourage private property rights, free enterprise and competition. In particular, in East Asian developing countries, GDP per head rose at 5.9% a year from 1975 to 2001 (according to 2003 Human Development Report of UNDP). Like this, the British economic journalist Martin Wolf says that incomes of poor developing countries, with more than half the world's population, grew substantially faster than those of the world's richest countries that remained relatively stable in its growth, leading to reduced international inequality and the incidence of poverty.

Certain demographic changes in the developing world after active economic liberalization and international integration resulted in rising general welfare and, hence, reduced inequality. According to Wolf, in the developing world as a whole, life expectancy rose by four months each year after 1970 and infant mortality rate declined from 107 per thousand in 1970 to 58 in 2000 due to improvements in standards of living and health conditions. Also, adult literacy in developing countries rose from 53% in 1970 to 74% in 1998 and much lower illiteracy rate among the young guarantees that rates will continue to fall as time passes. Furthermore, the reduction in fertility rate in the developing world as a whole from 4.1 births per woman in 1980 to 2.8 in 2000 indicates improved education level of women on fertility, and control of fewer children with more parental attention and investment. Consequently, more prosperous and educated parents with fewer children have chosen to withdraw their children from the labor force to give them opportunities to be educated at school improving the issue of child labor. Thus, despite seemingly unequal distribution of income within these developing countries, their economic growth and development have brought about improved standards of living and welfare for the population as a whole.

Per capita gross domestic product (GDP) growth among post-1980 globalizing countries accelerated from 1.4 percent a year in the 1960s and 2.9 percent a year in the 1970s to 3.5 percent in the 1980s and 5.0 percent in the 1990s. This acceleration in growth seems even more remarkable given that the rich countries saw steady declines in growth from a high of 4.7 percent in the 1960s to 2.2 percent in the 1990s. Also, the non-globalizing developing countries seem to fare worse than the globalizers, with the former's annual growth rates falling from highs of 3.3 percent during the 1970s to only 1.4 percent during the 1990s. This rapid growth among the globalizers is not simply due to the strong performances of China and India in the 1980s and 1990s—18 out of the 24 globalizers experienced increases in growth, many of them quite substantial.

The globalization of the late 20th and early 21st centuries has led to the resurfacing of the idea that the growth of economic interdependence promotes peace. This idea had been very powerful during the globalization of the late 19th and early 20th centuries, and was a central doctrine of classical liberals of that era, such as the young John Maynard Keynes (1883–1946).

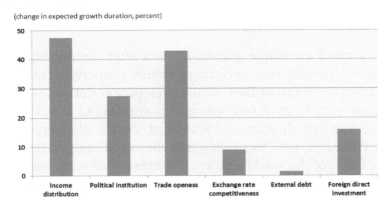

(change in expected growth duration, percent)

Of the factors influencing the duration of economic growth in both developed and developing countries, income equality has a more beneficial impact than trade openness, sound political institutions, and foreign investment.

Some opponents of globalization see the phenomenon as a promotion of corporatist interests. They also claim that the increasing autonomy and strength of corporate entities shapes the political policy of countries. They advocate global institutions and policies that they believe better address the moral claims of poor and working classes as well as environmental concerns. Economic arguments by fair trade theorists claim that unrestricted free trade benefits those with more financial leverage (i.e. the rich) at the expense of the poor.

Globalization allows corporations to outsource manufacturing and service jobs from high cost locations, creating economic opportunities with the most competitive wages and worker benefits. Critics of globalization say that it disadvantages poorer countries. While it is true that free trade encourages globalization among countries, some countries try to protect their domestic suppliers. The main export of poorer countries is usually agricultural productions. Larger countries often subsidize their farmers (e.g., the EU's Common Agricultural Policy), which lowers the market price for foreign crops.

Global Democracy

Democratic globalization is a movement towards an institutional system of global democracy that would give world citizens a say in political organizations. This would, in their view, bypass nation-states, corporate oligopolies, ideological Non-governmental organizations (NGO), political cults and mafias. One of its most prolific proponents is the British political thinker David Held. Advocates of democratic globalization argue that economic expansion and development should be the first phase of democratic globalization, which is to be followed by a phase of building global political institutions. Dr. Francesco Stipo, Director of the United States Association of the Club of Rome, advocates unifying nations under a world government, suggesting that it "should reflect the political and economic balances of world nations. A world confederation would not supersede the authority of the State governments but rather complement it, as both the States and the world authority would have power within their sphere of competence". Former Canadian Senator Douglas Roche, O.C., viewed globalization as inevitable and advocated creating institutions such as a directly elected United Nations Parliamentary Assembly to exercise oversight over unelected international bodies.

Global Civics

Monument to Multiculturalism by Francesco Perilli in Toronto, Ontario, Canada. Four identical sculptures are located in Buffalo City, South Africa; Changchun, China; Sarajevo, Bosnia and Sydney, Australia.

Global civics suggests that civics can be understood, in a global sense, as a social contract between global citizens in the age of interdependence and interaction. The disseminators of the concept define it as the notion that we have certain rights and responsibilities towards each other by the mere fact of being human on Earth. World citizen has a variety of similar meanings, often referring to a person who disapproves of traditional geopolitical divisions derived from national citizenship. An early incarnation of this sentiment can be found in Socrates, whom Plutarch quoted as saying: "I am not an Athenian, or a Greek, but a citizen of the world." In an increasingly interdependent world, world citizens need a compass to frame their mindsets and create a shared consciousness and sense of global responsibility in world issues such as environmental problems and nuclear proliferation.

Baha'i-inspired author Gregory Paul Meyjes embraces the single world community and emergent global consciousness but warns of globalization as a cloak for an expeditious economic, social, and cultural Anglo-dominance that may be insufficiently fertile to sustain the emergence of a world civilization. He proposes a process of "universalization" as an alternative.

Cosmopolitanism is the proposal that all human ethnic groups belong to a single community based on a shared morality. A person who adheres to the idea of cosmopolitanism in any of its forms is called a cosmopolitan or cosmopolite. A cosmopolitan community might be based on an inclusive morality, a shared economic relationship, or a political structure that encompasses different nations. The cosmopolitan community is one in which individuals from different places (e.g. nation-states) form relationships based on mutual respect. For instance, Kwame Anthony Appiah suggests the possibility of a cosmopolitan community in which individuals from varying locations (physical, economic, etc.) enter relationships of mutual respect despite their differing beliefs (religious, political, etc.).

Canadian philosopher Marshall McLuhan popularized the term *Global Village* beginning in 1962. His view suggested that globalization would lead to a world where people from all countries will become more integrated and aware of common interests and shared humanity.

International Cooperation

Military cooperation – Past examples of international cooperation exist. One example is the security cooperation between the United States and the former Soviet Union after the end of the Cold War, which astonished international society. Arms control and disarmament agreements, including the Strategic Arms Reduction Treaty and the establishment of NATO's Partnership for Peace, the Russia NATO Council, and the G8 Global Partnership against the Spread of Weapons and Materials of Mass Destruction, constitute concrete initiatives of arms control and de-nuclearization. The US–Russian cooperation was further strengthened by anti-terrorism agreements enacted in the wake of 9/11.

Environmental cooperation – One of the biggest successes of environmental cooperation has been the agreement to reduce chlorofluorocarbon (CFC) emissions, as specified in the Montreal Protocol, in order to stop ozone depletion. The most recent debate around nuclear energy and the non-alternative coal-burning power plants constitutes one more consensus on what not to do. Thirdly, significant achievements in IC can be observed through development studies.

Anti-globalization Movement

Anti-globalization, or counter-globalization, consists of a number of criticisms of globalization but, in general, is critical of the globalization of corporate capitalism. The movement is also commonly referred to as the alter-globalization movement, anti-globalist movement, anti-corporate globalization movement, or movement against neoliberal globalization. It can be explained as encompassing the ideologies present in the following other "movements", which will be discussed below: opposition to capital market integration, social injustice and inequality, anti-consumerism, anti-global governance and environmentalist opposition. Each of these ideologies can be framed around a specific strand of the anti-globalization movement, but in general the movement gears their efforts towards all of these primary principles. It is considered a rather new and modern day social movement, as the issues it is fighting against are relevant in today's time. However, the events that occurred which fuels the movement can be traced back through the lineage of the movement of a 500-year-old history of resistance against European colonialism and US imperialism. This refers to the continent of Africa being colonized and stripped of their resources by the Europeans in the 19th century. It is also related closely with the anti-Vietnam war mobilizations between 1960 and 1970, with worldwide protests against the adjustment of structure in Africa, Asia, and Latin America.

In general, opponents of globalization in developed countries are disproportionately middle-class and college-educated. This contrasts sharply with the situation in developing countries, where the anti-globalization movement has been more successful in enlisting a broader group, including millions of workers and farmers.

These supporters of the movement are aware of the unequal power and respect in terms of international trade between the developed and underdeveloped countries of the world. The activists that support the anti-globalism movement, as mentioned previously, can range in terms of the specific issue(s) that they oppose. Again, there are a few different dimensions of globalization: economic, political, cultural, ecological and ideological. The diverse subgroups that make up this movement include some of the following: trade unionists, environmentalists, anarchists, land rights and indigenous rights activists, organizations promoting human rights and sustainable development, opponents of privatization, and anti-sweatshop campaigners.

As summarized by Noam Chomsky:

The dominant propaganda systems have appropriated the term "globalization" to refer to the specific version of international economic integration that they favor, which privileges the rights of investors and lenders, those of people being incidental. In accord with this usage, those who favor a different form of international integration, which privileges the rights of human beings, become "anti-globalist." This is simply vulgar propaganda, like the term "anti-Soviet" used by the most disgusting commissars to refer to dissidents. It is not only vulgar, but idiotic. Take the World Social Forum (WSF), called "anti-globalization" in the propaganda system—which happens to include the media, the educated classes, etc., with rare exceptions. The WSF is a paradigm example of globalization. It is a gathering of huge numbers of people from all over the world, from just about every corner of life one can think of, apart from the extremely narrow highly privileged elites who meet at the competing World Economic Forum, and are called "pro-globalization" by the propaganda system.

In *The Revolt of the Elites and the Betrayal of Democracy*, Christopher Lasch analyzes the widening gap between the top and bottom of the social composition in the United States. For him, our epoch is determined by an social phenomenon: the revolt of the elites. According to Lasch, the new elites, ie those who are in the top 20% in terms of income, through to globalization, which allows total mobility of capital, no longer live in the same world as their fellow-citizens. In this, they oppose the old bourgeoisie of the nineteenth and twentieth centuries, which was constrained by its spatial stability to a minimum of rooting and civic obligations.Globalization, according to the sociologist, has turned elites into tourists in their own countries. The de-nationalisation of business enterprise tends to produce a class who see themselves as "world citizens, but without accepting ... any of the obligations that citizenship in a polity normally implies". Their ties to an international culture of work and leisure - of business, entertainment, information - make many of them deeply indifferent to the prospect of American national decline. Instead of financing public services, new elites are investing their money in improving their voluntary ghettos. They are happy to pay for private schools in their residential neighborhoods, for a private police, and for garbage collection systems; "they have succeeded, to a remarkable degree, in relieving themselves of the obligation to contribute to the public treasury". They have "withdrawn from common life and no longer want to pay for what they have stopped using". They have lost all contact with the people. Composed of those who control the international flows of capital and information, who preside over philanthropic foundations and institutions of higher education, manage the instruments of cultural production and thus fix the terms of public debate. This new class is distinguished by investment in education and information. He explains that the growing isolation of the elites means among other things that political ideologies lose all contact with the concerns of the ordinary citizen.The consequence is that the political debate is limited mainly to the dominant classes. However, the latter remain protected from the new problems affecting the working classes. The latter saw the decline of industrial activity and the resulting loss of employment; the decline of the middle class; increasing the number of the poor; the rising crime rate; growing drug trafficking; The urban crisis. The result of this split from the top of the scale is that no one has a likely solution to these inextricable problems and that there are furious ideological battles on related issues.

D.A. Snow et al. contend that the anti-globalization movement is an example of a new social movement, which uses tactics that are unique and use different resources than previously used before in other social movements. Actors of the movement participate in things such as disruptive tactics. These include flash mobs for example, which work extremely well in catching the attention of others and spreading awareness about the issue of globalization. There is also the spreading of information about the social movement through social media and word of mouth about NGOs, organizations and movement groups working to help alleviate the effects of globalization. Websites such as Twitter and Facebook have become a useful outlet for people to become aware of what is going on around the globe, any protests or tactics taking place and the progress of non-governmental organizations aiding in these impoverished countries.

One of the most infamous tactics of the movement is the Battle of Seattle in 1999, where there were protests against the World Trade Organization's Third Ministerial Meeting. All over the world, the movement has held protests outside meetings of institutions such as the WTO, the International Monetary Fund (IMF), the World Bank, the World Economic Forum, and the Group of Eight (G8). Within the Seattle demonstrations the protesters that participated used both creative and violent tactics to gain the attention towards the issue of globalization.

Opposition to Capital Market Integration

World Bank Protester, Jakarta, Indonesia

Capital markets have to do with raising and investing money in various human enterprises. Increasing integration of these financial markets between countries leads to the emergence of a global capital marketplace or a single world market. In the long run, increased movement of capital between countries tends to favor owners of capital more than any other group; in the short run, owners and workers in specific sectors in capital-exporting countries bear much of the burden of adjusting to increased movement of capital. It is not surprising that these conditions lead to political divisions about whether or not to encourage or increase international capital market integration.

Those opposed to capital market integration on the basis of human rights issues are especially disturbed by the various abuses which they think are perpetuated by global and international institutions that, they say, promote neoliberalism without regard to ethical standards. This can also be referred to as "corporate capitalism", as previous mentioned, which are money driven organizations such as the World Bank and the International Monetary Fund, along with many of the popular and competitive multinational corporations, like Nike and other institutions. Common targets include the World Bank (WB), International Monetary Fund (IMF), the Organisation for Economic Co-operation and Development (OECD) and the World Trade Organization (WTO) and free trade treaties like the North American Free Trade Agreement (NAFTA), Free Trade Area of the Americas (FTAA), the Multilateral Agreement on Investment (MAI) and the General Agreement on Trade in Services (GATS). In light of the economic gap between rich and poor countries, movement adherents claim "free trade" without measures in place to protect the under-capitalized will contribute only to the strengthening the power of industrialized nations (often termed the "North" in opposition to the developing world's "South"). Some of the powerful Northern corporations have implemented policies like privatizing public industry and reducing tariffs. By doing this it has created a growth in sweatshops in the developing world, where wages are minimal and unfair, and conditions are unsafe to the workers' health and psychological state. The global North can benefit from this by getting goods for a cheaper monetary amount. However, this is at the expense of these impoverished people and the community or country as a whole. Now, fair trade has been introduced in order to attempt to rebuild the economies of third world countries by paying employees, who work to produce goods to be exported, a fair price for their efforts.

Anti-corporatism and Anti-consumerism

Corporatist ideology, which privileges the rights of corporations (artificial or juridical persons) over those of natural persons, is an underlying factor in the recent rapid expansion of global commerce. In recent years, there have been an increasing number of books (Naomi Klein's 2000 *No Logo*, for example) and films (*e.g. The Corporation* & *Surplus*) popularizing an anti-corporate ideology to the public.

A related contemporary ideology, consumerism, which encourages the personal acquisition of goods and services, also drives globalization. Anti-consumerism is a social movement against equating personal happiness with consumption and the purchase of material possessions. Concern over the treatment of consumers by large corporations has spawned substantial activism, and the incorporation of consumer education into school curricula. Social activists hold materialism is connected to global retail merchandizing and supplier convergence, war, greed, anomie, crime, environmental degradation, and general social malaise and discontent. One variation on this topic is activism by *postconsumers*, with the strategic emphasis on moving *beyond* addictive consumerism.

Global Justice and Inequality

Global Justice

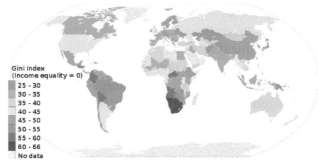

Differences in national income equality around the world as measured by
the national Gini coefficient, 2014.

The global justice movement is the loose collection of individuals and groups—often referred to as a "movement of movements"—who advocate fair trade rules and perceive current institutions of global economic integration as problems. The movement is often labeled an anti-globalization movement by the mainstream media. Those involved, however, frequently deny that they are anti-globalization, insisting that they support the globalization of communication and people and oppose only the global expansion of corporate power. The movement is based in the idea of social justice, desiring the creation of a society or institution based on the principles of equality and solidarity, the values of human rights, and the dignity of every human being. Social inequality within and between nations, including a growing global digital divide, is a focal point of the movement. Many nongovernmental organizations have now arisen to fight these inequalities that many in Latin America, Africa and Asia face. A few very popular and well known non-governmental organizations (NGOs) include: War Child, Red Cross, Free The Children and CARE International. They often create partnerships where they work towards improving the lives of those who live in developing countries by building schools, fixing infrastructure, cleaning water supplies, purchasing equipment and supplies for hospitals, and other aid efforts.

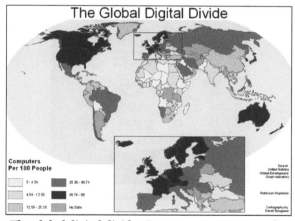

The global digital divide: Computers per 100 people.

Social Inequality

The economies of the world have developed unevenly, historically, such that entire geographical regions were left mired in poverty and disease while others began to reduce poverty and disease on a wholesale basis. From around 1980 through at least 2011, the GDP gap, while still wide, appeared to be closing and, in some more rapidly developing countries, life expectancies began to rise. If we look at the Gini coefficient for world income, since the late 1980s, the gap between some regions has markedly narrowed— between Asia and the advanced economies of the West, for example—but huge gaps remain globally. Overall equality across humanity, considered as individuals, has improved very little. Within the decade between 2003 and 2013, income inequality grew even in traditionally egalitarian countries like Germany, Sweden and Denmark. With a few exceptions—France, Japan, Spain—the top 10 percent of earners in most advanced economies raced ahead, while the bottom 10 percent fell further behind. By 2013, a tiny elite of multibillionaires, 85 to be exact, had amassed wealth equivalent to all the wealth owned by the poorest half (3.5 billion) of the world's total population of 7 billion.

Critics of globalization argue that globalization results in weak labor unions: the surplus in cheap labor coupled with an ever-growing number of companies in transition weakened labor unions in high-cost areas. Unions become less effective and workers their enthusiasm for unions when membership begins to decline. They also cite an increase in the exploitation of child labor: countries with weak protections for children are vulnerable to infestation by rogue companies and criminal gangs who exploit them. Examples include quarrying, salvage, and farm work as well as trafficking, bondage, forced labor, prostitution and pornography.

Immigrant rights march for amnesty, Los Angeles, on May Day, 2006.

Women often participate in the workforce in precarious work, including export-oriented employment. Evidence suggests that while globalization has expanded women's access to employment, the long-term goal of transforming gender inequalities remains unmet and appears unattainable without regulation of capital and a reorientation and expansion of the state's role in funding public goods and providing a social safety net.

Anti-global Governance

Beginning in the 1930s, opposition arose to the idea of a world government, as advocated by organizations such as the World Federalist Movement (WFM). Those who oppose global governance typically do so on objections that the idea is unfeasible, inevitably oppressive, or simply unnecessary. In general, these opponents are wary of the concentration of power or wealth that such governance might represent. Such reasoning dates back to the founding of the League of Nations and, later, the United Nations.

Environmentalist Opposition

Deforestation of the Madagascar Highland Plateau has led to extensive siltation and unstable flows of western rivers.

Environmentalism is a broad philosophy, ideology and social movement regarding concerns for environmental conservation and improvement of the health of the environment. Environmentalist concerns with globalization include issues such as global warming, climate change, global water supply and water crises, inequity in energy consumption and energy conservation, transnational air pollution and pollution of the world ocean, overpopulation, world habitat sustainability, deforestation, biodiversity and species extinction.

Another concern is labeled "environmental apartheid", which claims that the resources and wealth of society are typically appropriated by a small minority group of a privileged race or class, under much protection. Thus, the excluded majority never gets a chance to access to resources necessary for well-being and survival. In the pre-Rio conference period, it was the North that contributed most to the destruction of the environment. Globalization is restructuring control over resources in such a way that the natural resources of the poor are systematically taken over by the rich and the pollution promulgated by the rich is systematically dumped on the poor. For example, 90 percent of historic carbon dioxide emissions have been by the industrialized countries. The developed countries produce 90 percent of the hazardous wastes produced around the world every year. Global free trade has globalized this environmental destruction in an asymmetric pattern. Some argue the economy is controlled by Northern corporations and they are increasingly exploiting resources of less wealthy countries for their global activities while it is the South that is disproportionately bearing the environmental burden of the globalized economy. Globalization is thus leading to a type of environmental apartheid.

Helena Norberg-Hodge, the director and founder of Local Futures/International Society for Ecology and Culture, criticizes globalization in many ways. In her book *Ancient Futures*, Norberg-Hodge claims that "centuries of ecological balance and social harmony are under threat from the pressures of development and globalization." She also criticizes the standardization and rationalization of globalization, as it does not always yield the expected growth outcomes. Although globalization takes similar steps in most countries, scholars such as Hodge claim that it might not be effective to certain countries and that globalization has actually moved some countries backward instead of developing them.

A related area of concern is the pollution haven hypothesis, which posits that, when large industrialized nations seek to set up factories or offices abroad, they will often look for the cheapest option in terms of resources and labor that offers the land and material access they require. This often comes at the cost of environmentally sound practices. Developing countries with cheap resources and labor tend to have less stringent environmental regulations, and conversely, nations with stricter environmental regulations become more expensive for companies as a result of the costs associated with meeting these standards. Thus, companies that choose to physically invest in foreign countries tend to relocate to the countries with the lowest environmental standards or weakest enforcement.

Dimensions of Globalization

Manfred Steger, professor of Global Studies at the University of Hawaii at Manoa argues that globalization has four main dimensions: economic, political, cultural, ecological, with ideological aspects of each category. David Held's book *Global Transformations* is organized around the same dimensions, though the ecological is not listed in the title. This set of categories relates to the four-domain approach of circles of social life, and Circles of Sustainability.

Steger compares the current study of globalization to the ancient Buddhist parable of blind scholars and their first encounter with an elephant. Similar to the blind scholars, some globalization scholars are too focused on compacting globalization into a singular process and clashes over "which aspect of social life constitutes its primary domain" prevail.

Dimensions

Economic

Economic globalization is the intensification and stretching of economic interrelations around the globe. It encompasses such things as the emergence of a new global economic order, the internationalization of trade and finance, *the changing power of* transnational corporations, and the enhanced role of international economic institutions.

Political

Political globalization is the intensification and expansion of political interrelations around the globe. Aspects of political globalization include the modern-nation state system and its changing place in today's world, the role of global governance, and the direction of our global political systems.

Military

Military globalization, as subdomain of political globalization, is defined as the intensification and stretching of military power across the globe through various means of military power (nuclear military weapons, radiation weapons simply weapons of mass destruction). This form of globalization occurs across offensive and defensive uses of power and survival in international field. Beyond states, global organizations such as the United Nations also extend military means globally through support given by both Global North and South countries.

Cultural

Cultural globalization is the intensification and expansion of cultural flows across the globe. Culture is a very broad concept and has many facets, but in the discussion on globalization, Steger means it to refer to "the symbolic construction, articulation, and dissemination of meaning." Topics under this heading include discussion about the development of a global culture, or lack thereof, the role of the media in shaping our identities and desires, and the globalization of languages.

Ecological

Topics of ecological globalization include population growth, access to food, worldwide reduction in biodiversity, the gap between rich and poor as well as between the global North and global South, human-induced climate change, and global environmental degradation.

Ideologies

Globalization operates on a cross-cutting "ideological dimension" filled with a range of norms, claims, beliefs, and narratives about the phenomenon itself. According to Steger, there are three main types of globalisms (ideologies that endow the concept of globalization with particular values and meanings): market globalism, justice globalism, and religious globalisms. Steger defines them as follows:

- *Market globalism* seeks to endow 'globalization' with free-market norms and neoliberal meanings.

- *Justice globalism* constructs an alternative vision of globalization based on egalitarian ideals of global solidarity and distributive justice.

- *Religious globalisms* struggle against both market globalism and justice globalsm as they seek to mobilize a religious values and beliefs that are thought to be under severe attack by the forces of secularism and consumerism.

These ideologies of globalization (or globalisms) then relate to broader imaginaries and ontologies.

History of Globalization

Extent of the Silk Road and Spice trade routes blocked by the Ottoman
Empire in 1453 spurring exploration.

The historical origins of globalization are the subject of ongoing debate. Though several scholars situate the origins of globalization in the modern era, others regard it as a phenomenon with a long history. Some authors have argued that stretching the beginning of globalization far back in time renders the concept wholly inoperative and useless for political analysis.

Archaic Globalization

Perhaps the most extreme proponent of a deep historical origin for globalization was Andre Gunder Frank, an economist associated with dependency theory. Frank argued that a form of globalization has been in existence since the rise of trade links between Sumer and the Indus Valley Civilization in the third millennium BC Critics of this idea contend that it rests upon an over-broad definition of globalization.

Thomas L. Friedman divides the history of globalization into three periods: Globalization 1 (1492–1800), Globalization 2 (1800–2000) and Globalization 3 (2000–present). He states that Globalization 1 involved the globalization of countries, Globalization 2 involved the globalization of companies and Globalization 3 involves the globalization of individuals.

Even as early as the Prehistoric period, the roots of modern globalization could be found. Territorial expansion by our ancestors to all five continents was a critical component in establishing globalization. The development of agriculture furthered globalization by converting the vast majority of the world's population into a settled lifestyle. However, globalization failed to accelerate due to lack of long distance interaction and technology. The contemporary process of globalization likely occurred around the middle of the 19th century as increased capital and labor mobility coupled with decreased transport costs led to a smaller world.

An early form of globalized economics and culture, known as archaic globalization, existed during the Hellenistic Age, when commercialized urban centers were focused around the axis of Greek culture over a wide range that stretched from India to Spain, with such cities as Alexandria, Athens, and Antioch at its center. Trade was widespread during that period, and it is the first time the idea of a cosmopolitan culture (from Greek "Cosmopolis", meaning "world city") emerged. Others have perceived an early form of globalization in the trade links between the Roman Empire, the Parthian Empire, and the Han Dynasty. The increasing articulation of commercial links between these powers inspired the development of the Silk Road, which started in western China, reached the boundaries of the Parthian empire, and continued onwards towards Rome.

The Islamic Golden Age was also an important early stage of globalization, when Jewish and Muslim traders and explorers established a sustained economy across the Old World resulting in a globalization of crops, trade, knowledge and technology. Globally significant crops such as sugar and cotton became widely cultivated across the Muslim world in this period, while the necessity of learning Arabic and completing the Hajj created a cosmopolitan culture.

The advent of the Mongol Empire, though destabilizing to the commercial centers of the Middle East and China, greatly facilitated travel along the Silk Road. This permitted travelers and missionaries such as Marco Polo to journey successfully (and profitably) from one end of Eurasia to the other. The Pax Mongolica of the thirteenth century had several other notable globalizing effects. It witnessed the creation of the first international postal service, as well as the rapid transmission of epidemic diseases such as bubonic plague across the newly unified regions of Central Asia. These pre-modern phases of global or hemispheric exchange are sometimes known as archaic globalization. Up to the sixteenth century, however, even the largest systems of international exchange were limited to the Old World.

Proto-globalization

The next phase is known as proto-globalization. It was characterized by the rise of maritime European empires, in the 16th and 17th centuries, first the Portuguese and Spanish Empires, and later the Dutch and British Empires. In the 17th century, globalization became also a private business phenomenon when chartered companies like British East India Company (founded in 1600), often described as the first multinational corporation, as well as the Dutch East India Company (founded in 1602) were established.

The Age of Discovery brought a broad change in globalization, being the first period in which Eurasia and Africa engaged in substantial cultural, material and biologic exchange with the New World. It began in the late 15th century, when the two Kingdoms of the Iberian Peninsula – Portugal and Castile – sent the first exploratory voyages around the Cape of Good Hope and to the Americas, "discovered" in 1492 by Christopher Columbus. Shortly before the turn of the 16th century, Portuguese started establishing trading posts (factories) from Africa to Asia and Brazil, to deal with the trade of local products like gold, spices and timber, introducing an international business center under a royal monopoly, the House of India.

Global integration continued with the European colonization of the Americas initiating the Columbian Exchange, the enormous widespread exchange of plants, animals, foods, human populations (including slaves), communicable diseases, and culture between the Eastern and Western hemispheres. It was one of the most significant global events concerning ecology, agriculture, and culture in history. New crops that had come from the Americas via the European seafarers in the 16th century significantly contributed to the world's population growth.

Modern Globalization

Map showing Colonial empires evolution from 1492 to present.

The 19th century witnessed the advent of globalization approaching its modern form. Industrialization allowed cheap production of household items using economies of scale, while rapid population growth created sustained demand for commodities. Globalization in this period was decisively shaped by nineteenth-century imperialism. After the First and Second Opium Wars, which opened up China to foreign trade, and the completion of the British conquest of India, the vast populations of these regions became ready consumers of European exports. It was in this period that areas of sub-Saharan Africa and the Pacific islands were incorporated into the world system. Meanwhile, the conquest of new parts of the globe, notably sub-Saharan Africa, by Europeans yielded valuable natural resources such as rubber, diamonds and coal and helped fuel trade and investment between the European imperial powers, their colonies, and the United States.

The inhabitant of London could order by telephone, sipping his morning tea, the various products of the whole earth, and reasonably expect their early delivery upon his doorstep. Militarism and imperialism of racial and cultural rivalries were little more than the amusements of his daily newspaper. What an extraordinary episode in the economic progress of man was that age which came to an end in August 1914.

Between the globalization in the 19th and in the 20th there are significant differences. There are two main points on which the differences can be seen. One point is the global trade in this centuries as well as the capital, investment and the economy.

Global Trade

The global trade in the 20th century shows a higher share of trade in merchant production, a growth of the trade in services and the rise of production and trade by multinational firms. The production of merchant goods in the 20th century largely decreased from the levels seen in the 19th century. However, the amount of merchant goods that were produced for the merchandise trade grew. The trade in services also grew more important in the 20th compared to the 19th century. The last point that distinguishes the global trade in the 19th century compared to the global trade in the 20th century, is the extent of multinational cooperation. In the 20th century you can see a "quantum leap" in multinational cooperation compared to the 19th century. Before the 20th century began, there were just Portfolio investment, but no trade-related or production-relation Direct investment.

Commercial integration has improved since last century, barriers that inhibit trade are lower and transport costs have decreased. Multinational trade contracts and agreements have been signed, like the General Agreement on Tariffs and Trade (GATT), North American Free Trade Agreement (NAFTA), the European Union (EU) has been hugely involved in eliminating tariffs between member states, and the World Trade Organization. From 1890 and up to World War I instability in trade was a problem, but in the post war period there has mostly been economic expansion which leads to stability. Nations have to take care of their own products; they have to make sure that foreign goods do not suffocate their domestic products causing unemployment and maybe social instability. Technological changes have caused lower transporting costs; it takes just a few hours to transport goods between continents to-day, instead of weeks or even months in the nineteenth century.

By consideration financial crisis one key difference is the monetary regime. In the 19th century it occurred under the fixed exchange rates of the gold standard. But in the 20th century it took place in a regime of managed flexibility. Furthermore, in the 19th century countries had developed effective lenders of last resort, but the same was not true at the periphery and countries there suffered the consequences. A century later there was a domestic safety net in most emerging countries so that banking panics were changed into situations where the debts of an insolvent banking system were taken over by the government. The recovery from banking crisis is another key difference. It has tended to begin earlier in the recent period than in the typical crisis episode a hundred years ago. In the 19th century there were no international rescue packages available to emerging economies. But in the recent period such rescues were a typical component of the financial landscape all over the world.

The flows information were an important downside in 19th century. Prior to the Transatlantic cable and the Radiotelephone, it used to take very long for information to go from one place to another. So this means that it was very difficult to analyze the information. For instance, it was not so easy to distinguish good and bad credits. Therefore, the information asymmetry played a very important role in international investments. The railway bonds serve as a great example. There was also many contracting problems. It was very difficult for companies working overseas to manage their operations in other parts of the world, so this was clearly a big barrier to investment. Several macroeconomic factors such as exchange risks and uncertain monetary policies were a big barrier for international investments as well. The accounting standards in the U.S. were relatively underdeveloped in the 19th century. The British investors played a very important role in transferring their accounting practices to the new emerging markets.

Aftermath of World War I: Collapse of Globalization

The first phase of "modern globalization" began to break down at the beginning of the 20th century, with World War I. The European-dominated network were increasingly confronted with images and stories of 'others', thus, then took it upon themselves to take the role of world's guardians of universal law and morality. Racist and unequal practices became also part of their practices in search of materials and resources that from other regions of the world. The increase of world trade before beginning in 1850 right before World War I broke out in 1914 were incentives for bases of direct colonial rule in the global South. Since other European currencies were becoming quite largely circulated, the need to own resource bases became imperative. The novelist VM Yeates criticised the financial forces of globalization as a factor in creating World War I. Financial forces as a factor for creating World War 1 seem to be partly responsible. An example of this would be France's colonial rule over most of Africa during the 20th century. Before World War I broke out, there was no specific aims for the wars in Africa from the French, which left Africans in a "lost" state. Military potential of Africa was first to be emphasized unlike its economic potential...at least at first. France's interest in the military potential of French Africa took a while to be accepted. Africans in the French army were treated with feelings of inferiority from the French. As for the economic incentive for colonial rule came in 1917 when France's was faced with a crisis of food supply. This coming after the outbreak of the war which had left France without the ability to support itself agriculturally since France had a shortage of fertilizers and machinery in 1917.

Post-World War II: Globalization Resurgent

Globalization, since World War II, is partly the result of planning by politicians to break down borders hampering trade. Their work led to the Bretton Woods conference, an agreement by the world's leading politicians to lay down the framework for international commerce and finance, and the founding of several international institutions intended to oversee the processes of globalization. Globalization was also driven by the global expansion of multinational corporations based in the United States and Europe, and worldwide exchange of new developments in science, technology and products, with most significant inventions of this time having their origins in the Western world according to Encyclopædia Britannica. Worldwide export of western culture went through the new mass media: film, radio and television and recorded music. Development and growth of international transport and telecommunication played a decisive role in modern globalization.

These institutions include the International Bank for Reconstruction and Development (the World Bank), and the International Monetary Fund. Globalization has been facilitated by advances in technology which have reduced the costs of trade, and trade negotiation rounds, originally under the auspices of the General Agreement on Tariffs and Trade (GATT), which led to a series of agreements to remove restrictions on free trade.

Since World War II, barriers to international trade have been considerably lowered through international agreements – GATT. Particular initiatives carried out as a result of GATT and the World Trade Organization (WTO), for which GATT is the foundation, have included:

- Promotion of free trade:
  - Elimination of tariffs; creation of free trade zones with small or no tariffs
  - Reduced transportation costs, especially resulting from development of containerization for ocean shipping
  - Reduction or elimination of capital controls
  - Reduction, elimination, or harmonization of subsidies for local businesses
  - Creation of subsidies for global corporations
  - Harmonization of intellectual property laws across the majority of states, with more restrictions
  - Supranational recognition of intellectual property restrictions (e.g. patents granted by China would be recognized in the United States).

Cultural globalization, driven by communication technology and the worldwide marketing of Western cultural industries, was understood at first as a process of homogenization, as the global domination of American culture at the expense of traditional diversity. However, a contrasting trend soon became evident in the emergence of movements protesting against globalization and giving new momentum to the defense of local uniqueness, individuality, and identity.

The Uruguay Round (1986 to 1994) led to a treaty to create the WTO to mediate trade disputes and set up a uniform platform of trading. Other bilateral and multilateral trade agreements, including sections of Europe's Maastricht Treaty and the North American Free Trade Agreement (NAFTA) have also been signed in pursuit of the goal of reducing tariffs and barriers to trade.

World exports rose from 8.5% in 1970, to 16.2% of total gross world product in 2001.

In the 1990s, the growth of low cost communication networks allowed work done using a computer to be moved to low wage locations for many job types. This included accounting, software development, and engineering design.

In late 2000s, much of the industrialized world entered into a deep recession. Some analysts say the world is going through a period of deglobalization after years of increasing economic integration. China has recently become the world's largest exporter surpassing Germany.

Archaic Globalization

Archaic globalization is a phase in the history of globalization, and conventionally refers to globalizing events and developments from the time of the earliest civilizations until roughly 1600 (the following period is known as early modern globalization). This term is used to describe the relationships between communities and states and how they were created by the geographical spread of ideas and social norms at both local and regional levels.

States began to interact and trade with others within close proximity as a way to acquire coveted goods that were considered a luxury. This trade led to the spread of ideas such as religion, economic structure and political ideals. Merchants became connected and aware of others in ways that had not been apparent. Archaic globalization is comparable to present day globalization on a much smaller scale. It not only allowed the spread of goods and commodities to other regions, but it also allowed people to experience other cultures. Cities that partook in trading were bound together by sea lanes, rivers, and great overland routes, some of which had been in use since antiquity. Trading was broken up according to geographic location, with centers between flanking places serving as "break-in-bulk" and exchange points for goods destined for more distant markets. During this time period the subsystems were more self-sufficient than they are today and therefore less vitally dependent upon one another for everyday survival. While long distance trading came with many trials and tribulations, still so much of it went on during this early time period. Linking the trade together involved eight interlinked subsystems that were grouped into three large circuits, which encompassed the western European, the Middle Eastern, and the Far Eastern. This interaction during trading was early civilization's way to communicate and spread many ideas which caused modern globalization to emerge and allow a new aspect to present day society.

Defining Globalization

Globalization is the process of increasing interconnectedness between regions and individuals. Steps toward globalization include economic, political, technological, social, and cultural connections around the world. The term "archaic" can be described as early ideals and functions that were once historically apparent in society but may have disintegrated over time. There are three main prerequisites for globalization to occur. The first is the idea of Eastern Origins, which shows how Western states have adapted and implemented learned principles from the East. Without the traditional ideas from the East, Western globalization would not have emerged the way it did. The second is distance. The interactions amongst states were not on a global scale and most often were confined to Asia, North Africa, the Middle East and certain parts of Europe. With early globalization it was difficult for states to interact with others that were not within close proximity. Eventually, technological advances allowed states to learn of others existence and another phase of globalization was able to occur. The third has to do with interdependency, stability and regularity. If a state is not dependent on another then there is no way for them to be mutually affected by one another. This is one of the driving forces behind global connections and trade; without either globalization would not have emerged the way it did and states would still be dependent on their own production and resources to function. This is one of the arguments surrounding the idea of early globalization. It is argued that archaic globalization did not function in a similar manner to modern globalization because states were not as interdependent on others as they are today.

Emergence of a World System

Historians argue that a world system was in order before the rise of capitalism between the sixteenth and nineteenth centuries. This is referred to as the early age of capitalism where long-distance trade, market exchange and capital accumulation existed amongst states. In 800 AD Greek, Roman and Muslim empires emerged covering areas known today as China and the Middle East. Major religions such as Christianity, Islam and Buddhism spread to distant lands where many are still intact today. One of the most popular examples of distant trade routes can be seen with the silk route between China and the Mediterranean, movement and trade with art and luxury goods between Arab regions, South Asia and Africa. These relationships through trade mainly formed in the east and eventually led to the development of capitalism. It was at this time that power and land shifted from the nobility and church to the bourgeoisie and division of labor in production emerged. During the later part of the twelfth century and the beginning of the thirteenth century an international trade system was developed between states ranging from northwestern Europe to China.

During the 1500s other Asian empires emerged, which included trading over longer distances than before. During the early exchanges between states, Europe had little to offer with the exception of slaves, metals, wood and furs. The push for selling of items in the east drove European production and helped integrate them into the exchange. The European expansion and growth of opportunities for trade made possible by the Crusades increased the renaissance of agriculture, mining, and manufacturing. Rapid urbanization throughout Europe allowed a connection from the North Sea to Venice. Advances in industrialization coupled with the rouse of population growth and the growing demands of the eastern trade, led to the growth of true trading emporia with outlets to the sea.

There is a 'multi-polar' nature to archaic globalization, which involved the active participation of non-Europeans. Because it predated the Great Divergence of the nineteenth century, in which Western Europe pulled ahead of the rest of the world in terms of industrial production and economic output, archaic globalization was a phenomenon that was driven not only by Europe but also by other economically developed Old World centers such as Gujarat, Bengal, coastal China and Japan.

These pre-capitalist movements were regional rather than global and for the most part temporary. This idea of early globalization was proposed by the historian A.G. Hopkins in 2001. Hopkins main points on archaic globalization can be seen with trade, and diaspora that developed from this, as well as religious ideas and empires that spread throughout the region. This new interaction amongst states led to interconnections between parts of the world which led to the eventual interdependency amongst these state actors. The main actors that partook in the spreading of goods and ideas were kings, warriors, priests and traders. Hopkins also addresses that during this time period mini-globalizations were prominent and that some collapsed or became more insular. These mini-globalizations are referred to as episodic and ruptured, with empires sometimes overreaching and having to retract. These mini-globalizations left remnants that allowed the West to adopt these new ideals, leading to the idea of Western Capitalism. The adopted ideals can be seen in the Western monetary system and are central to systems like capitalism that define modernity and modern globalization.

The Three Principles of Archaic Globalization

Archaic globalization consists of three principles: universalizing kingship, expansion of religious movements, and medicinal understanding.

- The universalizing of kingship led soldiers and monarchs far distances to find honor and prestige. However, the crossing over foreign lands also gave the traveling men opportunity to exchange prized goods. This expanded trade between distant lands, which consequently increased the amount of social and economic relations.

- Despite the vast distances covered by monarchs and their companies, pilgrimages remain one of the greatest global movements of people.

- Finally, the desire for better health was the remaining push behind archaic globalization. While the trading of spices, precious stones, animals, and weapons remained of major importance, people began to seek medicine from faraway lands. This implemented more trade routes, especially to China for their tea.

Economic Exchange

With the increase in trade and state linkage, economic exchange extended through-out the region and caused actors to form new relationships. This early economic development can be seen in Champagne Fairs, which were outdoor markets where traveling merchants came to sell their products and make purchases. Traditionally, market fairs used barter as opposed to money, once larger itinerant merchants began to frequent them, the need for currency became greater and a money changer needed to be established. Some historical scholars argue that this was the beginning of the role of banker and the institution of credit. An example can be seen with one individual in need of an item the urban merchant does not ordinarily stock. The product seeker orders the item, which the merchant promises to bring him next time. The product seeker either gives credit to the merchant by paying them in ad-vance, gets credit from the merchant by promising to pay them once the item is in stock, or some type of concession is made through a down payment. If the product seeker does not have the amount required by the merchant he may borrow from the capital stored by the money changer or he may mortgage part of his expected har-vest, either from the money charger or the merchant he is seeking goods from. This lengthy transaction eventually resulted in a complex economic system and once the weekly market began to expand from barter to the monetized system required by long-distance trading.

A higher circuit of trade developed once urban traders from outside city limits trav-elled from distant directions to the market center in the quest to buy or sell goods. Merchants would then begin to meet at the same spot on a weekly basis allowing for them to arrange with other merchants to bring special items for exchange that were not demanded by the local agriculturalists but for markets in their home towns. When the local individuals placed advanced orders, customers from towns of different traders may begin to place order for items in a distant town that their trader can order from their counterpart. This central meeting point, becomes the focus of long-distance trade and how it began to increase.

Expansion of Long Distance Trade

In order for trade to be able to expand during this early time period, it required some basic functions of the market as well as the merchants. The first was security. Goods that were being transported began to have more value and the merchants needed to protect their coveted goods especially since they were often traveling through poor ar-eas where the risk of theft was high. To overcome this problem merchants began to travel in caravans as a way to ensure their personal safety as well as the safety of their goods. The second prerequisite to early long distant trade had to be an agreement on a rate of exchange. Since many of the merchants came from distant lands with different monetary systems a system had to be put into place as a way to enforce repayment of previous goods, repay previous debt and to ensure contracts were upheld. Expansion was also able to thrive so long as it had a motive for exchange as a way to promote trade amongst foreign lands. Also, outside merchants access to trading sites was a critical factor in trade route growth.

The Spread of Goods and Ideas

The most popular goods produced were spices, which were traded over short distances, while manufactured goods were central to the system and could not have been aided without them. The invention of money in the form of gold coins in Europe and Middle East and paper money in China around the thirteenth century allowed trade to move more easily between the different actors. The main actors involved in this system viewed gold, silver, and copper as valuable on different levels. Nevertheless, goods were transferred, prices set, exchange rates agreed upon, contracts entered into, credit extended, partnerships formed and agreements that were made were kept on record and honored. During this time of globalization, credit was also used as a means for trading. The use of credit began in the form of blood ties but later led to the emergence the "banker" as a profession.

With the spread of people came new ideas, religion and goods throughout the land, which had never been apparent in most societies before the movement. Also, this globalization lessened the degree of feudal life by transitioning from self-sufficient society to a money economy. Most of the trade connecting North Africa and Europe was controlled by the Middle East, China and India around 1400. Because of the danger and great cost of long-distance travel in the pre-modern period, archaic globalization grew out of the trade in high-value commodities which took up a small amount of space. Most of the goods that were produced and traded were considered a luxury and many considered those with these coveted items to have a higher place on the societal scale.

Examples of such luxury goods would include Chinese silks, exotic herbs, coffee, cotton, iron, Indian calicoes, Arabian horses, gems and spices or drugs such as nutmeg, cloves, pepper, ambergris and opium. The thirteenth century as well as present day favor luxury items due to the fact that small high-value goods can have high transport costs but still have a high value attached to them, whereas low-value heavy goods are not worth carrying very far. Purchases of luxury items such as these are described as archaic consumption since trade was largely popular for these items as opposed to everyday needs. The distinction between food, drugs and materia medica is often quite blurred in regards to these substances, which were valued not only for their rarity but because they appealed to humoral theories of health and the body that were prevalent throughout premodern Eurasia.

Major Trade Routes

During the time of archaic globalization there were three major trade routes which connected Europe, China and the Middle East. The northern most route went through mostly the Mongol Empire and was nearly 5000 miles long. Even though the route consisted of mostly vast stretches of desert with little to no resources, merchants still traveled it. The route was still traveled because during the 13th century Kubilai Khan united the Mongol Empire and charged only a small protective rent to travelers. Before the unification, merchants from the Middle East used the path but were stopped and taxed at nearly every village. The middle route went from the coast of Syria to Baghdad from there the traveler could follow the land route through Persia to India, or sail to India via the Persian Gulf. Between the 8th and 10th centuries, Baghdad was a world city but in the 11th century it began to decline due to natural disasters including floods, earthquakes, and fires. In 1258, Baghdad was taken over by the Mongols. The Mongols forced high taxes on the citizens of Baghdad which led to a decrease in production, causing merchants to bypass the city The third, southern most route, went though Mamluk controlled Egypt, After the fall of Baghdad, Cairo became the Islamic capital.

Some major cities along these trading routes were wealthy and provided services for merchants and the international markets. Palmyra and Petra which are located on the fringes of the Syrian Desert, flourished mainly as power centers of trading. They would police the trade routes and be the source of supplies for the merchants caravans. They also became places where people of different ethnic and cultural backgrounds could meet and interact. These trading routes were the communication highways for the ancient civilizations and their societies. New inventions, religious beliefs, artistic styles, languages, and social customs, as well as goods and raw materials, were transmitted by people moving from one place to another to conduct business.

Proto-globalization

Proto-globalization is the period following archaic globalization which occurred from the 17th through the 19th centuries. The global routes established within the period of archaic globalization gave way to more distinguished expanding routes and more complex systems of trade within the period of proto-globalization. Familiar trading arrangements such as the East India Company appeared within this period, making larger-scale exchanges possible. Slave trading was especially extensive and the associated mass-production of commodities on plantations is characteristic of this time.

As a result of a measurable amount of polyethnic regions due to these higher frequency trade routes, war became prominent. Such wars include the French and Indian War, American Revolutionary War. and the Anglo-Dutch War between England and the Dutch Republic.

Modern Globalization

The modern form of globalization began to take form during the 19th century. The evolving beginnings of this period were largely responsible for the expansion of the

West, capitalism and imperialism backed up by the nation-state and industrial technology. This began to emerge during the 1500s, continuing to expand exponentially over time as industrialization developed in the 18th century. The conquests of the British Empire and the Opium Wars added to the industrialization and formation of the growing global society because it created vast consumer regions.

World War I is when the first phase of modern globalization began to take force. It is said by VM Yeates that the economic forces of globalization were part of the cause of the war. Since World War I, globalization has expanded greatly. The evolving improvements of multinational corporations, technology, science, and mass media have all been results of extensive worldwide exchanges. In addition, institutions such as the World Bank, the World Trade Organization and many international telecommunication companies have also shaped modern globalization. The World Wide Web has also played a large role in modern globalization. The Internet provides connectivity across national and international borders, aiding in the enlargement of a global network.

Proto-globalization

Proto-globalization or early modern globalization is a period of the history of globalization roughly spanning the years between 1600 and 1800, following the period of archaic globalization. First introduced by historians A. G. Hopkins and Christopher Bayly, the term describes the phase of increasing trade links and cultural exchange that characterized the period immediately preceding the advent of so-called "modern globalization" in the 19th century.

Proto-globalization distinguished itself from modern globalization on the basis of expansionism, the method of managing global trade, and the level of information exchange. The period of proto-globalization is marked by such trade arrangements as the East India Company, the shift of hegemony to Western Europe, the rise of larger-scale conflicts between powerful nations such as the Thirty Year War, and a rise of new commodities—most particularly slave trade. The Triangular Trade made it possible for Europe to take advantage of resources within the western hemisphere. The transfer of plant and animal crops and epidemic diseases associated with Alfred Crosby's concept of The Columbian Exchange also played a central role in this process. Proto-globalization trade and communications involved a vast group including European, Muslim, Indian, Southeast Asian and Chinese merchants, particularly in the Indian Ocean region.

The transition from proto-globalization to modern globalization was marked with a more complex global network based on both capitalistic and technological exchange; however, it led to a significant collapse in cultural exchange.

Description

Although the 17th and 18th centuries saw a rise in Western Imperialism in the world system, the period of Proto-globalization involved increased interaction between

Western Europe and the systems that had formed between nations in East Asia and the Middle East. Proto-globalization was a period of reconciling the governments and traditional systems of individual nations, world regions, and religions with the "new world order" of global trade, imperialism and political alliances, what historian A.G. Hopkins called "the product of the contemporary world and the product of distant past."

Courtyard of the Amsterdam Stock Exchange, c. 1670

According to Hopkins, "globalization remains an incomplete process: it promotes fragmentation as well as uniformity; it may recede as well as advance; its geographical scope may exhibit a strong regional bias; its future direction and speed cannot be predicted with confidence—and certainly not by presuming that it has an 'inner logic' of its own. Before proto-globalization, globalizing networks were the product of "great kings and warriors searching for wealth and honor in fabulous lands, by religious wanderers, ... and by merchant princes". Proto-globalization held on to and matured many aspects of archaic globalization such as the importance of cities, migrants, and specialization of labor.

Proto-globalization was also marked by two main political and economic developments: "the reconfiguration of the state systems, and the growth of finance, services, and pre-industrial manufacturing". A number of states at the time began to "strengthen their connections between territory, taxation, and sovereignty" despite their continuing monopoly of loyalties from their citizens. The process of globalization during this time was heavily focused on material world and the labor needed for its production. The proto-globalization period was a time of "improved efficiency in the transactions sector" with the generation of goods such as sugar, tobacco, tea, coffee, and opium unlike anything the archaic globalization possessed. The improvement of economic management also spread to the expansion of transportation which created a complex set of connection between the West and East. The expansion of trade routes led to the "green revolution" based on the plantation system and slave exportation from Africa.

Precursors

During the pre-modern era early forms of globalization were already beginning to affect a world system, marking a period that historian A. G. Hopkins has called archaic globalization. The world system leading up to proto-globalization was one that hinged on one or more hegemonic powers assimilating neighboring cultures into their political system, waging war on other nations, and dominating world trade.

Representation of a sitting of the Roman Senate

A major hegemony in archaic globalization was the Roman Empire, which united the Greater Mediterranean Area and Western Europe through a long-running series of military and political campaigns expanding the Roman system of government and Roman values to more underdeveloped areas. Conquered areas became provinces of the empire and Roman military outposts in the provinces became cities with structures designed by the best Roman architects, which hastened the spread of Rome's "modern" way of life while absorbing the traditions and beliefs of these native cultures. Nationalist ideology as well as propaganda supporting the Roman Army and military success, bravery, and valor also strengthened the Roman Empire's spread across Western Europe and the Mediterranean Area. The Roman Empire's well-built aqueducts and cities and sturdy, effective naval fleets, ships and an organized system of paved roads also facilitated fast, easy travel and better networking and trade with neighboring nations and the provinces.

During the Han dynasty under Han Wudi (141–87 BCE), the Chinese government united and became powerful enough that China began to successfully indulge in imperialistic endeavors with its neighboring nations in East Asia. Han China's imperialism was a peaceful tributary system, which focused mainly on diplomatic and trade relations. The growth of the Han Empire facilitated trade and cultural exchange with virtually all of the known world as reached from Asia, and Chinese silks spread through Asia and Inner Asia and even to Rome. The early T'ang dynasty saw China as even more responsive to foreign influence and the T'ang dynasty becoming a great empire. Overseas trade with India and the Middle East grew rapidly, and China's East and Southern Coasts, once distant and unimportant regions, gradually became chief areas of foreign trade. During the Song Dynasty China's navy became more powerful thanks to technological improvements in shipbuilding and navigation, and China's maritime commerce also increased exponentially.

China's power began to decline in the 16th century when the rulers of the subsequent Ming Dynastyneglected the importance of China's trade from sea power. The Ming rulers let China's naval dominance and its grip on the Spice trade slacken, and the European powers stepped in. Portugal, with its technological advances in naval architecture, weaponry, seamanship and navigation, took over the Spice Trade and subdued China's navy. With this, European Imperialism and the age of European Hegemony was beginning, although China still retained power of many of its areas of trade.

Changes in Trade Systems

Batavia, capital of Dutch East Indies, c. 1661

One of the most significant differences between proto-globalization and archaic globalization was the switch from inter-nation trading of rarities to the trading of commodities. During the 12th and 13th centuries it was common to trade items that were foreign and rare to different cultures. A popular trade during archaic globalization involved European merchants sailing to areas of India or China in order to purchase luxury items such as porcelain, silk and spices. Traders of the pre-modern period also traded drugs and certain foods such as sugar cane and other crops. While these items were not rarities as such, the drugs and food traded were valued for the health and function of the human body. It was more common during proto-globalization to trade various commodities such as cotton, rice and tobacco. The shift into proto-globalization trade signified the "emergence of the modern international order" and the development of early capitalist expansion which began in the Atlantic during the 17th century and spread throughout the world by 1830.

Atlantic Slave Trade

One of the main reasons for the rise of commodities was the rise in the slave trade, specifically the Atlantic slave trade.

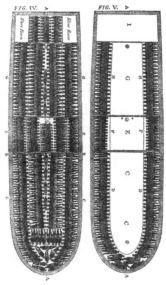

Diagram of a slave ship from the Atlantic slave trade. From an Abstract of Evidence delivered before a select committee of the House of Commons in 1790 and 1791.

The use of slaves prior to the 15th century was only a minor practice in the labor force and was not crucial in the development of products and goods; but, due to labor shortage, the use of slaves rose. After 1500, the settlement of island despots and plantation centers in Sao Tome began trade relations with the Kingdom of the Kongo, which brought West Central Africa into the Atlantic Slave Trade. The Portuguese maintained an export of slaves from Agadir, an Atlantic port, which they maintained for most of the early 16th century. Also the Portuguese settlement of the Brazilian subcontinent allowed the opening of the American slave market and slaves were shipped from Sao Tome directly to America. The Europeans also took use of the Atlantic Slave Trade in the first half of the century. The European slave ships took their slaves to the Iberian Peninsula, however slave owners in Europe were only seen in wealthy, aristocrat families due to the high costs of slaves and the cheap peasant labor available for agricultural uses, and as its name implies the first use of the African-American slaves in plantation work arose in the Atlantic islands not in the continental Europe. Approximately 10.2 million Africans survived the Atlantic crossing between 1450 and 1870. The large slave population thrived due to the demand for production from the Europeans who found it cheaper to import crops and goods rather than produce them on their own.

Many wars were fought during the 17th century between the slave trading companies for areas that were economically dependent on slaves. The West India Company gained many slaves through these wars (specifically with Portugal) by captains who had captured enemy ships; between 1623 and 1637, 2,336 were captured and sold in the New World by the West India Company. The selling of slaves to the New World opened up trading posts in North America; the Dutch opened their first on Manhattan Island in 1613. The West India Company had also opened a trading post in the Caribbean and the company was also carrying slaves to a colony of New Netherland. The use of slaves had many benefits to the economies and productions in the areas of trade. The emergent rise of coffee, tea, and chocolate in Europe led to the demand for the production of sugar; 70 percent of slaves were used solely for the labor-intensive production of crop. Slave trade was also beneficial to the trade voyages, because the constant sailing allowed investors to buy small shares of many ships at the same time. Hopkin states that many scholars, him among them, argue that slave trade was essential to the wealth of many nations, during and after proto-globalization, and without the trade production would have plummeted. The investment in ships and nautical technology was the catalyst to the complex trade networks developed throughout proto-globalization and into modern globalization.

Plantation Economy

Slaves processing tobacco in 17th-century Virginia

Consequently, the rise of slavery was due to the increasing rise of crops being produced and traded, more specifically the rise of the plantation economy The rise of the plantations was the main reason for the trade of commodities during proto-globalization. Plantations were used by the exporting countries (mainly America) to grow the raw materials needed to manufacture the goods which were traded back into the plantation economy. Commodities that grew in trade due to the plantation economy were mainly tobacco, cotton, sugar cane, and rubber.

Tobacco

During the second half of the 16th century, Europeans' interest in the New World revolved around gold and silver and not tobacco. The European lack of interest in tobacco was due to the fact that the Amerindians controlled the tobacco industry; as long as the Amerindians controlled the supply there was no need for the incorporation in European commercial capitalism.

The trading of tobacco was a new commodity and was in high popular demand in the 17th century due to the rise of the plantations. Tobacco began to be used a monetary standard, which is why the term "cash crop" was originated. The first export of tobacco from the then-colonies of the United States (specifically Virginia) to London showed fortunes in the English enterprise and by 1627, the Virginia tobacco was being shipped to London at 500,000 pounds a shipment. By 1637, tobacco had become the colony's currency and by 1639 Maryland was exporting 100,000 pounds of tobacco to London. English success with the production of tobacco caught the attention of many Europeans, specifically those colonized on Martinique and Guadeloupe, French islands. These islands soon became wealthy due to the tobacco production and by 1671 roughly one-third of the acreage devoted to the cash crops grown for the islands were for tobacco. While the cultivation of tobacco thrived, production saw severe depressions in later years due to the profits made from sugar. According to an account of the Barbadian exports 82 percent of the island's export value was due to sugar and less than one percent was accounted for by tobacco.

Nicotiana Tabacum

Sugar Cane

Another commodity that was a prominent source of trade was the production of sugar from the crop sugar cane. The original habitat of sugar was in India, where it was taken and planted in various islands. Once reaching to the people of the Iberian Peninsula, it was further migrated across the Atlantic Ocean. In the 16th century, the first plantations of sugar were started in the New World, marking the last great stage of migration of the cane to the West. Because of the conflict of transporting sugar in its raw form, sugar was not associated with commerce until the act of refining it came into play; this act became the center for industry. Venice was the center for refining during the Middle Ages, therefore making them the chief traders of sugar. Although, the Spanish and

Portuguese held the monopolies of the sugar cane fields in America, they were being supplied by Venice. In the 17th century, England dominated Venice and became the center for refining and cultivating sugar; this leadership was maintained until the rise of French industry. Sugar throughout the 17th century was still considered a luxury until the latter half of the 17th century when the sugar was being produced in mass quantities making it available to the mass of the English people. This turn of events made the sugar a commodity, because the crop was not being used in only special occasion, but in all daily meals.

Hostilities, War, and Imperialism

Map of colonial empires throughout the world in 1754

Proto-globalization differed from modern globalization in the practices of expansionism, methods of managing global trade, finances, as well as commercial innovation. With the shift of expansionism by large nations to Western Europe, nations began competing in an effort to achieve world domination. The rise of larger-scale conflicts between these powerful nations over expanding their wealth led to nations taking control over one another's territory and then moving products and the accumulated wealth of these conquered regions back to the sovereign country. Although conflicts occurred throughout the world between 1600 and 1800, European powers found themselves far more equipped to handle the pressures of war. A quote by Christopher Alan Bayly gives a better interpretation of these advantages by stating, "Europeans became much better at killing people. The European ideological wars of the 17th century had created links between war, finance, and commercial innovation which extended all these gains. It gave the Continent a brute advantage in world conflicts which broke out in the 18th century. Western European warfare was peculiarly complicated and expensive, partly because it was amphibious." These battle-tested nations fought for their own needs, but in reality their success increased European advancement in the global market. Whether a war was religious or commercial, its impact was greatly felt throughout the world. British victories during the Anglo-Dutch Wars led to their dominance in commercial shipping and naval power. The stage was set for future conflicts between Britain and foreign nations, as well as domestic frustration with "the motherland" on the North American continent. The French and Indian War, fought between the European powers of France and England, led to a British victory and resulted in continued dominance in maritime enterprise. The American Revolutionary War marked the beginning of the power shift for control over foreign markets.

English Civil War

The English Civil War was a battle over not only religious and political beliefs, but also economic and social as well. This war was between Parliamentarians and Royalists and took place from 1642 to 1651, but was broken into several separate engagements. Charles I and his supporters experienced the first two periods of the war, which resulted in King Charles I dissolving Parliament, which would not be called into session again for over ten years. Reasons for this dismissal were because supporters of Long Parliament tried to install two resolutions into English law. One called for consequences against individuals that taxed without the consent of Parliament and labeled them as enemies of England, while the other stated that innovations in religion would result in the same tag. Each of these policies was aimed at Charles I, in that he was inferior leader as well as a supporter of Catholicism. This prompted the Puritan Revolt and eventually led to the trial and execution of Charles I for treason. The final stage of the English Civil War came in 1649, and lasted until 1651. This time, King Charles II, the son of Charles I led supporters against Parliament. The Battle of Worcester, which took place in 1651, marked the end of the English Civil War. Charles II and other royalist forces were defeated by Parliamentarians and their leader Oliver Cromwell. This war began to take England in different directions regarding religious and political beliefs as well as economic and social. Also, the war constitutionally established that no British monarch was permitted to rule without first having been approved by Parliament.

Anglo-Dutch War

The Battle of Scheveningen, 10 August 1653 by Jan Abrahamsz Beerstraaten, painted c. 1654
shows the view of the battle from the Dutch shore where thousands gathered to watch.

The Anglo-Dutch War was a naval conflict between England and the Dutch Republic from 1652 to 1654 and was over the competition in commercial maritime and was focused mainly in the East Indies. The first Navigation Act, which forbade the import of goods unless they were transported either in English vessels or by vessels from the country of origin. This was a policy aimed against the Dutch, and fighting broke out on May 19, 1652 with a small skirmish between Dutch and English fleets. The War officially began in July and fighting continued for two years. The Battle of Scheveningen which is also referred to as Texel was the end of serious fighting in the war and took place in July 1653. The Treaty of Westminster was signed in April 1654 ending the war and obligated the Dutch Republic to respect the Navigation Act as well as compensate England for the war.

French and Indian War

Conference between the French and Indian leaders around a ceremonial fire by Émile Louis Vernier

The French and Indian War was between the nations of Great Britain and France, along with the numerous Native American Nations allied with both. The French and Indian war was the North American theater of the Seven Years' War being fought in Europe at the time. Growing population in British territory throughout North America forced expansion west; however, this was met with resistance from the French and their Native American allies. French forces began entering British territory, building numerous forts in preparation to defend the newly acquired land. The beginning of the war favored the French and their Native American allies, who were able to defeat British forces time and again, and it was not until 1756 that the British were able to hold off their opposition. Pittsburgh was a center for fighting during the French and Indian War, namely because of the geographical location at the center where three rivers unite: the Allegheny, the Monongahela and the Ohio. The location of present-day Pittsburgh provided an advantage in naval control. Ownership of this point provided not only naval dominance, but it also expanded economic ventures, enabling shipments to be sent and received with relative ease. French and British forces both claimed ownership to this region; the French installing Fort Duquesne and the British with Fort Pitt. Fort Pitt was established in 1758 after French forces abandoned and destroyed Fort Duquesne. The French and Indian War came to an end in 1763, after British forces were able to secure Quebec and Montreal from the French and on February 10, the Treaty of Paris was signed. The French were forced to surrender their territory in North America, giving England control all the way to the Mississippi River. The effects of this war were heavily felt in the North American British colonies. England imposed many taxes on colonists in order to control the newly acquired territory. These tensions would soon culminate into a war for independence as well as a shift in power for dominance in the economic world.

American Revolutionary War

Emanuel Leutze's stylized depiction of *Washington Crossing the Delaware* (1851).

The American Revolutionary War was a war between the nation of England and the 13 colonies in the North American continent. This war lasted from 1775 to 1783 and began with the Battle of Bunker Hill, where over 1,150 British soldiers were killed or wounded. This equated to almost half of the entire British army that were present at the engagement. American casualties were far less severe, totaling an estimated at 450 killed and wounded. The British, however, were able to take the ground and push the newly formed Continental Army back to the city of Boston, which also soon fell to British forces. Before the Battle of Bunker Hill, the Battles of Lexington and Concord in April, 1775, saw British troops begin their assault into the American colonies. British troops were searching for colonist supply depots, however, were met by heavy resistance and the British forces were turned around at Concord by outnumbering Minutemen forces. On July 4, 1776 the Declaration of Independence was signed by the Second Continental Congress and officially declared the colonies of North America to be a sovereign nation, free from England's rule. Also, the Congress permitted funding for a Continental Army, which is the first instance of an American political body handling military affairs. The British were dominating in the beginning of the war, holding off Continental regulars and militia and gaining vast amounts of territory throughout North America. However, the tide began to turn for the colonists in 1777 with their first major victory over British forces at the Battle of Saratoga. Victory for the rest of the war pushed back and forth between the British and colonists, but the alliance with France in 1778 by the American colonists leveled the playing field and aided in the final push for the defeat of the British Army and Navy. In 1781, American and French forces were able to trap the escaping southern British Army at Yorktown, thus ending the major fighting of the Revolution. The Treaty of Paris was signed in 1783, and recognized the American colonies as an independent nation. The newly formed United States would undergo numerous transitions to becoming one of the top economic and military powers in the world.

Treaties and Agreements

The expanded East India House, Leadenhall Street, London, as rebuilt 1799–1800, Richard Jupp, architect (as seen c. 1817; demolished in 1929).

Much of the trading during the proto-globalization time period was regulated by Europe. Globalization from an economic standpoint relied on the East India Company. The East India Company was a number of enterprises formed in western Europe in the 17th and 18th centuries, initially created to further trade in the East Indies. The company controlled trading from India to East and Southeast Asia.

One of the key contributors to globalization was the *Triangular Trade* and how it connected the world. The Triangular Trade or Triangle Trade was a system used to connect three areas of the world through trade. Once traded, items and goods were shipped to other parts of the world, making the triangle trade a key to global trade. The Triangle Trade system was run by Europeans, increasing their global power.

Europeans would sail to the West African coast and trade African kings manufactured goods (rifles and ammunition) for slave. From there slaves would be sent to the West Indies or the east coast of North America to be used for labor. Goods such as cotton, molasses, sugar, tobacco would be sent from these places back to Europe. Europe would also use their goods and trade with Asian countries for tea, cloth and spices. The triangle trade in a sense was an agreement for established trade routes, that led to greater global integration, which ultimately contributed to globalization.

Along with the control Europe gained, as far as global trade, came several treaties and laws. In 1773, the Regulating Act was passed, regulating affairs of the company in India and London. In 1748, the Treaty of Aix-la-Chapelle ended the War of the Austrian Succession, but failed to settle the commercial struggle between England and France in the West Indies, Africa and India. The treaty was an attempt at regulating trade and market expansion between the two regions, but was ultimately unsuccessful.

Globalization at this time was hindered by war, diseases and population growth in certain areas. The Corn Laws were established to regulate imports and exports of grains in England, thus restricting trade and the expansion of globalization. The Corn Crop Laws hindered the market economy and globalization based on tariffs and import restrictions. Eventually, the Ricardian theory of economics became prominent and allowed for improved trade regulations, specifically with Portugal.

Transition Into Modern Globalization

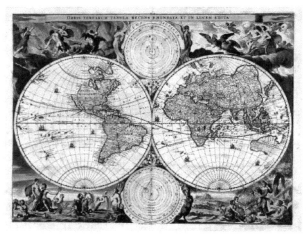

A 1657 world map. Several regions of the globe, notably western
North America and Australia, remain mostly blank.

According to Sebastian Conrad, proto-globalization is marked with a "rise of national chauvinism, racism, Social Darwinism, and genocidal thinking" which came to be with relations to the "establishment of a world economy". Beginning in the 1870s, the global trade cycle started to cement itself so that more nations' economies depended on one another than in any previous era. Domino effects in this new world trade cycle lead to both worldwide recessions and world economic booms. Modelski describes the late period of proto-globalization as a "thick range of global networks extending throughout the world at high speed and covering all components of society". By the 1750s, Europe, Africa, Asia, and America's contact had grown into a stable multilateral interdependency which was echoed in the modern globalization period.

Shift in Capital

Although the North Atlantic World dominated the global system before proto-globalization, a more "multipolar global economy" started taking form around the early 19th century, and capital was becoming highly mobile. By the end of the 19th century, British capital wealth was 17% overseas, and the level of capital invested overseas nearly doubled by 1913 to 33%. Germany invested one-fifth of their total domestic savings in 1880, and, like Britain, increased their wealth tremendously in the early 20th century. The net foreign investment of total domestic savings abroad was 35% in 1860, 47% in 1880, and 53% in the years prior to the Great War. Global investments were taking a steady rise throughout societies, and those able to invest thrust more and more of their domestic savings into international investments.

The ability to mobilize capital was due to the development of the Industrial Revolution and the beginnings of mechanical production (most prominent in Great Britain). During proto-globalization, "merchant capitalists in many societies quickly became aware of potential markets and new producers and began to link them together in new patterns of world trade. The expansion of the slave production and the exploitation of the Americas put Europeans on the top of the economic network. During the modern globalization period, mass production allowed the development of a stronger, more complex global network of trade. Another element of European success between 1750 and 1850 was the limitation and "relative 'failure'" of the Afro-Asian Industrial Revolution. The movement into modern globalization was marked with the economic drain of capital into Europe.

Shift in Culture

Like capital, the end of proto-globalization was filled with mobility of individuals. The time of proto-globalization was one filled with "mutual influence, hybridization, and cross-cultural entanglement". Many historians blame this web of national entanglements and agreements as the cause for the intensity and vast involvement during World War I. Between 1750-1880, the expansion of worldwide integration was influenced by the new capacities in production, transportation, and communication. The end of proto-globalization also marked the final phase of "great domestication". After the 1650s, the process of regular and intensive agrarian exploitation was complete. Human population began to increase almost exponentially with the end of the great pandemics. At the end of the proto-globalization and the cusp of modern globalization, population began to "recover in Central and South America," where at the beginning of proto-globalization, European-imported illnesses had savagely decreased indigenous populations. The importation of nutritious varieties from Central and South America created a more fertile and resilient population to forge ahead into modern globalization. The greater population pushed individuals in high populated areas to "spill into less populous forested and grazing lands, and bring them under cultivation". This development lead to an influx in produce production and exported trade.

Another development that lead to the shift to modern globalization was the development of a more politicized system. Proto-globalization period marked a steady expansion of larger states from the Indonesian islands to northern Scandinava. The settlement of these individuals made it easier for governments to tax, develop an army, labor force, and create a sustainable economy. The development and streamlining of these cultural aspects lead to an increase in peripheral players in the game of globalization. The stable legal institutions developed in the late proto-globalization and early modern globalization period established economic advances, intellectual property rights (more predominantly in England), general geographical stability, and generational societal improvement.

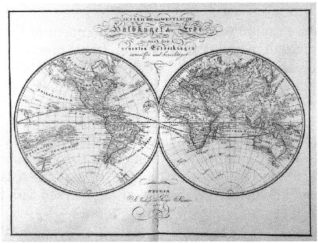

An 1817 Perspective of the world consistent with the view point of
Modern Globalization. Notice the amount of details.

The shift in exchange of technological advancements was another reason for modern globalization. In the early 19th century, European civilizations traveled the world to accumulate an "impressive knowledge about languages, religions, customs, and political orders of other countries. By the end of the 19th century, Europe was no longer receiving any significant technological innovations from Asia.

Shift in Global Networks

The developed global networks lead to the creation of new networks leading to new production. By 1880, there was a renewed thrust of European colonial expansion. The shift to modern globalization was slow, overlapping and interacting. Mid-19th century, noncompeting goods were exchanged between continents and markets for widely used commodities developed. Also, labor was becoming globally integrated. Modern globalization came to be as the movement of general expansion of socio-economic networks became more elaborate. An example of this is the development and establishment of free masonry. The "existing trading networks grew, capital and commodity flows intensified. The permanence of long-term interdependencies was unchanged. By the beginning of the modern globalization period, the European colonial expansion retreats into itself. National societies began to regret the economic integration and attempted to limit the effects. Bayly, Hopkins and others stress that proto-globalization's transformation into modern globalization was a complex process that took place at different times in different regions,and involved the hold-over of older notions of value and rarity which had their origins in the pre-modern period. Thus leading to the age of economic deglobalization and world wars which ended after 1945.

Democratic Globalization

Democratic globalisation is a social movement towards an institutional system of global democracy. This would, in their view, bypass nation-states, corporate oligopolies, ideological NGOs, cults and mafias. One of its most prolific proponents is the British political thinker David Held. In the last decade he published a dozen books regarding the spread of democracy from territorially defined nation states to a system of global governance that encapsulates the entire world. For some, democratic mundialisation is a variant of democratic globalisation stressing the need for the direct election of world leaders and members of global institutions by citizens worldwide; for others, it is just another name for democratic globalisation.

These proponents state that democratic globalisation's purpose is to:

- Expand globalisation and make people closer and more united. This expansion should differ from economic globalization and "make people closer, more united and protected"; because of a variety of opinions and proposals it is still unclear what this would mean in practice and how it could be realized.

- Have it reach all fields of activity and knowledge, including governmental and economic, since the economic one is crucial to develop the well-being of world citizens; and

- Give world citizens democratic access and a say in those global activities. For example, presidential voting for United Nations Secretary-General by citizens and direct election of members of a United Nations Parliamentary Assembly.

Supporters of the democratic globalization movement draw a distinction between their movement and the one most popularly known as the 'anti-globalization' movement, claiming that their movement avoids ideological agenda about economics and social matters. Democratic globalization supporters state that the choice of political orientations should be left to the world citizens, via their participation in world democratic institutions. Some proponents in the "anti-globalization movement" do not necessarily disagree with this position. For example, George Monbiot, normally associated with the anti-globalization movement (who prefers the term Global Justice Movement) in his work *Age of Consent* has proposed similar democratic reforms of most major global institutions, suggesting direct democratic elections of such bodies, and suggests a form of "world government."

Background

Democratic globalization supports the extension of political democratization to economic and financial globalization. It is based upon an idea that free international transactions benefit the global society as a whole. They believe in financially open economies, where the government and central bank must be transparent in order to retain the confidence of the markets, since transparency spells doom for autocratic regimes. They promote democracy that makes leaders more accountable to the citizenry through the removal of restrictions on such transactions.

Social Movements

The democratic globalization movement started to get public attention when New York Times reported its demonstration to contest a World Trade Organization (WTO) in Seattle, Washington, November 1999. This gathering was to criticize unfair trade and undemocratic globalization of the WTO, World Bank, World Economic Forum (WEF), the International Monetary Fund. Its primary tactics were public rallies, street theater and civil disobedience.

Democratic globalization, proponents claim, would be reached by creating democratic global institutions and changing international organizations (which are currently intergovernmental institutions controlled by the nation-states), into global ones controlled by world citizens. The movement suggests to do it gradually by building a limited number of democratic global institutions in charge of a few crucial fields of common interest. Its long-term goal is that these institutions federate later into a full-fledged democratic world government.

Global Democracy

Thus, it supports the International Campaign for the Establishment of a United Nations Parliamentary Assembly, that would allow for participation of member nations' legislators and, eventually, direct election of United Nations (UN) parliament members by citizens worldwide.

Difference to Anti-globalization

Some supporters of the democratic globalization movement draw a distinction between their movement and the one most popularly known as the 'anti-globalization' movement, claiming that their movement avoids ideological agenda about economics and social matters although, in practice, it is often difficult to distinguish between the two camps. Democratic globalization supporters state that the choice of political orientations should be left to the world citizens, via their participation in world democratic institutions and direct vote for world presidents.

Some supporters of the "anti-globalization movement" do not necessarily disagree with this position. For example, George Monbiot, normally associated with the anti-globalization movement (who prefers the term Global Justice Movement) in his work *Age of Consent* has proposed similar democratic reforms of most major global institutions, suggesting direct democratic elections of such bodies by citizens, and suggests a form of "federal world government".

Procedure

Democratic globalization, proponents claim, would be reached by creating democratic global institutions and changing international organizations (which are currently inter-governmental institutions controlled by the nation-states), into global ones controlled by voting by the citizens. The movement suggests to do it gradually by building a limited number of democratic global institutions in charge of a few crucial fields of common interest. Its long-term goal is that these institutions federate later into a full-fledged democratic world government.

They propose the creation of world services for citizens, like world civil protection and prevention (from natural hazards) services.

Proponents

The concept of democratic globalization has supporters from all fields. Many of the campaigns and initiatives for global democracy, such as the UNPA campaign, list quotes by and names of their supporters on their websites.

Academics

Some of the most prolific proponents are the British political thinker David Held and the Italian political theorist Daniele Archibugi. In the last decade they published several books regarding the spread of democracy from territorially defined nation states to a system of global governance that encapsulates the entire planet. Richard Falk has developed the idea from an international law perspective, Ulrich Beck from a sociological approach and Jürgen Habermas has elaborate the normative principles.

Politicians

- In 2003 Bob Brown, the leader of the Australian Green Party, has tabled a move for global democracy in the Australian Senate: "I move: That the Senate supports global democracy based on the principle of `one person, one vote, one value'; and supports the vision of a global parliament which empowers all the world's people equally to decide on matters of international significance."

- The current President of Bolivia Evo Morales and the Bolivian UN Ambassador Pablo Solón Romero have demanded a democratisation of the UN on many occasions. For example, Evo Morales at the United Nations, May 7, 2010: "The response to global warming is global democracy for life and for the Mother Earth. we have two paths: to save capitalism, or to save life and Mother Earth."

- Graham Watson (Member of the European Parliament and former leader of the Alliance of Liberals and Democrats for Europe) and Jo Leinen (Member of the European Parliament) are strong supporter of global democracy. They were among those presenting the "Brussels Declaration on Global Democracy" on February 23, 2010, at an event inside the European Parliament.

- The appeals of the campaign for a United Nations Parliamentary Assembly has already been endorsed by more than 700 parliamentarians from more than 90 countries.

Grassroot Movements

Jim Stark has initiated a process for a Democratic World Parliament through a Global Referendum. As of August 20, 2013, 22,126 people have voted. So far, the votes are 95.3% in favor of creating a democratic world parliament. Portable voting booths are available. Online voting at Mr. Stark's website is online. Mr. Stark has published a companion book to the online referendum entitled "Rescue Plan for Planet Earth".

Environmental Globalization

The official logo of the Mount Everest Earth Day 20 International Peace Climb. Initiatives like Earth Day promote international cooperation on pro-environmental initiatives, or in other words – promote environmental globalization.

Environmental globalization refers to the internationally coordinated practices and regulations (often in the form of international treaties) regarding environmental protection. An example of environmental globalization would be the series of International Tropical Timber Agreement treaties (1983, 1994, 2006), establishing International Tropical Timber Organization and promoting sustainable management of tropical forests. Environmental globalization is usually supported by non-governmental organizations and governments of developed countries, but opposed by governments of developing countries which see pro-environmental initiatives as hindering their economic development.

Definitions and Characteristics

Karl S. Zimmerer defined it as "the increased role of globally organized management institutions, knowledge systems and monitoring, and coordinated strategies aimed at resource, energy, and conservation issues." Alan Grainger in turn wrote that it can be understood as "an increasing spatial uniformity and contentedness in regular environmental management practices". Steven Yearley has referred to this concept as "globalization of environmental concern". Grainger also cited a study by Clark (2000), which he noted was an early treatment of the concept, and distinguished three aspects of environmental globalization: "global flows of energy, materials and organisms; formulation and global acceptance of ideas about global environment; and environmental governance" (a growing web of institutions concerned with global environment).

Environmental globalization is related to economic globalization, as economic development on a global scale has environmental impacts on such scale, which is of concern to numerous organizations and individuals. While economic globalization has environmental impacts, those impacts should not be confused with the concept of environmental globalization. In some regards, environmental globalization is in direct opposition to economic globalization, particularly when the latter is described as encouraging trade, and the former, as promoting pro-environment initiatives that are an impediment to trade. For that reason, an environmental activists might might be opposed to economic globalization, but advocate environmental globalization.

History

Grainger has discussed that environmental globalization in the context of international agreements on pro-environmental initiatives. According to him, precursors to modern environmental globalization can be found in the colonial era scientific forestry (research into how to create and restore forests). Modern initiatives contributing to environmental globalization include the 1972 United Nations Conference on the Human Environment, came from the World Bank 1980s requirements that development projects need to protect indigenous peoples and conserve biodiversity. Other examples of such initiative include treaties such as the series of International Tropical Timber Agreement treaties (1983, 1994, 2006). Therefore, unlike other main forms of globalization economic, political and cultural which were already strong in the 19th century, environmental globalization is a more recent phenomena, one that begun in earnest only in the later half of the 20th century. Similarly, Steven Yearley states that it was around that time that the environmental movement started to organize on the international scale focus on the global dimension of the issues (the first Earth Day was celebrated on 1970).

Supporters and Opponents

According to Grainger, environmental globalization (in the form of pro-environmental international initiatives) is usually supported by various non-governmental organizations and governments of developed countries, and opposed by governments of developing countries (Group of 77), which see pro-environmental initiatives as hindering their economic development. Governmental resistance to environmental globalization takes form or policy ambiguity (exemplified by countries which sign international pro-environmental treaties and pass domestic pro-environmental laws, but then proceed to not enforce them) and collective resistance in forums such as United Nations to projects that would introduce stronger regulations or new institutions policing environmental issues worldwide (such as opposition to the forest-protection agreement during the Earth Summit in 1992, which was eventually downgraded from a binding to a non-binding set of Forest Principles).

World Trade Organization has also been criticized as focused on economic globalization (liberalizing trade) over concerns of environmental protection, which are seen as impeding the trade. Steven Yearley states that WTO should not be described as "anti-environmental", but its decisions have major impact on environment worldwide, and they are based primarily on economic concerns, with environmental concerns being given secondary weight.

Global Regionalization

Global regionalization is a process which is parallel to globalization. The most important feature of the global community is globalization of many processes and phenomena of the development of international relations, strengthening relationships and interdependence of modern states in the second half of the 20th century. Globalization is evident not only globally, but also regionally. An important component of international relations in the 21st century is regional development and cooperation. In this regard, the importance of regional significant factor in current international relations. Most of the changes which is observed in today's world are associated with the development of the information sphere. There were predictable transformation and give rise to the beginning of the entry of humanity into a global information society. The researchers are note five definitions of information society-related parameters identification newness of the world which are technological, economic, concerning employment, spatial or cultural nature. The significance of the information society in terms of its impact on system are consisting of international relations. In 2000 G-8 Summit in Okinawa adopted a Charter on Global Information Society, which are reflected to the changes in the world information. The same issues in lot of attention were paid to the Millennium Summit.

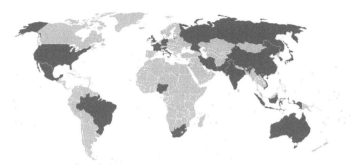

Global Regional Powers

Regionalization as a Trend of Global Development

The driving forces of regionalization are not only state, but also non-governmental structure (the economic "interest groups", NGOs, political parties, etc.). World regionalism is one of the manifestations of globalization and at the same time it is the opposite trend. Globalization is accompanied by a regionalization of international relations, transfer of public functions to sub-national or international level. Regions helps to protect public relations of globalization from negative impact and act as an independent subject of international relations. Many developing countries see in regionalization attempt to confront global competition. In the context of globalization acquires special relevance selective protectionism - gradual global economic integration, combining openness to the outside world with the protection of national interests. Universal theories of regions are exist on the theories of the problem, type, goals and objectives of the study. The following theoretical concepts are reflect to the processes of regionalism, which is a consequence of globalization. They are can be as : Multipolar world theory, the theory of large spaces, the theory of convergence and regional joint doctrine. In the study of regionalism are analyzed the regionalization emerging in response to the challenges of globalization, regionalization, such as institutional integration of the process of interpenetration merging national productions which are combine together social and political institutional structure of the state. There are different forms and types of integration. They are characterized by the degree of freedom of movement within groups factors of production. Currently there are mentioned forms of regional economic integration as: free trade area (FTA); Customs Union (CU); single or common market (BP); Economic Union (EU); Economic and Monetary Union (EMU) and others.

Information Society and International Relations

Increased of exposure information changes on the international relations caused by a number of features of the information. The first feature - information not only decreases or disappears in his large-scale use but it is starting point for the formation of new species and new qualities. The second feature - information is a fundamental principle for the development and decision-making at all levels of government, including the level of global governance. Third - feature information is "Oedipus effect", is the ability to influence the mind and behavior of individuals and society in general. Developing of the global information society are influenced by the progress of new information and communication technologies (ICT) in conjunction with the globalization of markets, both within individual countries and internationally. As a result, the harmonious joining the information society and respecting the necessary balance required coordinating efforts by the state as a body that can fully express the interests of society. Creating of a global information society are requires to the overcoming informational imbalances that exist in the world between different countries and regions, as well as information imbalances existing within themselves, for example, between different social groups. Because of these disparities, the task of building the information society acquire varying degrees of importance for different countries. Due to the intensification of information exchange and its interplay with economic imbalances interaction available information provided to the growing influence of politics, economics and culture.

In 1993 the Vice President of US - A. Gore used the term "information superhighway." In the field of information, the states like Singapore, Finland, Sweden, Denmark, Canada, Switzerland, Norway, Australia and Iceland are according to the United States. In the information technology ratings Russia is in the sixth place in the top ten. Below - Morocco, Egypt, Sri Lanka, Bulgaria, Vietnam, the Philippines, Peru, Tanzania. In 1996 was adopted the programme " Participation in international cultural exchange" by the Federal Law. To stay among the countries that affect global politics and largely define it, needs to strengthen active in shaping the global information society. At the end of 2001 Russia issued to the First Committee of the UN General Assembly resolution "Developments in the field of information and telecommunications in the context of international security". However, according to the Institute of the Information Society, 64% of the population of Russia does not feel the need to use the Internet. This figure was the result of adding Methodology Center for International Development at Harvard University "Ready for the networked world" (Readiness for the Networked World) and Russian realities which is relevant to the assessment: human capital, business climate and using of ICT in culture. It appears to the "effect resource economy." It is most clearly seen when comparing the two global markets: the global oil market which is estimated at 650 billion dollars, (Russia's share in it - 16%); ICT world market - about $1 trillion share in it represents the hundredths of a percent (Vaganov, 2004). The impact which formed of global information society on international relations has not only positive but also negative effects. Thus, the importance of international cooperation is often less important for the media industry, which allows for requests of the audience. Everywhere we are seeing a decline in international news programs, very costly and have a constant audience for stories related to the consumption and criminal chronicle (Atlas Monde diplomatique, 2007). Media increasingly contribute to the formation of world opinion, laying patterns to assess the achievements of globalization as well as risks and challenges of globalization. For example, growth media publications about the terrorist threat is much ahead of terrorist activity in the world (Chernikov, 2002).

However, there is no sufficient information on such global issues as water crisis, or human trafficking. All this points are need for the transformation of information policy.

Unrecognized States

The list of current unrecognized states in scientific publications is large. It includes the Republic of China on Taiwan and the Turkish Republic of Northern Cyprus. Often can be added the Republic of Somaliland, Tamil Eelam (Ceylon), and more recently - the Islamic State of Waziristan, whose independence was proclaimed in February 2006. Occasionally in this context refers to Southern Sudan, Kashmir, Western Sahara, Palestine, Kurdistan and some other areas (e.g. exotic Sealand). Consequently, the unrecognized state - it is the common name of public entities who are possessing all the attributes of statehood (control of territory, control system, the actual sovereignty) at the same time deprived of full or partial international diplomatic recognition and thus can not de jure act as in international relations. They should not be confused with self-declared republics (- it is education, which is itself declared, but no more). Some authors believe that the term of "unrecognized state" - incorrect (they believe that unrecognized state - is education that passed even though the short period of statehood, it ended in failure) and prefer the term "State de facto". International legal conflict between the right of nations and self-determination are enshrined in the famous decision of the UN General Assembly on decolonization in 1960. The principle of territorial integrity of States - is the principle of inviolability of borders which is officially recognized by all European countries, USA and Canada in the Conference on Security and Cooperation in Europe in Helsinki in 1975. Uncertainty state by the international community negatively affects its legal status and operational capabilities. Such a state can not be in active economic activities can not conclude trade contracts and implement multilateral investment and infrastructure projects. The area relies only on the international community to humanitarian aid, social and cultural projects, cooperation with various countries and regions in its infancy. Thus the political and legal recognition of any territory depends for its existence and development. Top prospects in terms of possible transformations is the current status of Kosovo. It is about independence in some form, as this concerned the United States and the European Union. Apparently, Serbia will only be able to postpone such a decision or to bargain for themselves some political and economic concessions (integration of Serbia into the EU or Kosovo section). On the other hand, if the recognition of Kosovo be qualified as a unique case (a unique case) it could provoke a serious precedent in countries where the problem of ethnic separatism. Abkhazia, Transnistria and South Ossetia can rely on partial, incomplete recognition of Russia, but their future prospects far from obvious. This "half independence" will not be recognized by the United States, European Union, India, China and many other countries. There is the slightest chance of changing the status of Nagorno Karabakh. This situation is mainly determined by the position of the US, EU, Russia, Iran and Turkey. To effectively address the problem of unrecognized states is likely to develop the clear international legal criteria under which after a certain period unrecognized state formation can count on international recognition. With all the reservations can be stated that unrecognized independent state players are the regional and international politics. Their influence on political processes is quite noticeable. Globalization has created additional opportunities for long-term existence of unrecognized states without their formal recognition by other countries. It is gradually becoming the norm.

Globality

Globality is the end-state of globalization – a hypothetical condition in which the process of globalization is complete or nearly so, barriers have fallen, and "a new global reality" is emerging.

The term was used in 1998 by author and economist Daniel Yergin in a *Newsweek* article that described the end-state of the globalization process, and in his book, *Commanding Heights: The Battle for the World Economy*. Though Yergin was credited with having coined it, the word is in fact much older. William Safire traces the etymology of "globality" in his book *No Uncertain Terms* and identifies a range of citations as far back as 1942, when it was used as a synonym for "global." Current use of "globality" as it applies to business – as a description of the current competitive state of world commerce – was not adopted until recently. The book: Globality: Competing with Everyone from Everywhere for Everything, Hal Sirkin Jim Hemerling Arindam Bhattacharya June 11, 2008, elaborates on how 'challenger' businesses from rapidly developing economies abroad are aggressively and inventively overtaking existing 'incumbent' nations.

The term has been described by William J. Holstein in the *New York Times* as "a new buzzword [that] doesn't work — it merely describes trends that have been under way for at least two decades under a very similar name."

Characteristics

According to all these authors, globality is what comes next after globalization: a new state of worldwide hyper-competition. Sirkin et al. (2008) further detail globality's three main features as they apply to commerce and business:

1. A significant structural shift in the flow of commerce: companies from every part of the world are now competing with each other for "everything" – customers, suppliers, partners, capital, intellectual property, raw materials, distribution systems, manufacturing capabilities, and most important, talent. In this competitive free-for-all, products and services flow from many locations to many destinations.

2. A breakdown in the established hierarchy of commercial power and influence: power is shifting away from traditional centers of influence in developed mar-

kets in the United States, Europe, and Japan, as companies from rapidly developing economies (RDEs) are quickly assuming leadership positions in global markets, forcing established leaders to compete on new terms.

3. The emergence of new business and governance practices better suited to a truly global and decentralized business environment. To compete successfully in a world of globality, established industry leaders from developed markets are being forced to learn from competitors in developing markets. The practices include shifting autonomy and decision making outward to satellite operations; redeploying assets to build commerce within emerging regions; and expanding quickly into new markets to match the speed and scale with which challengers are rising.

History

Yergin's chief distinction between globality and globalization is conceptual – he says that former is a "condition" while the latter is a "process." He describes globality as the end-state of the process of globalization:

The borders that constrained commerce – but also protected companies from the full brunt of competition – are eroding. Governments are retreating from control of the commanding heights of their economies: they are privatizing and deregulating. Barriers to trade and investment are coming down rapidly. Ever-cheaper communications and ever-faster computers, along with the Internet, are facilitating the flow of goods and services, as well as knowledge and information. Increasingly, companies are integrating their global strategies with global capital markets.

In their book, Sirkin et al. (2008) focus on the business conditions that emerge – and the challenges for management – once the state of globality is established. They distinguish globality from globalization based on the emergence of a new set of competitive dynamics between established leaders from developed economies and challenger companies from developing economies. With respect to global business, they argue that the three fundamental characteristics of globalization were these:

1. Established industry leaders – known as "incumbents" – from the developed economies of the United States, Europe, and Japan – relocated their manufacturing activities to developing countries in order to lower the cost of production and, accordingly, reduce the price of their goods offered in their home markets.

2. The incumbents also began to sell their offerings – usually with few if any modifications for local consumers – into the low-cost markets and enjoyed incremental sales gains, as the consumer economies began to grow in these countries.

3. Local companies in developing economies acted primarily as suppliers, jobbers, and local distribution partners, to these established industry leaders.

In this traditional model of globalization, the flow of commerce was predominantly from West to East and followed established Western business practices.

According to Sirkin et al., globality is a totally different kind of environment – one in which the competitive landscape has changed dramatically. In today's new phase of worldwide trade and economic development, companies are "competing with everyone from everywhere for everything." And while there is no ultimate model for success, no surefire strategy for innovation and growth, emerging-market challengers have evolved new management and governance structures that are ideally suited to this new competitive reality.

References

- Alan Grainger (31 October 2013). "Environmental Globalization and Tropical Forests". In Jan Oosthoek; Barry K. Gills. The Globalization of Environmental Crisis. Routledge. p. 54. ISBN 978-1-317-96896-2

- Steve Yearly (15 April 2008). "Globalization and the Environment". In George Ritzer. The Blackwell Companion to Globalization. John Wiley & Sons. p. 250. ISBN 978-0-470-76642-2

- Відкриті очі (2016-10-17). "Відкриті Очі: Вплив Глобалізації На Розвиток Сучасного Світу". Vidkryti-ochi.org.ua. Retrieved 2017-03-06

- Steger, Manfred (2009). Globalization: A Very Short Introduction. New York: Oxford University Press. ISBN 978-0-19-955226-9

- Karl S. Zimmerer (2006). Globalization & New Geographies of Conservation. University of Chicago Press. p. 1. ISBN 978-0-226-98344-8

Theories Related to Globalization

Modernization theory discusses the pattern of social evolution and argues for a relatively similar development of urbanization and industrialization. Postmodernism, globalism and global citizenship are other themes discussed here. The topics elaborated in this chapter will help in gaining a better perspective about the theories related to globalization.

Modernization Theory

Modernization theory is used to explain the process of modernization within societies. Modernization refers to a model of a progressive transition from a 'pre-modern' or 'traditional' to a 'modern' society. Modernization theory originated from the ideas of German sociologist Max Weber (1864–1920), which provided the basis for the modernization paradigm developed by Harvard sociologist Talcott Parsons (1902–1979). The theory looks at the internal factors of a country while assuming that with assistance, "traditional" countries can be brought to development in the same manner more developed countries have been. Moderniziation theory was a dominant paradigm in the social sciences in the 1950s and 1960s, then went into a deep eclipse. It made a comeback after 1990 but remains a controversial model.

Overview

Modernization theory both attempts to identify the social variables that contribute to social progress and development of societies and seeks to explain the process of social evolution. Modernization theory is subject to criticism originating among socialist and free-market ideologies, world-systems theorists, globalization theorists and dependency theorists among others. Modernization theory stresses not only the process of change but also the responses to that change. It also looks at internal dynamics while referring to social and cultural structures and the adaptation of new technologies. Modernization theory maintains that traditional societies will develop as they adopt more modern practices. Proponents of modernization theory claim that modern states are wealthier and more powerful and that their citizens are freer to enjoy a higher standard of living. Developments such as new data technology and the need to update traditional methods in transport, communication and production, it is argued, make modernization necessary or at least preferable to the status quo. That view makes critique of modernization difficult since it implies that such developments control the limits of human interaction, not vice versa. It also implies that human agency controls the speed and severity of modernization. Supposedly, instead of being dominated by tradition, societies undergoing the process of modernization typically arrive at forms of governance dictated by abstract principles. Traditional religious beliefs and cultural traits, according to the theory, usually become less important as modernization takes hold.

Historians link modernization to the processes of urbanization and industrialization and the spread of education. As Kendall (2007) notes, "Urbanization accompanied modernization and the rapid process of industrialization." In sociological critical theory, modernization is linked to an overarching process of rationalisation. When modernization increases within a society, the individual becomes increasingly important, eventually replacing the family or community as the fundamental unit of society.

Sociological theories of the late 19th century such as Social Darwinism provided a basis for asking what were the laws of evolution of human society. The current modernization theory originated with the ideas of German sociologist Max Weber (1864–1920) regarding the role of rationality and irrationality in the transition from traditional to modern society. Weber's approach provided the basis for the modernization paradigm as popularized by Harvard sociologist Talcott Parsons (1902–1979), who translated Weber's works into English in the 1930s and provided his own interpretation.

After 1945 the Parsonian version became widely used in sociology and other social sciences. By the late 1960s opposition developed because the theory was too general and did not fit all societies in quite the same way.

Globalization and Modernization

Globalization can be defined as the integration of economic, political and social cultures and, it is argued that is related to the spreading of modernization across borders.

Global trade has grown continuously since the European discovery of new continents in the Early modern period; it increased particularly as a result of the Industrial Revolution and the mid-20th century adoption of the shipping container.

Annual trans-border tourist arrivals rose to 456 million by 1990 and are expected to double again, to 937 million per annum, by 2010. Communication is another major area that has grown due to modernization. Communication industries have enabled capitalism to spread throughout the world. Telephony, television broadcasts, news services and online service providers have played a crucial part in globalization.

With the many apparent positive attributes to globalization there are also negative consequences. The dominant, neoliberal model of globalization often increases disparities between a society's rich and its poor. In major cities of developing countries there exist pockets where technologies of the modernised world, computers, cell phones and satellite television, exist alongside stark poverty. Globalists are globalization modernization theorists and argue that globalization is positive for everyone, as its benefits must eventually extend to all members of society, including vulnerable groups such as women and children.

Democratization and Modernization

The relationship between modernization and democracy is one of the most researched studies in comparative politics. There is academic debate over the drivers of democracy because there are theories that support economic growth as both a cause and effect of the institution of democracy. "Lipset's observation that democracy is related to economic development, first advanced in 1959, has generated the largest body of research on any topic in comparative politics," (Przeworski and Limongi, 1997).

Larry Diamond and Juan Linz, who worked with Lipset in the book, Democracy in Developing Countries: Latin America, argue that economic performance affects the development of democracy in at least three ways. First, they argue that economic growth is more important for democracy than given levels of socioeconomic development. Second, socioeconomic development generates social changes that can potentially facilitate democratization. Third, socioeconomic development promotes other changes, like organization of the middle class, which is conducive to democracy.

As Seymour Martin Lipset put it, "All the various aspects of economic development — industrialization, urbanization, wealth and education — are so closely interrelated as to form one major factor which has the political correlate of democracy". In the 1960s, some critics argued that the link between modernization and democracy was based too much on the example of European history and neglected the Third World. Recent demonstrations of the emergence of democracy in South Korea, Taiwan and South Africa have been cited as support for Lipset's thesis."

The argument also appears in Walt W. Rostow, *Politics and the Stages of Growth* (1971); A. F. K. Organski, *The Stages of Political Development* (1965); and David Apter, *The Politics of Modernization* (1965). In the 1960s, some critics argued that the link between modernization and democracy was based too much on the example of European history and neglected the Third World. Recent demonstrations of the emergence of democracy in South Korea, Taiwan and South Africa have been cited as support for Lipset's thesis.

One historical problem with that argument has always been Germany whose economic modernization in the 19th century came long before the democratization after 1918. Berman, however, concludes that a process of democratization was underway in Imperial Germany, for "during these years Germans developed many of the habits and mores that are now thought by political scientists to augur healthy political development".

Ronald Inglehart and Christian Welzel (2009) contend that the realization of democracy is not based solely on an expressed desire for that form of government, but democracies are born as a result of the admixture of certain social and cultural factors. They argue the ideal social and cultural conditions for the foundation of a democracy are born of significant modernization and economic development that result in mass political participation.

Peerenboom (2008) explores the relationships among democracy, the rule of law and their relationship to wealth by pointing to examples of Asian countries, such as Taiwan and South Korea, which have successfully democratized only after economic growth reached relatively high levels and to examples of countries such as the Philippines, Bangladesh, Cambodia, Thailand, Indonesia and India, which sought to democratize at lower levels of wealth but have not done as well.

Adam Przeworski and others have challenged Lipset's argument. They say political regimes do not transition to democracy as per capita incomes rise. Rather, democratic transitions occur randomly, but once there, countries with higher levels of gross domestic product per capita remain democratic. Epstein et al. (2006) retest the modernization hypothesis using new data, new techniques, and a three-way, rather than dichotomous, classification of regimes. Contrary to Przeworski, this study finds that the modernization hypothesis stands up well. Partial democracies emerge as among the most important and least understood regime types.

Highly contentious is the idea that modernization implies more human rights, with China in the 21st century being a major test case.

Technology

New technology is a major source of social change. Since modernization entails the social transformation from agrarian societies to industrial ones, it is important to look at the technological viewpoint; however, new technologies do not change societies by itself. Rather, it is the *response* to technology that causes change. Frequently, technology is recognized but not put to use for a very long time such as the ability to extract metal from rock. Although that initially went unused, it later had profound implications for the developmental course of societies. Technology makes it possible for a more innovated society and broad social change. That dramatic change through the centuries that has evolved socially, industrially, and economically, can be summed up by the term modernization. Cell phones, for example, have changed the lives of millions throughout the world. That is especially true in Africa and other parts of the Middle East, where there is a low cost communication infrastructure. With cell phone technology, widely dispersed populations are connected, which facilitates business-to-business communication and provides internet access to remoter areas, with a consequential rise in literacy.

Development and Modernization

Development, like modernization, has become the orienting principle of modern times. Countries that are seen as modern are also seen as developed, which means that they are generally more respected by institutions such as the United Nations and even as possible trade partners for other countries. The extent to which a country has modernized or developed dictates its power and importance on the international level.

Modernization of the health sector of developing nations recognizes that transitioning from 'traditional' to 'modern' is not merely the advancement in technology and the introduction of Western practices; implementing modern healthcare requires the reorganization of political agenda and, in turn, an increase in funding by feeders and resources towards public health. However, rather than replicating the stages of developed nations, whose roots of modernization are found with the context of industrialization or colonialism, underdeveloped nations should apply proximal interventions to target rural communities and focus on prevention strategies rather than curative solutions. That has been successfully exhibited by the Christian Medical Commission and in China through 'barefoot doctors'. Additionally, a strong advocate of the DE-emphasis of medical institutions was Halfdan T. Mahler, the WHO General Director from 1973 to 1988. Related ideas have been proposed at international conferences such as Alma-Ats and the "Health and Population in Development" conference, sponsored by the Rockefeller Foundation in Italy in 1979, and selective primary healthcare and GOBI were discussed (although they have both been strongly criticized by supporters of comprehensive healthcare). Overall, however, this is not to say that the nations of the Global South can function independently from Western states; significant funding is received from well-intention programs, foundations, and charities that target epidemics such as HIV/AIDS, malaria, and tuberculosis that have substantially improved the lives of millions of people and impeded future development.

Modernization theorists often saw traditions as obstacles to economic growth. According to Seymour Martin Lipset, economic conditions are heavily determined by the cultural, social values present in that given society. Furthermore, while modernization might deliver violent, radical change for traditional societies, it was thought worth the price. Critics insist that traditional societies were often destroyed without ever gaining the promised advantages if, among other things, the economic gap between advanced societies and such societies actually increased. The net effect of modernization for some societies was therefore the replacement of traditional poverty by a more modern form of misery, according to these critics. Others point to improvements in living standards, physical infrastructure, education and economic opportunity to refute such criticisms.

Criticism

From the 1960s, modernization theory has been criticized by numerous scholars, including Andre Gunder Frank (1929 – 2005) and Immanuel Wallerstein (born 1930). In this model, the modernization of a society required the destruction of the indigenous culture and its replacement by a more Westernized one. By one definition, *modern* simply refers to the present, and any society still in existence is therefore modern. Proponents of modernization typically view only Western society as being truly modern and argue that others are primitive or unevolved by comparison. That view sees unmodernized societies as inferior even if they have the same standard of living as western societies. Opponents argue that modernity is independent of culture and can be adapted to any society. Japan is cited as an example by both sides. Some see it as proof that a thoroughly modern way of life can exist in a non western society. Others argue that Japan has become distinctly more western as a result of its modernization.

As Tipps has argued, by conflating modernization with other processes, with which theorists use interchangeably (democratization, liberalization, development), the term becomes imprecise and therefore difficult to disprove.

The theory has also been criticised empirically, as modernization theorists ignore external sources of change in societies. The binary between traditional and modern is unhelpful, as the two are linked and often interdependent, and 'modernization' does not come as a whole.

Modernization theory has also been accused of being Eurocentric, as modernization began in Europe, with the Industrial Revolution, the French Revolution and the Revolutions of 1848 (Macionis 953) and has long been regarded as reaching its most advanced stage in Europe. Anthropologists typically make their criticism one step further and say that the view is ethnocentric and is specific to Western culture.

Dependency Theory

One alternative model on the left is Dependency theory. It emerged in the 1950s and argues that the underdevelopment of poor nations in the Third World derived from systematic imperial and neo-colonial exploitation of raw materials. Its proponents argue that resources typically flow from a "periphery" of poor and underdeveloped states to a "core" of wealthy states, enriching the latter at the expense of the former. It is a central contention of dependency theorists such as Andre Gunder Frank that poor states are impoverished and rich ones enriched by the way poor states are integrated into the "world system".

Dependency models arose from a growing association of southern hemisphere nationalists (from Latin America and Africa) and Marxists. It was their reaction against modernization theory, which held that all societies progress through similar stages of development, that today's underdeveloped areas are thus in a similar situation to that of today's developed areas at some time in the past, and that, therefore, the task of helping the underdeveloped areas out of poverty is to accelerate them along this supposed common path of development, by various means such as investment, technology transfers, and closer integration into the world market. Dependency theory rejected this view, arguing that underdeveloped countries are not merely primitive versions of developed countries, but have unique features and structures of their own; and, importantly, are in the situation of being the weaker members in a world market economy.

Postmodernism

Postmodernism describes a broad movement that developed in the mid- to late 20th century across philosophy, the arts, architecture and criticism which marked a departure from modernism. While encompassing a broad range of ideas, postmodernism is typically defined by an attitude of skepticism, irony or distrust toward grand narratives, ideologies and various tenets of universalism, including objective notions of reason, human nature, social progress, moral universalism, absolute truth, and objective reality. Instead, it asserts to varying degrees that claims to knowledge and truth are products of social, historical or political discourses or interpretations, and are therefore contextual or socially constructed. Accordingly, postmodern thought is broadly characterized by tendencies to epistemological and moral relativism, pluralism, irreverence and self-referentiality.

The term *postmodernism* has been applied both to the era following modernity and to a host of movements within that era (mainly in art, music, and literature) that reacted against tendencies in modernism. Postmodernism includes skeptical critical interpretations of culture, literature, art, philosophy, history, linguistics, economics, architecture, fiction, feminist theory, and literary criticism. Postmodernism is often associated with schools of thought such as deconstruction and post-structuralism, as well as philosophers such as Jean-François Lyotard and Frederic Jameson.

Term

The term *postmodern* was first used around the 1880s. John Watkins Chapman suggested "a Postmodern style of painting" as a way to depart from French Impressionism. J. M. Thompson, in his 1914 article in *The Hibbert Journal* (a quarterly philosophical review), used it to describe changes in attitudes and beliefs in the critique of religion: "The raison d'etre of Post-Modernism is to escape from the double-mindedness of Modernism by being thorough in its criticism by extending it to religion as well as theology, to Catholic feeling as well as to Catholic tradition."

In 1921 and 1925, postmodernism had been used to describe new forms of art and music. In 1942 H. R. Hays described it as a new literary form. However, as a general theory for a historical movement it was first used in 1939 by Arnold J. Toynbee: "Our own Post-Modern Age has been inaugurated by the general war of 1914–1918".

Portland Building (1982), by architect Michael Graves, an example of Postmodern architecture

In 1949 the term was used to describe a dissatisfaction with modern architecture, and led to the postmodern architecture movement, and a response to the modernist architectural movement known as the International Style. Postmodernism in architecture was initially marked by a re-emergence of surface ornament, reference to surrounding buildings in urban settings, historical reference in decorative forms (eclecticism), and non-orthogonal angles.

Peter Drucker suggested the transformation into a post modern world happened between 1937 and 1957 (when he was writing). He described an as yet "nameless era" which he characterised as a shift to conceptual world based on pattern purpose and process rather than mechanical cause, outlined by four new realities: the emergence of Educated Society, the importance of international development, the decline of the nation state, and the collapse of the viability of non-Western cultures.

In 1971, in a lecture delivered at the Institute of Contemporary Art, London, Mel Bochner described "post-modernism" in art as having started with Jasper Johns, "who first rejected sense-data and the singular point-of-view as the basis for his art, and treated art as a critical investigation."

More recently, Walter Truett Anderson described postmodernism as belonging to one of four typological world views, which he identifies as either (a) Postmodern-ironist, which sees truth as socially constructed, (b) Scientific-rational, in which truth is found through methodical, disciplined inquiry, (c) Social-traditional, in which truth is found in the heritage of American and Western civilization, or (d) Neo-Romantic, in which truth is found through attaining harmony with nature and/or spiritual exploration of the inner self.

Postmodernist ideas in philosophy and the analysis of culture and society expanded the importance of critical theory and has been the point of departure for works of literature, architecture, and design, as well as being visible in marketing/business and the interpretation of history, law and culture, starting in the late 20th century. These developments— re-evaluation of the entire Western value system (love, marriage, popular culture, shift from industrial to service economy) that took place since the 1950s and 1960s, with a peak in the Social Revolution of 1968—are described with the term "postmodernity", as opposed to *Postmodernism*, a term referring to an opinion or movement. Postmodernism has also been used interchangeably with the term post-structuralism out of which postmodernism grew; a proper understanding of postmodernism or doing justice to the postmodernist concept demands an understanding of the poststructuralist movement and the ideas of its advocates. Post-structuralism resulted similarly to postmodernism by following a time of structuralism. It is characterized by new ways of thinking through structuralism, contrary to the original form. "Postmodernist" describes part of a movement; "Postmodern" places it in the period of time since the 1950s, making it a part of contemporary history.

Influential Postmodernist Ideas

Martin Heidegger

Martin Heidegger rejected the philosophical basis of the concepts of "subjectivity" and "objectivity" and asserted that similar grounding oppositions in logic ultimately refer to one another. Instead of resisting the admission of this paradox in the search for understanding, Heidegger requires that we embrace it through an active process of elucidation he called the "hermeneutic circle". He stressed the historicity and cultural construction of concepts while simultaneously advocating the necessity of an atemporal and immanent apprehension of them. In this vein, he asserted that it was the task of contemporary philosophy to recover the original question of (or "openness to") *Dasein* (translated as Being or Being-there) present in the Presocratic philosophers but normalized, neutered, and standardized since Plato. This was to be done, in part, by tracing the record of *Dasein's* sublimation or forgetfulness through the history of philosophy which meant that we were to ask again what constituted the grounding conditions in ourselves and in the World for the affinity between beings and between the many usages of the term "being" in philosophy. To do this, however, a non-historical and, to a degree, self-referential engagement with whatever set of ideas, feelings or practices would permit (both the non-fixed concept and reality of) such a continuity was required—a continuity permitting the possible experience, possible existence indeed not only of beings but of all differences as they appeared and tended to develop.

Such a conclusion led Heidegger to depart from the phenomenology of his teacher Husserl and prompt instead an (ironically anachronistic) return to the yet-unasked questions of Ontology, a return that in general did not acknowledge an intrinsic distinction between phenomena and noumena or between things in themselves (*de re*) and things as they appear: Being-in-the-world, or rather, the openness to the process of *Dasein*'s becoming was to bridge the age-old gap between these two. In this latter premise, Heidegger shares an affinity with the late Romantic philosopher, Friedrich Nietzsche, another principal forerunner of post-structuralist and postmodernist thought. Influential to thinkers associated with Postmodernism are Heidegger's critique of the subject–object or sense–knowledge division implicit in Rationalism, Empiricism, and methodological naturalism, his repudiation of the idea that facts exist outside or separately from the process of thinking and speaking them (however, Heidegger is not specifically a nominalist), his related admission that the possibilities of philosophical and scientific discourse are wrapped up in the practices and expectations of a society and that concepts and fundamental constructs are the expression of a lived, historical exercise rather than simple derivations of external, *a priori* conditions independent from historical mind and changing experience, and his instrumentalist and negativist notion that Being (and, by extension, reality) is an action, method, tendency, possibility, and question rather than a discrete, positive, identifiable state, answer, or entity.

Jacques Derrida

Jacques Derrida re-examined the fundamentals of writing and its consequences on philosophy in general; sought to undermine the language of "presence" or metaphysics in an analytical technique which, beginning as a point of departure from Heidegger's notion of *Destruktion*, came to be known as Deconstruction. Derrida utilized, like Heidegger, references to Greek philosophical notions associated with the Skeptics and the Presocratics, such as Epoché and Aporia to articulate his notion of implicit circularity between premises and conclusions, origins and manifestations, but—in a manner analogous in certain respects to Gilles Deleuze—presented a radical re-reading of canonical philosophical figures such as Plato, Aristotle, and Descartes as themselves being informed by such "destabilizing" notions.

Michel Foucault

Michel Foucault introduced concepts such as 'discursive regime', or re-invoked those of older philosophers like 'episteme' and 'genealogy' in order to explain the relationship between meaning, power, and social behavior within social orders. In direct contradiction to what have been typified as modernist perspectives on epistemology, Foucault asserted that rational judgment, social practice, and what he called "biopower" are not only inseparable but co-determinant. While Foucault himself was deeply involved in a number of progressive political causes and maintained close personal ties with members of the far-left, he was also controversial with leftist thinkers of his day, including those associated with various Marxist tendencies, proponents of left-libertarianism (such as Noam Chomsky), and supporters of humanism (like Jürgen Habermas), for his rejection of what he deemed to be Enlightenment concepts of freedom, liberation, self-determination, and human nature. Instead, Foucault focused on the ways in which such constructs can foster cultural hegemony, violence, and exclusion.

In line with his rejection of such "positive" tenets of Enlightenment-era human-ism, he was active—with Gilles Deleuze and Félix Guattari—in the anti-psychiatry movement, considering much of institutionalized psychiatry and, in particular, Freud's concept of repression central to Psychoanalysis (which was still very influ-ential in France during the 1960s and 1970s), to be both harmful and misplaced. Foucault was known for his controversial aphorisms, such as "language is oppres-sion", meaning that language functions in such a way as to render nonsensical, false, or silent tendencies that might otherwise threaten or undermine the distri-butions of power backing a society's conventions—even when such distributions purport to celebrate liberation and expression or value minority groups and per-spectives. His writings have had a major influence on the larger body of postmod-ern academic literature.

Jean-François Lyotard

Jean-François Lyotard identified in *The Postmodern Condition* a crisis in the "dis-courses of the human sciences" latent in modernism but catapulted to the fore by the advent of the "computerized" or "telematic" era. This crisis, insofar as it pertains to academia, concerns both the motivations and justification procedures for making research claims: unstated givens or values that have validated the basic efforts of academic research since the late 18th century might no longer be valid—particularly, in social science and humanities research, though examples from mathematics are given by Lyotard as well. As formal conjecture about real-world issues becomes in-extricably linked to automated calculation, information storage, and retrieval, such knowledge becomes increasingly "exteriorised" from its knowers in the form of in-formation. Knowledge thus becomes materialized and made into a commodity ex-changed between producers and consumers; it ceases to be either an idealistic end-in-itself or a tool capable of bringing about liberty or social benefit; it is stripped of its humanistic and spiritual associations, its connection with education, teaching, and human development, being simply rendered as "data"—omnipresent, material, unending, and without any contexts or pre-requisites. Furthermore, the "diversity" of claims made by various disciplines begins to lack any unifying principle or intu-ition as objects of study become more and more specialized due to the emphasis on specificity, precision, and uniformity of reference that competitive, database-orient-ed research implies.

The value-premises upholding academic research have been maintained by what Ly-otard considers to be quasi-mythological beliefs about human purpose, human reason, and human progress—large, background constructs he calls "metanarratives". These metanarratives still remain in Western society but are now being undermined by rapid Informatization and the commercialization of the university and its functions. The shift of authority from the presence and intuition of knowers—from the good faith of reason to seek diverse knowledge integrated for human benefit or truth fidelity—to the automated database and the market had, in Lyotard's view, the power to unravel the very idea of "justification" or "legitimation" and, with it, the rationale for research altogether, especially in disciplines pertaining to human life, society, and meaning. We are now controlled not by binding extra-linguistic value paradigms defining notions of collective identity and ultimate purpose, but rather by our automatic responses to different species of "language games" (a concept Lyotard imports from J. L. Austin's theory of speech acts). In his vision of a solution to this "vertigo", Lyotard opposes the assumptions of universality, consensus, and generality that he identified within the thought of humanistic, Neo-Kantian philosophers like Jürgen Habermas, and proposes a continuation of experimentation and diversity to be assessed pragmatically in the context of language games rather than via appeal to a resurrected series of transcendentals and metaphysical unities.

Richard Rorty

Richard Rorty argues in *Philosophy and the Mirror of Nature* that contemporary analytic philosophy mistakenly imitates scientific methods. In addition, he denounces the traditional epistemological perspectives of representationalism and correspondence theory that rely upon the independence of knowers and observers from phenomena and the passivity of natural phenomena in relation to consciousness. As a proponent of anti-foundationalism and anti-essentialism within a pragmatist framework, he echoes the postmodern strain of conventionalism and relativism, but opposes much of postmodern thinking with his commitment to social liberalism.

Jean Baudrillard

Jean Baudrillard, in *Simulacra and Simulation*, introduced the concept that reality or the principle of "The Real" is short-circuited by the interchangeability of signs in an era whose communicative and semantic acts are dominated by electronic media and digital technologies. Baudrillard proposes the notion that, in such a state, where subjects are detached from the outcomes of events (political, literary, artistic, personal, or otherwise), events no longer hold any particular sway on the subject nor have any identifiable context; they therefore have the effect of producing widespread indifference, detachment, and passivity in industrialized populations. He claimed that a constant stream of appearances and references without any direct consequences to viewers or readers could eventually render the division between appearance and object indiscernible, resulting, ironically, in the "disappearance" of mankind in what is, in effect, a virtual or holographic state, composed only of appearances. For Baudrillard, "simulation is no longer that of a territory, a referential being or a substance. It is the generation by models of a real without origin or a reality: a hyperreal.

Fredric Jameson

Fredric Jameson set forth one of the first expansive theoretical treatments of postmodernism as a historical period, intellectual trend, and social phenomenon in a series of lectures at the Whitney Museum, later expanded as *Postmodernism, or The Cultural Logic of Late Capitalism* (1991). Eclectic in his methodology, Jameson has continued a sustained examination of the role that periodization continues to play as a grounding assumption of critical methodologies in humanities disciplines. He has contributed extensive effort to explicating the importance of concepts of Utopia and Utopianism as driving forces in the cultural and intellectual movements of modernity, and outlining the political and existential uncertainties that may result from the decline or suspension of this trend in the theorized state of postmodernity. Like Susan Sontag, Jameson served to introduce a wide audience of American readers to key figures of the 20th century continental European intellectual left, particularly those associated with the Frankfurt School, structuralism, and post-structuralism. Thus, his importance as a "translator" of their ideas to the common vocabularies of a variety of disciplines in the Anglo-American academic complex is equally as important as his own critical engagement with them.

Douglas Kellner

In *Analysis of the Journey*, a journal birthed from postmodernism, Douglas Kellner insists that the "assumptions and procedures of modern theory" must be forgotten. His terms defined in the depth of postmodernism are based on advancement, innovation, and adaptation. Extensively, Kellner analyzes the terms of this theory in real-life experiences and examples. Kellner used science and technology studies as a major part of his analysis; he urged that the theory is incomplete without it. The scale was larger than just postmodernism alone; it must be interpreted through cultural studies where science and technology studies play a huge role. The reality of the September 11 attacks on the United States of America is the catalyst for his explanation. This catalyst is used as a great representation due to the mere fact of the planned ambush and destruction of "symbols of globalization", insinuating the World Trade Center.

One of the numerous yet appropriate definitions of postmodernism and the qualm aspect aids this attribute to seem perfectly accurate. In response, Kellner continues to examine the repercussions of understanding the effects of the September 11 attacks. He questions if the attacks are only able to be understood in a limited form of postmodern theory due to the level of irony. In further studies, he enhances the idea of semiotics in alignment with the theory. Similar to the act of September 11 and the symbols that were interpreted through this postmodern ideal, he continues to even describe this as "semiotic systems" that people use to make sense of their lives and the events that occur in them. Kellner's adamancy that signs are necessary to understand one's culture is what he analyzes from the evidence that most cultures have used signs in place of existence.

Finally, he recognizes that many theorists of postmodernism are trapped by their own cogitations. He finds strength in theorist Baudrillard and his idea of Marxism. Kellner acknowledges Marxism's end and lack of importance to his theory.

The conclusion he depicts is simple: postmodernism, as most utilize it today, will decide what experiences and signs in one's reality will be one's reality as they know it.

Deconstruction

One of the most well-known postmodernist concerns is "deconstruction," a theory for philosophy, literary criticism, and textual analysis developed by Jacques Derrida. The notion of a "deconstructive" approach implies an analysis that questions the already evident understanding of a text in terms of presuppositions, ideological underpinnings, hierarchical values, and frames of reference. A deconstructive approach further depends on the techniques of close reading without reference to cultural, ideological, moral opinions or information derived from an authority over the text such as the author. At the same time Derrida famously writes: "Il n'y a pas d'hors-texte (*there is no such thing as outside-of-the-text*)." Derrida implies that the world follows the grammar of a text undergoing its own deconstruction. Derrida's method frequently involves recognizing and spelling out the different, yet similar interpretations of the meaning of a given text and the problematic implications of binary oppositions within the meaning of a text. Derrida's philosophy inspired a postmodern movement called deconstructivism among architects, characterized by the intentional fragmentation, distortion, and dislocation of architectural elements in designing a building. Derrida discontinued his involvement with the movement after the publication of his collaborative project with architect Peter Eisenmann in *Chora L Works: Jacques Derrida and Peter Eisenman.*

Postmodernism and Structuralism

Structuralism was a philosophical movement developed by French academics in the 1950s, partly in response to French Existentialism. It has been seen variously as an expression of Modernism, High modernism, or postmodernism. "Post-structuralists" were thinkers who moved away from the strict interpretations and applications of structuralist ideas. Many American academics consider post-structuralism to be part of the broader, less well-defined postmodernist movement, even though many post-structuralists insisted it was not. Thinkers who have been called structuralists include the anthropologist Claude Lévi-Strauss, the linguist Ferdinand de Saussure, the Marxist philosopher Louis Althusser, and the semiotician Algirdas Greimas. The early writings of the psychoanalyst Jacques Lacan and the literary theorist Roland Barthes have also been called structuralist. Those who began as structuralists but became post-structuralists include Michel Foucault, Roland Barthes, Jean Baudrillard, Gilles Deleuze. Other post-structuralists include Jacques Derrida, Pierre Bourdieu, Jean-François Lyotard, Julia Kristeva, Hélène Cixous, and Luce Irigaray. The American cultural theorists, critics and intellectuals whom they influenced include Judith Butler, John Fiske, Rosalind Krauss, Avital Ronell, and Hayden White.

Post-structuralism is not defined by a set of shared axioms or methodologies, but by an emphasis on how various aspects of a particular culture, from its most ordinary, everyday material details to its most abstract theories and beliefs, determine one another. Post-structuralist thinkers reject Reductionism and Epiphenomenalism and the idea that cause-and-effect relationships are top-down or bottom-up. Like structuralists, they start from the assumption that people's identities, values and economic conditions determine each other rather than having *intrinsic* properties that can be understood in isolation. Thus the French structuralists considered themselves to be espousing Relativism and Constructionism. But they nevertheless tended to explore how the subjects of their study might be described, reductively, as a set of *essential* relationships, schematics, or mathematical symbols. (An example is Claude Lévi-Strauss's algebraic formulation of mythological transformation in "The Structural Study of Myth"). Post-structuralists thinkers went further, questioning the existence of any distinction between the nature of a thing and its relationship to other things.

Post-postmodernism

The connection between postmodernism, posthumanism, and cyborgism has led to a challenge of postmodernism, for which the terms "postpostmodernism" and "postpoststructuralism" were first coined in 2003:

> "In some sense, we may regard postmodernism, posthumanism, poststructuralism, etc., as being of the 'cyborg age' of mind over body. Deconference was an exploration in post-cyborgism (i.e. what comes after the postcorporeal era), and thus explored issues of postpostmodernism, postpoststructuralism, and the like. To understand this transition from 'pomo' (cyborgism) to 'popo' (post-cyborgism) we must first understand the cyborg era itself."

More recently metamodernism, post-postmodernism and the "death of postmodernism" have been widely debated: in 2007 Andrew Hoberek noted in his introduction to a special issue of the journal *Twentieth Century Literature* titled "After Postmodernism" that "declarations of postmodernism's demise have become a critical commonplace". A small group of critics has put forth a range of theories that aim to describe culture or society in the alleged aftermath of postmodernism, most notably Raoul Eshelman (performatism), Gilles Lipovetsky (hypermodernity), Nicolas Bourriaud (altermodern), and Alan Kirby (digimodernism, formerly called pseudo-modernism). None of these new theories and labels have so far gained very widespread acceptance. The exhibition *Postmodernism – Style and Subversion 1970–1990* at the Victoria and Albert Museum (London, 24 September 2011 – 15 January 2012) was billed as the first show to document postmodernism as a historical movement.

Influence on Art

Architecture

Neue Staatsgalerie (1977-84), Stuttgart, Germany, by James Stirling and Michael Wilford, showing the eclectic mix of classical architecture and colourful ironic detailing.

The idea of Postmodernism in architecture began as a response to the perceived blandness and failed Utopianism of the Modern movement. Modern Architecture, as established and developed by Walter Gropius and Le Corbusier, was focused on the pursuit of a perceived ideal perfection, and attempted harmony of form and function, and dismissal of "frivolous ornament," as well as arguing for an architecture that represented the spirit of the age as depicted in cutting-edge technology, be it airplanes, cars, ocean liners or even supposedly artless grain silos. Critics of modernism argued that the attributes of perfection and minimalism themselves were subjective, and pointed out anachronisms in modern thought and questioned the benefits of its philosophy. Definitive postmodern architecture such as the work of Michael Graves and Robert Venturi rejects the notion of a 'pure' form or 'perfect' architectonic detail, instead conspicuously drawing from all methods, materials, forms and colors available to architects.

Modernist Ludwig Mies van der Rohe is associated with the phrase "less is more"; in contrast Venturi famously said, "Less is a bore." Postmodernist architecture was one of the first aesthetic movements to openly challenge Modernism as antiquated and "totalitarian", favoring personal preferences and variety over objective, ultimate truths or principles.

The intellectual scholarship regarding postmodernism and architecture is closely linked with the writings of critic-turned-architect Charles Jencks, beginning with lectures in the early 1970s and his essay "The rise of post-modern architecture" from 1975. His *magnus opus*, however, is the book *The Language of Post-Modern Architecture*, first published in 1977, and since running to seven editions. Jencks makes the point that Post-Modernism (like Modernism) varies for each field of art, and that for architecture it is not just a reaction to Modernism but what he terms *double coding*: "Double Coding: the combination of Modern techniques with something else (usually traditional building) in order for architecture to communicate with the public and a concerned minority, usually other architects." Furthermore, Post-Modern architects would for economic reasons by compelled to make use of contemporary technology, hence distinguishing such architects from mere revivalists. Among the Post-Modern architects championed by Jencks were Robert Venturi, Robert Stern, Charles Moore, Michael Graves, Leon Krier, and James Stirling.

Urban Planning

Postmodernism is a rejection of 'totality', of the notion that planning could be 'comprehensive', widely applied regardless of context, and rational. In this sense, Postmodernism is a rejection of its predecessor: Modernism. From the 1920s onwards, the Modern movement sought to design and plan cities which followed the logic of the new model of industrial mass production; reverting to large-scale solutions, aesthetic standardisation and prefabricated design solutions (Goodchild 1990). Postmodernism also brought a break from the notion that planning and architecture could result in social reform, which was an integral dimension of the plans of Modernism (Simonsen 1990). Furthermore, Modernism eroded urban living by its failure to recognise differences and aim towards homogenous landscapes (Simonsen 1990, 57). Within Modernism, urban planning represented a 20th-century move towards establishing something stable, structured, and rationalised within what had become a world of chaos, flux and change (Irving 1993, 475). The role of planners predating Postmodernism was one of the 'qualified professional' who believed they could find and implement one single 'right way' of planning new urban establishments (Irving 1993). In fact, after 1945, urban planning became one of the methods through which capitalism could be managed and the interests of developers and corporations could be administered (Irving 1993, 479).

Considering Modernism inclined urban planning to treat buildings and developments as isolated, unrelated parts of the overall urban ecosystems created fragmented, isolated, and homogeneous urban landscapes (Goodchild, 1990). One of the greater problems with Modernist-style of planning was the disregard of resident or public opinion, which resulted in planning being forced upon the majority by a minority consisting of affluent professionals with little to no knowledge of real 'urban' problems characteristic of post-Second World War urban environments: slums, overcrowding, deteriorated infrastructure, pollution and disease, among others (Irving 1993). These were precisely the 'urban ills' Modernism was meant to 'solve', but more often than not, the types of 'comprehensive', 'one size fits all' approaches to planning made things worse., and residents began to show interest in becoming involved in decisions which had once been solely entrusted to professionals of the built environment. Advocacy planning and participatory models of planning emerged in the 1960s to counter these traditional elitist and technocratic approaches to urban planning (Irving 1993; Hatuka & D'Hooghe 2007). Furthermore, an assessment of the 'ills' of Modernism among planners during the 1960s, fuelled development of a participatory model that aimed to expand the range of participants in urban interventions (Hatuka & D'Hooghe 2007, 21).

Jane Jacobs' 1961 book *The Death and Life of Great American Cities* was a sustained critique of urban planning as it had developed within Modernism and marked a transition from modernity to postmodernity in thinking about urban planning (Irving 1993, 479). However, the transition from Modernism to Postmodernism is often said to have happened at 3:32pm on 15 July in 1972, when Pruitt Igoe; a housing development for low-income people in St. Louis designed by architect Minoru Yamasaki, which had been a prize-winning version of Le Corbusier's 'machine for modern living' was deemed uninhabitable and was torn down (Irving 1993, 480). Since then, Postmodernism has involved theories that embrace and aim to create diversity, and it exalts uncertainty, flexibility and change (Hatuka & D'Hooghe 2007). Postmodern planning aims to accept pluralism and heighten awareness of social differences in order to accept and bring to light the claims of minority and disadvantaged groups (Goodchild 1990). It is important to note that urban planning discourse within Modernity and Postmodernity has developed in different contexts, even though they both grew within a capitalist culture. Modernity was shaped by a capitalist ethic of Fordist-Keynesian paradigm of mass, standardized production and consumption, while postmodernity was created out of a more flexible form of capital accumulation, labor markets and organisations (Irving 1993, 60). Also, there is a distinction between a postmodernism of 'reaction' and one of 'resistance'. A postmodernism of 'reaction' rejects Modernism and seeks to return to the lost traditions and history in order to create a new cultural synthesis, while Postmodernity of 'resistance' seeks to deconstruct Modernism and is a critique of the origins without necessarily returning to them (Irving 1993, 60). As a result of Postmodernism, planners are much less inclined to lay a firm or steady claim to there being one single 'right way' of engaging in urban planning and are more open to different styles and ideas of 'how to plan' (Irving 474).

Literature

Orhan Pamuk, winner of the 2006 Nobel Prize in Literature.

Literary postmodernism was officially inaugurated in the United States with the first issue of *boundary 2*, subtitled "Journal of Postmodern Literature and Culture", which appeared in 1972. David Antin, Charles Olson, John Cage, and the Black Mountain College school of poetry and the arts were integral figures in the intellectual and artistic exposition of postmodernism at the time. *boundary 2* remains an influential journal in postmodernist circles today.

Jorge Luis Borges' (1939) short story *Pierre Menard, Author of the Quixote*, is often considered as predicting postmodernism and conceiving the ideal of the ultimate parody. Samuel Beckett is sometimes seen as an important precursor and influence. Novelists who are commonly connected with postmodern literature include Vladimir Nabokov, William Gaddis, Umberto Eco, John Hawkes, William S. Burroughs, Giannina Braschi, Kurt Vonnegut, John Barth, Jean Rhys, Donald Barthelme, E.L. Doctorow, Richard Kalich, Jerzy Kosinski, Don DeLillo, Thomas Pynchon (Pynchon's work has also been described as "high modern"), Ishmael Reed, Kathy Acker, Ana Lydia Vega, Jachym Topol and Paul Auster.

In 1971, the Arab-American scholar Ihab Hassan published *The Dismemberment of Orpheus: Toward a Postmodern Literature,* an early work of literary criticism from a postmodern perspective, in which the author traces the development of what he calls "literature of silence" through Marquis de Sade, Franz Kafka, Ernest Hemingway, Beckett, and many others, including developments such as the Theatre of the Absurd and the nouveau roman. In 'Postmodernist Fiction' (1987), Brian McHale details the shift from modernism to postmodernism, arguing that the former is characterized by an epistemological dominant, and that postmodern works have developed out of modernism and are primarily concerned with questions of ontology. In *Constructing Postmodernism* (1992), McHale's second book, he provides readings of postmodern fiction and of some of the contemporary writers who go under the label of cyberpunk. McHale's "What Was Postmodernism?" (2007), follows Raymond Federman's lead in now using the past tense when discussing postmodernism.

Music

Composer Henryk Górecki.

Postmodern music is either music of the postmodern era, or music that follows aesthetic and philosophical trends of postmodernism. As the name suggests, the postmodernist movement formed partly in reaction to the ideals of the modernist. Because of this, postmodern music is mostly defined in opposition to modernist music, and a work can either be modernist, or postmodern, but not both. Jonathan Kramer posits the idea (following Umberto Eco and Jean-François Lyotard) that postmodernism (including *musical* postmodernism) is less a surface style or historical period (i.e., condition) than an *attitude*.

The postmodern impulse in classical music arose in the 1960s with the advent of musical minimalism. Composers such as Terry Riley, Henryk Górecki, Bradley Joseph, John Adams, Steve Reich, Philip Glass, Michael Nyman, and Lou Harrison reacted to the perceived elitism and dissonant sound of atonal academic modernism by producing music with simple textures and relatively consonant harmonies, whilst others, most notably John Cage challenged the prevailing narratives of beauty and objectivity common to Modernism. Some composers have been openly influenced by popular music and world ethnic musical traditions.

Postmodern classical music as well is not a musical *style*, but rather refers to music of the postmodern era. It bears the same relationship to postmodernist music that postmodernity bears to postmodernism. Postmodern music, on the other hand, shares characteristics with postmodernist art—that is, art that comes *after* and reacts *against* modernism.

Though representing a general return to certain notions of music-making that are often considered to be classical or romantic, not all postmodern composers have eschewed the experimentalist or academic tenets of modernism. The works of Dutch composer Louis Andriessen, for example, exhibit experimentalist preoccupation that is decidedly anti-romantic. Eclecticism and freedom of expression, in reaction to the rigidity and aesthetic limitations of modernism, are the hallmarks of the postmodern influence in musical composition.

Author on postmodernism, Dominic Strinati, has noted, it is also important "to include in this category the so-called 'art rock' musical innovations and mixing of styles associated with groups like Talking Heads, and performers like Laurie Anderson, together with the self-conscious 'reinvention of disco' by the Pet Shop Boys".

Graphic Design

Postmodern designers were in the beginning stages of what we now refer to as "graphic design". They created works beginning in the 1970s without any set adherence to rational order and formal organization. They also seemed to entirely pay no attention to traditional conventions such as legibility. Another characteristic of postmodern graphic design is that "retro, techno, punk, grunge, beach, parody, and pastiche were all conspicuous trends. Each had its own sites and venues, detractors and advocates". Yet, while postmodern design did not consist of one unified graphic style, the movement was an expressive and playful time for designers who searched for more and more ways to go against the system. Key influential postmodern graphic designers include Wolfgang Weingart, April Greiman, Tibor Kalman, and Jamie Reid.

Criticisms

Criticisms of postmodernism are intellectually diverse, including the assertions that postmodernism is meaningless and promotes obscurantism. For example, Noam Chomsky has argued that postmodernism is meaningless because it adds nothing to analytical or empirical knowledge. He asks why postmodernist intellectuals do not respond like people in other fields when asked, "what are the principles of their theories, on what evidence are they based, what do they explain that wasn't already obvious, etc.? If these requests an't be met, then I'd suggest recourse to Hume's advice in similar circumstances: 'to the flames'."

Christian apologist and philosopher William Lane Craig has noted "The idea that we live in a postmodern culture is a myth. In fact, a postmodern culture is an impossibility; it would be utterly unliveable. People are not relativistic when it comes to matters of science, engineering, and technology; rather, they are relativistic and pluralistic in matters of religion and ethics. But, of course, that's not postmodernism; that's modernism!"

Formal, academic critiques of postmodernism can also be found in works such as *Beyond the Hoax* and *Fashionable Nonsense*.

However, as for continental philosophy, American academics have tended to label it "postmodernist", especially practitioners of "French Theory". Such a trend might derive from U.S. departments of Comparative Literature. It is interesting to note that Félix Guattari, often considered a "postmodernist", rejected its theoretical assumptions by arguing that the structuralist and postmodernist visions of the world were not flexible enough to seek explanations in psychological, social and environmental domains at the same time.

Philosopher Daniel Dennett declared, "Postmodernism, the school of 'thought' that proclaimed 'There are no truths, only interpretations' has largely played itself out in absurdity, but it has left behind a generation of academics in the humanities disabled by their distrust of the very idea of truth and their disrespect for evidence, settling for 'conversations' in which nobody is wrong and nothing can be confirmed, only asserted with whatever style you can muster."

Globalism

Globalism is a group of ideologies that advocate the concept of globalization. It tends to advocate for such policies as increases in immigration, interventionism and global governance. Economically, globalism varies between free trade and lowering tariffs to Marxist proletarian internationalism. It is typically viewed as opposite of nationalism, and has become increasingly divisive in politics in many developed countries, such as the United States.

Definitions and Interpretations

Paul James defines *globalism* at least in its more specific use ... as the [dominant ideology] and subjectivity associated with different historically-dominant formations of global extension. The definition thus implies that there were pre-modern or traditional forms of globalism and globalisation long before the driving force of capitalism sought to colonise every corner of the globe, for example, going back to the Roman Empire in the second century AD and perhaps to the Greeks of the fifth century BC.

Manfred Steger distinguishes between different globalisms such as justice globalism, jihad globalism, and market globalism. Market globalism includes the ideology of neoliberalism. In some hands, the reduction of globalism to the single ideology of market globalism and neoliberalism has led to confusion. For example, in his 2005 book *The Collapse of Globalism and the Reinvention of the World*, Canadian philosopher John Ralston Saul treated globalism as coterminous with neoliberalism and neoliberal globalization. He argued that, far from being an inevitable force, globalization is already breaking up into contradictory pieces and that citizens are reasserting their national interests in both positive and destructive ways.

Alternatively, American political scientist Joseph Nye, co-founder of the international relations theory of neoliberalism, generalized the term to argue that *globalism* refers to any description and explanation of a world which is characterized by networks of connections that span multi-continental distances; while globalization refers to the increase or decline in the degree of globalism. This use of the term originated in, and continues to be used, in academic debates about the economic, social, and cultural developments that is described as globalization. The term is used in a specific and narrow way to describe a position in the debate about the historical character of globalization (i.e. whether globalization is unprecedented or not).

History of the Concept

The word itself came into widespread usage, first and foremost in the United States, from the early 1940s. This was the period when US global power was at its peak: the country was the greatest economic power the world had ever known, with the greatest military machine in human history. Or, as George Kennan's Policy Planning Staff put it in February 1948: "We have about 50% of the world's wealth but only 6.3% of its population. Our real task in the coming period is to devise a pattern of relationships which will permit us to maintain this position of disparity". America's allies and foes in Eurasia were, of course, at this time suffering the dreadful effects of World War II.

In their position of unprecedented power, US planners formulated policies to shape the kind of postwar world they wanted, which, in economic terms, meant a globe-spanning capitalist order centered exclusively upon the United States.

The first person in the United States to use the term *economic integration* in its modern sense (i.e. combining separate economies into larger economic regions) did so at this time: one John S. de Beers, an economist in the US Treasury Department, towards the end of 1941. By 1948, *economic integration* was appearing in an increasing number of American documents and speeches. Paul Hoffman, then head of the Economic Cooperation Administration, made the most marked use of the term in a 1949 speech to the Organisation for European Economic Co-operation. As *The New York Times* put it,

> Mr Hoffmann used the word 'integration' fifteen times or almost once to every hundred words of his speech. It is a word that rarely if ever has been used by European statesmen having to do with the Marshall Plan to describe what should happen to Europe's economies. It was remarked that no such term or goal was included in the commitments the European nations gave in agreeing to the Marshall Plan. Consequently it appeared to the Europeans that "integration" was an American doctrine that had been superimposed upon the mutual engagements made when the Marshall Plan began ...

While ideologies of the global have a long history, globalism emerged as a dominant set of associated ideologies across the course of the late twentieth century. As these ideologies settled, and as various processes of globalization intensified, they contributed to the consolidation of a connecting global imaginary. In their recent writings, Manfred Steger and Paul James have theorized this process in terms of four levels of change: changing ideas, ideologies, imaginaries and ontologies.

Global Citizenship

Global citizenship is the rights, responsibilities and duties that come with being a member of the global entity as a citizen of a particular nation or place. The idea is that one's identity transcends geography or political borders and that responsibilities or rights are or can be derived from membership in a broader class: "humanity". This does not mean that such a person denounces or waives their nationality or other, more local identities, but such identities are given "second place" to their membership in a global community. Extended, the idea leads to questions about the state of global society in the age of globalization. In general usage, the term may have much the same meaning as "world citizen" or cosmopolitan, but it also has additional, specialized meanings in differing contexts.

Usage

Education

In education, the term is most often used to describe a worldview or a set of values toward which education is oriented (for example, the priorities of the *Global Education First Initiative* led by the Secretary-General of the United Nations). The term "global society" is sometimes used to indicate a global studies set of learning objectives for students to prepare them for global citizenship (for example, the Global Studies Center at the University of Pittsburgh).

Global Citizenship Education

Within the educational system, the concept of global citizenship education (GCED) is beginning to supersede or overarch movements such as multicultural education, peace education, human rights education, Education for Sustainable Development and international education. Additionally, GCED rapidly incorporates references to the aforementioned movements. The concept of global citizenship has been linked with awards offered for helping humanity. Teachers are being given the responsibility of being social change agents. Audrey Osler, director of the *Centre for Citizenship and Human Rights Education*, the University of Leeds, affirms that "Education for living together in an interdependent world is not an optional extra, but an essential foundation".

With GCED gaining attention, scholars are investigating the field and developing perspectives. The following are a few of the more common perspectives:

- *Critical and transformative perspective.* Citizenship is defined by being a member with rights and responsibilities. Therefore, GCED must encourage active involvement. GCED can be taught from a critical and transformative perspective, whereby students are thinking, feeling, and doing. In this approach, GCED requires students to be politically critical and personally transformative. Teachers provide social issues in a neutral and grade-appropriate way for students to understand, grapple with, and do something about.

- *Worldmindedness.* Graham Pike and David Selby view GCED as having two strands. Worldmindedness, the first strand, refers to understanding the world as one unified system and a responsibility to view the interests of individual nations with the overall needs of the planet in mind. The second strand, Child-centeredness, is a pedagogical approach that encourages students to explore and discover on their own and addresses each learner as an individual with inimitable beliefs, experiences, and talents.

- *Holistic Understanding.* The Holistic Understanding perspective was founded by Merry Merryfield, focusing on understanding the self in relation to a global community. This perspective follows a curriculum that attends to human values and beliefs, global systems, issues, history, cross-cultural understandings, and the development of analytical and evaluative skills.

Philosophy

Global citizenship, in some contexts, may refer to a brand of ethics or political philosophy in which it is proposed that the core social, political, economic and environmental realities of the world today should be addressed at all levels—by individuals, civil society organizations, communities and nation states—through a global lens. It refers to a broad, culturally- and environmentally-inclusive worldview that accepts the fundamental interconnectedness of all things. Political, geographic borders become irrelevant and solutions to today's challenges are seen to be beyond the narrow vision of national interests. Proponents of this philosophy often point to Diogenes of Sinope (c. 412 B.C.) as an example, given his reported declaration that "I am a citizen of the world (κοσμοπολίτης, *cosmopolites*)" in response to a question about his place of origin. A Sanskrit term, *Vasudhaiva Kutumbakam*, has the meaning of "the world is one family". The earliest reference to this phrase is found in the Hitopadesha, a collection of parables. In the Mahopanishad VI.71-73, ślokas describe how one finds the Brahman (the one supreme, universal Spirit that is the origin and support of the phenomenal universe). The statement is not just about peace and harmony among the societies in the world, but also about a truth that somehow the whole world has to live together like a family.

Psychological Studies

Recently, global pollsters and psychologists have studied individual differences in the sense of global citizenship. Beginning in 2005, the World Values Survey, administered across almost 100 countries, included the statement, "I see myself as a world citizen." For smaller studies, several multi-item scales have been developed, including Sam McFarland and colleagues' Identification with All Humanity scale (e.g., "How much do you identify with (that is, feel a part of, feel love toward, have concern for) . . . all humans everywhere?"), Anna Malsch and Alan Omoto's Psychological Sense of Global Community (e.g., "I feel a sense of connection to people all over the world, even if I don't know them personally"), Gerhard Reese and colleagues' Global Social Identity scale (e.g. "I feel strongly connected to the world community as a whole."), and Stephen Reysen and Katzarska-Miller's global citizenship identification scale (e.g., "I strongly identify with global citizens."). These measures are strongly related to one another, but they are not fully identical.

Studies of the psychological roots of global citizenship have found that persons high in global citizenship are also high on the personality traits of openness to experience and agreeableness from the Big Five personality traits and high in empathy and caring. Oppositely, the authoritarian personality, the social dominance orientation and psychopathy are all associated with less global human identification. Some of these traits are influenced by heredity as well as by early experiences, which, in turn, likely influence individuals' receptiveness to global human identification.

Not surprisingly, those who are high in global human identification are less prejudiced toward many groups, care more about international human rights, worldwide inequality, global poverty and human suffering. They attend more actively to global concerns, value the lives of all human beings more equally, and give more in time and money to international humanitarian causes. They tend to be more politically liberal on both domestic and international issues. They want their countries to do more to alleviate global suffering.

Following a social identity approach, Reysen and Katzarska-Miller tested a model showing the antecedents and outcomes of global citizenship identification (i.e., degree of psychological connection with global citizens). Individuals' normative environment (the cultural environment in which one is embedded contains people, artifacts, cultural patterns that promote viewing the self as a global citizen) and global awareness (perceiving oneself as aware, knowledgeable, and connected to others in the world) predict global citizenship identification. Global citizenship identification then predicts six broad categories of prosocial behaviors and values, including: intergroup empathy, valuing diversity, social justice, environmental sustainability, intergroup helping, and a felt responsibility to act. Subsequent research has examined variables that influence the model such as: participation in a college course with global components, perception of one's global knowledge, college professors' attitudes toward global citizenship, belief in an intentional worlds view of culture, participation in a fan group that promotes the identity, use of global citizen related words when describing one's values, possible self as a global citizen, religiosity and religious orientation, threat to one's nation, interdependent self-construal prime, perception of the university environment, and social media usage.

Aspects

Geography, Sovereignty, and Citizenship

At the same time that globalization is reducing the importance of nation-states, the idea of global citizenship may require a redefinition of ties between civic engagement and geography. Face-to-face town hall meetings seem increasingly supplanted by electronic "town halls" not limited by space and time. Absentee ballots opened the way for expatriates to vote while living in another country; the Internet may carry this several steps further. Another interpretation given by several scholars of the changing configurations of citizenship due to globalization is the possibility that citizenship becomes a changed institution; even if situated within territorial boundaries that are national, if the meaning of the national itself has changed, then the meaning of being a citizen of that nation changes.

Tension Among Local, National, and Global Forces

An interesting feature of globalization is that, while the world is being internationalized, it's also being localized at the same time. The world shrinks as the local community (village, town, city) takes on greater and greater importance. This is reflected in the term glocalization, a portmanteau of the words "global" and "local". Mosco (1999) noted this feature and saw the growing importance of technopoles. If this trend is true, it seems global citizens may be the glue that holds these separate entities together. Put another way, global citizens are people who can travel within these various boundaries and somehow still make sense of the world through a global lens.

Human Rights

The lack of a universally recognized world body can put the initiative upon global citizens themselves to create rights and obligations. Rights and obligations as they arose at the formation of nation-states (e.g. the right to vote and obligation to serve in time of war) are being expanded. Thus, new concepts that accord certain "human rights" which arose in the 20th century are increasingly being universalized across nations and governments. This is the result of many factors, including the Universal Declaration of Human Rights by the United Nations in 1948, the aftermath of World War II and the Holocaust and growing sentiments towards legitimizing marginalized peoples (e.g., pre-industrialized peoples found in the jungles of Brazil and Borneo). Couple this with growing awareness of our impact on the environment, and there is the rising feeling that citizen rights may extend to include the right to dignity and self-determination. If national citizenship does not foster these new rights, then global citizenship may seem more accessible.

One cannot overestimate the importance of human rights discourse in shaping public opinion. What are the rights and obligations of human beings trapped in conflicts? Or, incarcerated as part of ethnic cleansing? Equally striking, are the pre-industrialized tribes newly discovered by scientists living in the depths of dense jungle? These rights can be equated with the rise of global citizenship as normative associations, indicating a national citizenship model that is more closed and a global citizenship one that is more flexible and inclusive. If true, this places a strain in the relationship between national and global citizenship.

UN General Assembly

On 10 December 1948, the UN General Assembly Adopted Resolution 217A (III), also known as "The Universal Declaration of Human Rights."

Article 1 states that "All human beings are born free and equal in dignity and rights. They are endowed with reason and conscience and should act towards one another in a spirit of brotherhood."

Article 2 states that "Everyone is entitled to all the rights and freedoms set forth in this Declaration, without distinction of any kind, such as race, colour, sex, language, religion, political or other opinion, national or social origin, property, birth or other status. Furthermore, no distinction shall be made on the basis of the political, jurisdictional or international status of the country or territory to which a person belongs, whether it be independent, trust, non-self-governing or under any other limitation of sovereignty."

Article 13(2) states that "Everyone has the right to leave any country, including his own, and to return to his country."

As evidence in today's modern world, events such as the Trial of Saddam Hussein have proven what British jurist A. V. Dicey said in 1885, when he popularized the phrase "rule of law" in 1885. Dicey emphasized three aspects of the rule of law :

1. No one can be punished or made to suffer except for a breach of law proved in an ordinary court.

2. No one is above the law and everyone is equal before the law regardless of social, economic, or political status.

3. The rule of law includes the results of judicial decisions determining the rights of private persons.

US Declaration of Independence

The opening of the United States Declaration of Independence, written by Thomas Jefferson in 1776, states as follows:

We hold these truths to be self-evident, that all men are created equal, that they are endowed by their Creator with certain unalienable Rights, that among these are Life, Liberty, and the Pursuit of Happiness. That to secure these rights, Governments are instituted among Men, deriving their just powers from the consent of the governed;

"Global citizenship in the United States" was a term used by U.S. President Barack Obama in 2008 in a speech in Berlin.

Support for Global Government

In contrast to questioning definitions, a counter-criticism can be found on the World Alliance of YMCA's website. An online article in *YMYCA World* emphasizes the importance of fostering global citizenship and global justice, and states, "Global citizenship might sound like a vague concept for academics but in fact it's a very practical way of looking at the world which anyone, if given the opportunity, can relate to." The author acknowledges the positive and negative outlooks towards globalization, and states, "In the context of globalisation, thinking and acting as global citizens is immensely important and can bring real benefits, as the YMCA experience shows."

Social Movements

World Citizen

World Citizen flag by Garry Davis

In general, a world citizen is a person who places global citizenship above any nationalistic or local identities and relationships. An early expression of this value is found in Diogenes of Sinope (c. 412 B.C.; mentioned above), the founding father of the Cynic movement in Ancient Greece. Of Diogenes it is said: "Asked where he came from, he answered: 'I am a citizen of the world (kosmopolitês)'". This was a ground-breaking concept because the broadest basis of social identity in Greece at that time was either the individual city-state or the Greeks (Hellenes) as a group. The Tamil poet Kaniyan Poongundran wrote in *Purananuru*, "To us all towns are one, all men our kin." In later years, political philosopher Thomas Paine would declare, "my country is the world, and my religion is to do good." Today, the increase in worldwide globalization has led to the formation of a "world citizen" social movement under a proposed world government. In a non-political definition, it has been suggested that a world citizen may provide value to society by using knowledge acquired across cultural contexts.

World Citizen badge

Albert Einstein described himself as a world citizen and supported the idea throughout his life, famously saying "Nationalism is an infantile disease. It is the measles of mankind." World citizenship has been promoted by distinguished people including Garry Davis, who lived for 60 years as a citizen of no nation, only the world. Davis founded the World Service Authority in Washington, DC, which issues the World Passport, a fantasy passport to world citizens. In 1956 Hugh J. Schonfield founded the Commonwealth of World Citizens, later known by its Esperanto name "Mondcivitana Respubliko", which also issued a world passport; it declined after the 1980s.

The Bahá'í faith promotes the concept through its founder's proclamation (in the late 19th century) that "The Earth is but one country, and mankind its citizens." As a term defined by the Bahá'í International Community in a concept paper shared at the 1st session of the United Nations Commission on Sustainable Development, New York, U.S.A. on 14–25 June 1993. "World citizenship begins with an acceptance of the oneness of the human family and the interconnectedness of the nations of 'the earth, our home.' While it encourages a sane and legitimate patriotism, it also insists upon a wider loyalty, a love of humanity as a whole. It does not, however, imply abandonment of legitimate loyalties, the suppression of cultural diversity, the abolition of national autonomy, nor the imposition of uniformity. Its hallmark is 'unity in diversity.' World citizenship encompasses the principles of social and economic justice, both within and between nations; non-adversarial decision making at all levels of society; equality of the sexes; racial, ethnic, national and religious harmony; and the willingness to sacrifice for the common good. Other facets of world citizenship—including the promotion of human honour and dignity, understanding, amity, co-operation, trustworthiness, compassion and the desire to serve—can be deduced from those already mentioned."

Mundialization

Philosophically, mundialization (French, *mondialisation*) is seen as a response to globalization's "dehumanisation through [despatialised] planetarisation" (Teilhard de Chardin quoted in Capdepuy 2011). An early use of *mondialisation* was to refer to the act of a city or a local authority declaring itself a "world citizen" city, by voting a charter stating its awareness of global problems and its sense of shared responsibility. The concept was promoted by the self-declared World Citizen Garry Davis in 1949, as a logical extension of the idea of individuals declaring themselves world citizens, and promoted by Robert Sarrazac, a former leader of the French Resistance who created the Human Front of World Citizens in 1945. The first city to be officially mundialised was the small French city of Cahors (only 20,000 in 2006), the capital city of the Département of Lot in central France, on 20 July 1949. Hundreds of cities mundialised themselves over a few years, most of them in France, and then it spread internationally, including to many German cities and to Hiroshima and Nagasaki. In less than a year, 10 General Councils (the elected councils of the French "Départements"), and hundreds of cities in France covering 3.4 million inhabitants voted mundialisation charters. One of the goals was to elect one delegate per million inhabitants to a People's World Constitutional Convention given the already then historical failure of the United Nations in creating a global institution able to negotiate a final world peace. To date, more than 1000 cities and towns have declared themselves World cities, including Beverly Hills, Los Angeles, Minneapolis, St. Louis, Philadelphia, Toronto, Hiroshima, Tokyo, Nivelles, and Königswinter.

As a social movement, mundialization expresses the solidarity of populations of the globe and aims to establish institutions and supranational laws of a federative structure common to them, while respecting the diversity of cultures and peoples. The movement advocates for a new political organization governing all humanity, involving the transfer of certain parts of national sovereignty to a Federal World Authority, Federal World Government and Federal World Court. Basing its authority on the will of the people, and developing new systems to draw the highest and best wisdom of all humanity into the task of governing our world, the collaborative governing system would be capable of solving the problems which call into question the future of man, such as hunger, water, war, peace-keeping, pollution and energy. The mundialization movement includes the declaration of specified territory - a city, town, or state, for example - as world territory, with responsibilities and rights on a world scale. Currently the nation-state system and the United Nations offer no way for the people of the world to vote for world officials or participate in governing our world. International treaties or agreements lack the force of law. Mundialization seeks to address this lack by presenting a way to build, one city at a time, such a system of true World Law based upon the sovereignty of the whole.

Earth Anthem

Author Shashi Tharoor feels that an Earth Anthem sung by people across the world can inspire planetary consciousness and global citizenship among people.

Criticisms

Not all interpretations of global citizenship are positive. For example, Parekh advocates what he calls globally oriented citizenship, and states, "If global citizenship means being a citizen of the world, it is neither practicable nor desirable." He argues that global citizenship, defined as an actual membership of a type of worldwide government system, is impractical and dislocated from one's immediate community. He also notes that such a world state would inevitably be "remote, bureaucratic, oppressive, and culturally bland."

Parekh presents his alternate option with the statement: "Since the conditions of life of our fellow human beings in distant parts of the world should be a matter of deep moral and political concern to us, our citizenship has an inescapable global dimension, and we should aim to become what I might call a globally oriented citizen." Parekh's concept of globally oriented citizenship consists of identifying with and strengthening ties towards one's political regional community (whether in its current state or an improved, revised form), while recognizing and acting upon obligations towards others in the rest of the world.

Michael Byers, a professor in Political Science at the University of British Columbia, questions the assumption that there is one definition of global citizenship, and unpacks aspects of potential definitions. In the introduction to his public lecture, the UBC Internalization website states, "'Global citizenship' remains undefined. What, if anything, does it really mean? Is global citizenship just the latest buzzword?" Byers notes the existence of stateless persons, whom he remarks ought to be the primary candidates for global citizenship, yet continue to live without access to basic freedoms and citizenship rights.

Byers does not oppose the concept of global citizenship, however he criticizes potential implications of the term depending on one's definition of it, such as ones that provide support for the "ruthlessly capitalist economic system that now dominates the planet." Byers states that global citizenship is a "powerful term" because "people that invoke it do so to provoke and justify action," and encourages the attendees of his lecture to re-appropriate it in order for its meaning to have a positive purpose, based on idealistic values.

Neither is criticism of global citizenship anything new. Gouverneur Morris, a delegate to the Constitutional Convention (United States), criticized "citizens of the world" while he was on the floor of the convention; August 9, 1787. "As to those philosophical gentlemen, those Citizens of the World as they call themselves, He owned he did not wish to see any of them in our public Councils. He would not trust them. The men who can shake off their attachments to their own Country can never love any other. These attachments are the wholesome prejudices which uphold all Governments, Admit a Frenchman into your Senate, and he will study to increase the commerce of France: an Englishman, and he will feel an equal biass in favor of that of England."

References

- Theda Skocpol, "Wallerstein's world capitalist system: a theoretical and historical critique." American Journal of Sociology (1977) 82#5 pp. 1075–90

- Sachs, Wolfgang (1992). The Development Dictionary: A Guide to Knowledge as Power. Zed Books. ISBN 1-85649-044-0

- Cairncross, A. K. (1961). "The Stages of Economic Growth". The Economic History Review. 13 (3): 450–458. doi:10.1111/j.1468-0289.1959.tb01829.x

- ""Dependency Theory: An Introduction," Vincent Ferraro, Mount Holyoke College, July 1966". Mtholyoke.edu. Retrieved 2013-05-24

- Tausch, Arno (2003). "Social Cohesion, Sustainable Development and Turkey's Accession to the European Union: Implications from a Global Model". Alternatives: Turkish Journal of International Relations

- Benoît Peeters, Derrida: A Biography, pp. 377–8, translated by Andrew Brown, Polity Press, 2013, ISBN 9780745656151

- Stewart, Frances (1 January 1989). "Basic Needs Strategies, Human Rights, and the Right to Development". Human Rights Quarterly. 11 (3): 347–374. JSTOR 762098. doi:10.2307/762098

- One of the earliest formulations of the notion of a postmodern level of the economy was John Hinkson, 'Postmodern Economy: Value, Self-Formation and Intellectual Practice', Arena Journal, New Series, no. 1, 1993, pp. 23–44

- Drucker, Johanna and Emily McVarish (2008). Graphic Design History. Pearson. pp. 305–306. ISBN 978-0132410755

- Yilmaz, K (2010). "Postmodernism and its Challenge to the Discipline of History: Implications for History Education". Educational Philosophy & Theory. 42 (7): 779–795. doi:10.1111/j.1469-5812.2009.00525.x

An Integrated Study of Cultural Globalization

Cultural globalization is the spreading of ideas and values globally. Cultural imperialism, cultural appropriation, Cross-cultural communication, multiculturalism and multiculturalism are some significant and important topics related to cultural globalization. The following chapter unfolds its crucial aspects in a critical yet systematic manner.

Cultural Globalization

Painting of a turn-of-century trading fair, *Hessisches Volksfest*
(*Hessian Folk Festival*), 1887, Louis Toussaint (1826-1887), Öl auf Leinwand.

Cultural globalization refers to the transmission of ideas, meanings and values around the world in such a way as to extend and intensify social relations. This process is marked by the common consumption of cultures that have been diffused by the Internet, popular culture media, and international travel. This has added to processes of commodity exchange and colonization which have a longer history of carrying cultural meaning around the globe. The circulation of cultures enables individuals to partake in extended social relations that cross national and regional borders. The creation and expansion of such social relations is not merely observed on a material level. Cultural globalization involves the formation of shared norms and knowledge with which people associate their individual and collective cultural identities. It brings increasing interconnectedness among different populations and cultures.

Cultural globalization integrates scholars from several disciplines, such as anthropolo-

gy, sociology, communication, cultural studies, geography, political ⸬
national relations. The field is notably broad as there are several con
be perceived as cultural or transnational.

A visible aspect of the cultural globalization is the diffusion of certain cu
American fast food chains. The two most successful global food and bev
McDonald's and Starbucks, are American companies often cited as examp⸬
ization, with over 36,000 and 24,000 locations operating worldwide respecti
2015. The Big Mac Index is an informal measure of purchasing power parity
world currencies.

Cultural globalization is one of the three main dimensions of globalization commo
ly found in academic literature, with the two other being economic globalization an
political globalization. However, unlike economic and political globalization, cultural
globalization has not been the subject of extensive research.

Measurement

There have been numerous attempts to measure globalization, typically using indices
that capture quantitative data for trade flows, political integration, and other measures.
The two most prominent are the AT Kearney/Foreign Policy Globalization index and
the KOF Globalization Index. Cultural globalization, however, is much more difficult
to capture using quantitative data, because it is difficult to find easily verifiable data of
the flow of ideas, opinions, and fashions. One attempt to do so was the Cultural Globalization Index, proposed by Randolph Kluver and Wayne Fu in 2004, and initially published by Foreign Policy Magazine. This effort measured cultural flow by using global
trade in media products (books, periodicals, and newspapers) as a proxy for cultural
flow. Kluver and Fu followed up with an extended analysis, using this method to measure cultural globalization in Southeast Asia.

Perspectives

Hybridization

Many writers suggest that cultural globalization is a long-term historical process of
bringing different cultures into interrelation. Jan Pieterse suggest that cultural globalization is involving human integration and hybridization, arguing that it is possible
to detect cultural mixing across continents and regions going back many centuries.
They refer, for example, to the movement of religious practices, language and culture
brought by Spanish colonization of the Americas. The Indian experience, to take another example, reveals both the pluralization of the impact of cultural globalization and its
long-term history. The work of such cultural historians qualifies the lineage of writers—
predominantly economists and sociologists—who trace the origins of globalization to
recent capitalism, facilitated through technological advances.

:spective on cultural globalization emphasizes the transfiguration of
ity into a pandemic of Westernized consumer culture. Some critics
ominance of American culture influencing the entire world will ulti-
the end of cultural diversity. Such cultural globalization may lead to a
culture. This process, understood as cultural imperialism, is associated
ruction of cultural identities, dominated by a homogenized and western-
ner culture. The global influence of American products, businesses and cul-
er countries around the world has been referred to as Americanization. This
is represented through that of American-based television programs which
adcast throughout the world. Major American companies such as McDonald's
a-Cola have played a major role in the spread of American culture around the
erms such as Coca-colonization have been coined to refer to the dominance of
an products in foreign countries, which some critics of globalization view as a
to the cultural identity of these nations.

nflict Intensification

Another alternative perspective argues that in reaction to the process of cultural globalization, a "Clash of Civilizations" might appear. Indeed, Samuel Huntington emphasizes the
fact that while the world is becoming smaller and interconnected, the interactions between
peoples of different cultures enhance the civilization consciousness that in turn invigorate
differences. Indeed, rather than reaching a global cultural community, the differences in
culture sharpened by this very process of cultural globalization will be a source of conflict.
While not many commentators agree that this should be characterized as a 'Clash of Civilizations', there is general concurrence that cultural globalization is an ambivalent process
bringing an intense sense of local difference and ideological contestation.

Alternatively, Benjamin Barber in his book *Jihad vs. McWorld* argues for a different
"cultural division" of the world. In his book the McWorld represents a world of globalization and global connectivity and interdependence, looking to create a "commercially
homogeneous global network". This global network is divided into four imperatives;
Market, Resource, Information-Technology and the Ecological imperative. On the other hand, "Jihad" represents traditionalism and maintaining one's identity. Whereas
"Clash of Civilizations" portrays a world with five coalitions of nation-states, "Jihad vs.
McWorld" shows a world where struggles take place on a sub-national level. Although
most of the western nations are capitalist and can be seen as "McWorld" countries, societies within these nations might be considered "Jihad" and vice versa.

Cultural Homogenization

Cultural homogenisation is an aspect of cultural globalisation, listed as one of its main
characteristics, and refers to the reduction in cultural diversity through the populari-

sation and diffusion of a wide array of cultural symbols—not only p
customs, ideas and values. O'Connor defines it as "the process by w
are transformed or absorbed by a dominant outside culture". Cultura
has been called "perhaps the most widely discussed hallmark of globa
ory, homogenization could result in the breakdown of cultural barrie
assimilation of a single culture.

Cultural homogenization can impact national identity and culture, wh
"eroded by the impact of global cultural industries and multinational medi
is usually used in the context of Western culture dominating and destroyin
tures. The process of cultural homogenization in the context of the domina
Western (American), capitalist culture is also known as McDonaldization, co
zation,Americanization or Westernization and criticized as a form of cultural i
ism and neo-colonialism. This process has been resented by many indigenous o
However, while some scholars, critical of this process, stress the dominance of Ar
culture and corporate capitalism in modern cultural homogenization, others no
the process of cultural homogenization is not one-way, and in fact involves a numb
cultures exchanging various elements. Critics of cultural homogenization theory p
out that as different cultures mix, homogenization is less about the spread of a sin
culture as about the mixture of different cultures, as people become aware of other cu
tures and adopt their elements. Examples of non-Western culture affecting the West
include world music and the popularization of non-Western television (Latin American
telenovelas, Japanese anime, Indian Bollywood), religion (Islam, Buddhism), food, and
clothing in the West, though in most cases insignificant in comparison to the Western
influence in other countries. The process of adoption of elements of global culture to
local cultures is known as glocalization or cultural heterogenization.

Some scholars like Arjun Appadurai note that "the central problem of today's global
interaction is the tension between cultural homogenization and cultural heterogenization".

Perspectives

The debate regarding the concept of cultural homogenization consists of two separate
questions:

- whether homogenization is occurring or not

- whether it is good or not.

John Tomlinson says, "It is one thing to say that cultural diversity is being destroyed,
quite another to lament the fact."

Tomlinson argues that globalization leads to homogenization. He comments on Cees
Hamelink, "Hamelink is right to identify cultural synchronization as an unprecedented

odernity." However, unlike Hamelink, he believes in the idea that
not a bad thing in itself and that benefits of homogenization may
s of cultural diversity.

vledging the concept of homogenization, still provides an alternative
enization. He says that " the homogenization argument subspeciates
gument about Americanization or an argument about commoditiza-
arguments fail to consider is that at least as rapidly as forces from
olises are brought into new societies, they tend to become indigenized."

re is more to be explored on the dynamics of indigenization, examples
onesianization in Irian Jaya and Indianization in Sri Lanka show the possi-
ernatives to Americanization.

homogenization is viewed negatively, as it leads to the "reduction in cultural
." However, some scholars have a positive view on homogenization, especially
rea of education. They say that it "produces consistent norms of behavior across
f modern institutions, thus tying institutions such as the modern nation state and
al education together in a tight political sphere."

uching universal values such as rationality by mass schooling is a part of the positive
enefits that can be generated from homogenization.

Maps

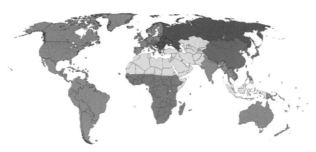

Global governance and identity as influenced by cultural homogenization.

Cultural Imperialism

Cultural imperialism comprises the cultural aspects of imperialism. Imperialism here
refers to the creation and maintenance of unequal relationships between civilizations,
favoring the more powerful civilization. Thus, cultural imperialism is the practice of promoting and imposing a culture, usually that of a politically powerful nation, over a less
powerful society; in other words, the cultural hegemony of industrialized or economically influential countries which determine general cultural values and standardize civ-

ilizations throughout the world. The term is employed especially in the fields of history, cultural studies, and postcolonial theory. It is usually used in a pejorative sense, often in conjunction with calls to reject such influence. Cultural imperialism can take various forms, such as an attitude, a formal policy, or military action, insofar as it reinforces cultural hegemony.

Background and Definitions

Although the *Oxford English Dictionary* has a 1921 reference to the "cultural imperialism of the Russians", John Tomlinson, in his book on the subject, writes that the term emerged in the 1960s and has been a focus of research since at least the 1970s. Terms such as "media imperialism", "structural imperialism", "cultural dependency and domination", "cultural synchronization", "electronic colonialism", "ideological imperialism", and "economic imperialism" have all been used to describe the same basic notion of cultural imperialism.

Various academics give various definitions of the term. American media critic Herbert Schiller wrote: "The concept of cultural imperialism today best describes the sum of the processes by which a society is brought into the modern world system and how its dominating stratum is attracted, pressured, forced, and sometimes bribed into shaping social institutions to correspond to, or even promote, the values and structures of the dominating centre of the system. The public media are the foremost example of operating enterprises that are used in the penetrative process. For penetration on a significant scale the media themselves must be captured by the dominating/penetrating power. This occurs largely through the commercialization of broadcasting."

Tom McPhail defined "Electronic colonialism as the dependency relationship established by the importation of communication hardware, foreign-produced software, along with engineers, technicians, and related information protocols, that vicariously establish a set of foreign norms, values, and expectations which, in varying degrees, may alter the domestic cultures and socialization processes." Sui-Nam Lee observed that "communication imperialism can be defined as the process in which the ownership and control over the hardware and software of mass media as well as other major forms of communication in one country are singly or together subjugated to the domination of another country with deleterious effects on the indigenous values, norms and culture." Ogan saw "media imperialism often described as a process whereby the United States and Western Europe produce most of the media products, make the first profits from domestic sales, and then market the products in Third World countries at costs considerably lower than those the countries would have to bear to produce similar products at home."

Downing and Sreberny-Mohammadi state: "Imperialism is the conquest and control of one country by a more powerful one. Cultural imperialism signifies the dimensions of the process that go beyond economic exploitation or military force. In the history of colonialism, (i.e., the form of imperialism in which the government of the colony is run directly by foreigners), the educational and media systems of many Third World countries have been set up as replicas of those in Britain, France, or the United States and carry their values. Western advertising has made further inroads, as have architectural and fashion styles. Subtly but powerfully, the message has often been insinuated that Western cultures are superior to the cultures of the Third World." Needless to say, all these authors agree that cultural imperialism promotes the interests of certain circles within the imperial powers, often to the detriment of the target societies.

The issue of cultural imperialism emerged largely from communication studies. However, cultural imperialism has been used as a framework by scholars to explain phenomena in the areas of international relations, anthropology, education, science, history, literature, and sports.

Theoretical Foundations

Many of today's academics that employ the term, *cultural imperialism,* are heavily informed by the work of Foucault, Derrida, Said, and other poststructuralist and postcolonialist theorists. Within the realm of postcolonial discourse, *cultural imperialism* can be seen as the cultural legacy of colonialism, or forms of social action contributing to the continuation of Western hegemony. To some outside of the realm of this discourse, the term is critiqued as being unclear, unfocused, and/or contradictory in nature.

Michel Foucault

The work of French philosopher and social theorist Michel Foucault has heavily influenced use of the term *cultural imperialism,* particularly his philosophical interpretation of power and his concept of governmentality.

Following an interpretation of power similar to that of Machiavelli, Foucault defines power as immaterial, as a "certain type of relation between individuals" that has to do with complex strategic social positions that relate to the subject's ability to control its environment and influence those around itself. According to Foucault, power is intimately tied with his conception of truth. "Truth," as he defines it, is a "system of ordered procedures for the production, regulation, distribution, circulation, and operation of statements" which has a "circular relation" with systems of power. Therefore, inherent in systems of power, is always "truth," which is culturally specific, inseparable from ideology which often coincides with various forms of hegemony. *Cultural imperialism* may be an example of this.

Foucault's interpretation of governance is also very important in constructing theories of transnational power structure. In his lectures at the Collège de France, Foucault often defines governmentality as the broad art of "governing," which goes beyond the traditional conception of governance in terms of state mandates, and into other realms such as governing "a household, souls, children, a province, a convent, a religious order, a family". This relates directly back to Machiavelli's The Prince, and Foucault's aforementioned conceptions of truth and power. (i.e. various subjectivities are created through power relations that are culturally specific, which lead to various forms of culturally specific governmentality such as neoliberal governmentality).

Edward Saïd

Informed by the works of Noam Chomsky, Foucault, and Antonio Gramsci, Edward Saïd is a founding figure of postcolonialism, established with the book *Orientalism* (1978), a humanist critique of The Enlightenment, which criticizes Western knowledge of "The East" — specifically the English and the French constructions of what is and what is not "Oriental". Whereby said "knowledge" then led to cultural tendencies towards a binary opposition of the Orient vs. the Occident, wherein one concept is defined in opposition to the other concept, and from which they emerge as of unequal value. In *Culture and Imperialism* (1993), the sequel to *Orientalism*, Saïd proposes that, despite the formal end of the "age of empire" after the Second World War (1939–45), colonial imperialism left a cultural legacy to the (previously) colonized peoples, which remains in their contemporary civilizations; and that said *cultural imperialism* is very influential in the international systems of power.

Gayatri Chakravorty Spivak

A self-described "practical Marxist-feminist-deconstructionist" Gayatri Chakravorty Spivak has published a number of works challenging the "legacy of colonialism" including *A Critique of Postcolonial Reason: Towards a History of the Vanishing Present* (1999), *Other Asias* (2005), and "Can the Subaltern Speak?" (1988).

In "Can the Subaltern Speak?" Spivak critiques common representations in the West of the Sati, as being controlled by authors other than the participants (specifically English colonizers and Hindu leaders). Because of this, Spivak argues that the subaltern, referring to the communities that participate in the Sati, are not able to represent themselves through their own voice. Spivak says that cultural imperialism has the power to disqualify or erase the knowledge and mode of education of certain populations that are low on the social hierarchy.

Throughout "Can the Subaltern Speak?", Spivak is cites the works of Karl Marx, Michel Foucault, Walter Benjamin, Louis Althusser, Jacques Derrida, and Edward Said, among others.

In *A critique of Postcolonial Reason*, Spivak argues that Western philosophy has a history of not only exclusion of the subaltern from discourse, but also does not allow them to occupy the space of a fully human subject.

Contemporary Ideas and Debate

Cultural imperialism can refer to either the forced acculturation of a subject population, or to the voluntary embracing of a foreign culture by individuals who do so of their own free will. Since these are two very different referents, the validity of the term has been called into question.

Cultural influence can be seen by the "receiving" culture as either a threat to or an enrichment of its cultural identity. It seems therefore useful to distinguish between cultural imperialism as an (active or passive) attitude of superiority, and the position of a culture or group that seeks to complement its own cultural production, considered partly deficient, with imported products.

The imported products or services can themselves represent, or be associated with, certain values (such as consumerism). According to one argument, the "receiving" culture does not necessarily perceive this link, but instead absorbs the foreign culture passively through the use of the foreign goods and services. Due to its somewhat concealed, but very potent nature, this hypothetical idea is described by some experts as *"banal imperialism."* For example, it is argued that while "American companies are accused of wanting to control 95 percent of the world's consumers", "cultural imperialism involves much more than simple consumer goods; it involved the dissemination of American principles such as freedom and democracy", a process which "may sound appealing" but which "masks a frightening truth: many cultures around the world are disappearing due to the overwhelming influence of corporate and cultural America".

Some believe that the newly globalised economy of the late 20th and early 21st century has facilitated this process through the use of new information technology. This kind of cultural imperialism is derived from what is called "soft power". The theory of electronic colonialism extends the issue to global cultural issues and the impact of major multi-media conglomerates, ranging from Viacom, Time-Warner, Disney, News Corp, to Google and Microsoft with the focus on the hegemonic power of these mainly United States-based communication giants.

Cultural Diversity

One of the reasons often given for opposing any form of cultural imperialism, voluntary or otherwise, is the preservation of cultural diversity, a goal seen by some as analogous to the preservation of ecological diversity. Proponents of this idea argue either that such diversity is valuable in itself, to preserve human historical heritage and knowledge, or instrumentally valuable because it makes available more ways of solving problems and responding to catastrophes, natural or otherwise.

Ideas Relating to African Colonization

Of all the areas of the world that scholars have claimed to be adversely affected by imperialism, Africa is probably the most notable. In the expansive "age of imperialism" of the nineteenth century, scholars have argued that European colonization in Africa has led to the elimination of many various cultures, worldviews, and epistemologies. This, arguably has led to uneven development, and further informal forms of social control having to do with culture and imperialism. A variety of factors, scholars argue, lead to the elimination of cultures, worldviews, and epistemologies, such as "de-linguicization" (replacing native African languages with European ones) and devaluing ontologies that are not explicitly individualistic. One scholar, Ali A. Obdi, claims that imperialism inherently "involves extensively interactive regimes and heavy contexts of identity deformation, misrecognition, loss of self-esteem, and individual and social doubt in self-efficacy."(2000: 12) Therefore, all imperialism would always, already be cultural.

Ties to Neoliberalism

Neoliberalism is often critiqued by sociologists, anthropologists, and cultural studies scholars as being culturally imperialistic. Critics of neoliberalism, at times, claim that it is the newly predominant form of imperialism. Other Scholars, such as Elizabeth Dunn and Julia Elyachar have claimed that neoliberalism requires and creates its own form of governmentality.

In Dunn's work, *Privatizing Poland*, she argues that the expansion of the multinational corporation, Gerber, into Poland in the 1990s imposed Western, neoliberal governmentality, ideologies, and epistemologies upon the post-soviet persons hired. Cultural conflicts occurred most notably the company's inherent individualistic policies, such as promoting competition among workers rather than cooperation, and in its strong opposition to what the company owners claimed was bribery.

In Elyachar's work, *Markets of Dispossession*, she focuses on ways in which, in Cairo, NGOs along with INGOs and the state promoted neoliberal governmentality through schemas of economic development that relied upon "youth microentrepreneurs." Youth microentrepreneurs would receive small loans to build their own businesses, similar to the way that microfinance supposedly operates. Elyachar argues though, that these programs not only were a failure, but that they shifted cultural opinions of value (personal and cultural) in a way that favored Western ways of thinking and being.

Ties to Development Studies

Often, methods of promoting development and social justice to are critiqued as being imperialistic, in a cultural sense. For example, Chandra Mohanty has critiqued Western feminism, claiming that it has created a misrepresentation of the "third world woman" as being completely powerless, unable to resist male dominance. Thus, this leads to the often critiqued narrative of the "white man" saving the "brown woman" from the "brown man." Other, more radical critiques of development studies, have to do with the field of study itself. Some scholars even question the intentions of those developing the field of study, claiming that efforts to "develop" the Global South were never about the South itself. Instead, these efforts, it is argued, were made in order to advance Western development and reinforce Western hegemony.

Ties to Media Effects Studies

The core of cultural imperialism thesis is integrated with the political-economy traditional approach in media effects research. Critics of cultural imperialism commonly claim that non-Western cultures, particularly from the Third World, will forsake their traditional values and lose their cultural identities when they are solely exposed to Western media. Nonetheless, Michael B. Salwen, in his book *Critical Studies in Mass Communication* (1991), claims that cross-consideration and integration of empirical findings on cultural imperialist influences is very critical in terms of understanding mass media in the international sphere. He recognizes both of contradictory contexts on cultural imperialist impacts. The first context is where cultural imperialism imposes socio-political disruptions on developing nations. Western media can distort images of foreign cultures and provoke personal and social conflicts to developing nations in some cases. Another context is that peoples in developing nations resist to foreign media and preserve their cultural attitudes. Although he admits that outward manifestations of Western culture may be adopted, but the fundamental values and behaviors remain still. Furthermore, positive effects might occur when male-dominated cultures adopt the "liberation" of women with exposure to Western media and it stimulates ample exchange of cultural exchange.

Criticisms of "Cultural Imperialism Theory"

Critics of scholars who discuss cultural imperialism have a number of critiques. *Cultural imperialism* is a term that is only used in discussions where cultural relativism and constructivism are generally taken as true. (One cannot critique promoting Western values if one believes that said values are absolutely correct. Similarly, one cannot argue that Western epistemology is unjustly promoted in non-Western societies if one believes that those epistemologies are absolutely correct.) Therefore, those who disagree with cultural relativism and/or constructivism may critique the employment of the term, *cultural imperialism* on those terms.

John Tomlinson provides a critique of cultural imperialism theory and reveals major problems in the way in which the idea of cultural, as opposed to economic or political, imperialism is formulated. In his book *Cultural Imperialism: A Critical Introduction*, he delves into the much debated "media imperialism" theory. Summarizing research on the Third World's reception of American television shows, he challenges the cultural imperialism argument, conveying his doubts about the degree to which US shows in developing nations actually carry US values and improve the profits of US companies. Tomlinson suggests that cultural imperialism is growing in some respects, but local transformation and interpretations of imported media products propose that cultural diversification is not at an end in global society. He explains that one of the fundamental conceptual mistakes of cultural imperialism is to take for granted that the distribution of cultural goods can be considered as cultural dominance. He thus supports his argument highly criticizing the concept that Americanization is occurring through global overflow of American television products. He points to a myriad of examples of television networks who have managed to dominate their domestic markets and that domestic programs generally top the ratings. He also doubts the concept that cultural agents are passive receivers of information. He states that movement between cultural/ geographical areas always involves translation, mutation, adaptation, and the creation of hybridity.

Other major critiques are that the term is not defined well, and employs further terms that are not defined well, and therefore lacks explanatory power, that *cultural imperialism* is hard to measure, and that the theory of a legacy of colonialism is not always true.

Rothkopf on Dealing with Cultural Dominance

David Rothkopf, managing director of Kissinger Associates and an adjunct professor of international affairs at Columbia University (who also served as a senior US Commerce Department official in the Clinton Administration), wrote about cultural imperialism in his provocatively titled *In Praise of Cultural Imperialism?* in the summer 1997 issue of *Foreign Policy* magazine. Rothkopf says that the United States should embrace "cultural imperialism" as in its self-interest. But his definition of cultural imperialism stresses spreading the values of tolerance and openness to cultural change in order to avoid war and conflict between cultures as well as expanding accepted technological and legal standards to provide free traders with enough security to do business with more countries. Rothkopf's definition almost exclusively involves allowing individuals in other nations to accept or reject foreign cultural influences. He also mentions, but only in passing, the use of the English language and consumption of news and popular music and film as cultural dominance that he supports. Rothkopf additionally makes the point that globalization and the Internet are accelerating the process of cultural influence.

Culture is sometimes used by the organizers of society — politicians, theologians, academics, and families — to impose and ensure order, the rudiments of which change over time as need dictates. One need only look at the 20th century's genocides. In each one, leaders used culture as a political front to fuel the passions of their armies and other minions and to justify their actions among their people.

Rothkopf then cites genocide and massacres in Armenia, Russia, the Holocaust, Cambodia, Bosnia and Herzegovina, Rwanda and East Timor as examples of culture (in some cases expressed in the ideology of "political culture" or religion) being misused to justify violence. He also acknowledges that cultural imperialism in the past has been guilty of forcefully eliminating the cultures of natives in the Americas and in Africa, or through use of the Inquisition, *"and during the expansion of virtually every empire."*.The most important way to deal with cultural influence in any nation, according to Rothkopf, is to promote tolerance and allow, or even promote, cultural diversities that are compatible with tolerance and to eliminate those cultural differences that cause violent conflict:

Successful multicultural societies, be they nations, federations, or other conglomerations of closely interrelated states, discern those aspects of culture that do not threaten union, stability, or prosperity (such as food, holidays, rituals, and music) and allow them to flourish. But they counteract or eradicate the more subversive elements of culture (exclusionary aspects of religion, language, and political/ideological beliefs). History shows that bridging cultural gaps successfully and serving as a home to diverse peoples requires certain social structures, laws, and institutions that transcend culture. Furthermore, the history of a number of ongoing experiments in multiculturalism, such as in the European Union, India, South Africa, Canada and the United States, suggests that workable, if not perfected, integrative models exist. Each is built on the idea that tolerance is crucial to social well-being, and each at times has been threatened by both intolerance and a heightened emphasis on cultural distinctions. The greater public good warrants eliminating those cultural characteristics that promote conflict or prevent harmony, even as less-divisive, more personally observed cultural distinctions are celebrated and preserved.

Cultural Imperialism in History

Although the term was popularized in the 1960s, and was used by its original proponents to refer to cultural hegemonies in a post-colonial world, cultural imperialism has also been used to refer to times further in the past.

Ancient Rome

The Roman empire has been seen as an early example of cultural imperialism.

Early Rome, in its conquest of Italy, assimilated the people of Etruria by replacing the Etruscan language with Latin, which led to the demise of that language and many aspects of Etruscan civilization.

Cultural Romanization was imposed on many parts of Rome's empire by "many regions receiving Roman culture unwillingly, as a form of cultural imperialism." For example, when Greece was conquered by the Roman armies, Rome set about altering the culture of Greece to conform with Roman ideals. For instance, the Greek habit of stripping naked, in public, for exercise, was looked on askance by Roman writers, who considered the practice to be a cause of the Greeks' effeminacy and enslavement.

The Pax Romana was secured in the empire, in part, by the "forced acculturation of the culturally diverse populations that Rome had conquered."

British Empire

British worldwide expansion in the 18th and 19th centuries was an economic and political phenomenon. However, "there was also a strong social and cultural dimension to it, which Rudyard Kipling termed the 'white man's burden'." One of the ways this was carried out was by religious proselytising, by, amongst others, the London Missionary Society, which was "an agent of British cultural imperialism." Another way, was by the imposition of educational material on the colonies for an "imperial curriculum". Morag Bell writes, "The promotion of empire through books, illustrative materials, and educational syllabuses was widespread, part of an education policy geared to cultural imperialism". This was also true of science and technology in the empire. Douglas M. Peers and Nandini Gooptu note that "Most scholars of colonial science in India now prefer to stress the ways in which science and technology worked in the service of colonialism, as both a 'tool of empire' in the practical sense and as a vehicle for cultural imperialism. In other words, science developed in India in ways that reflected colonial priorities, tending to benefit Europeans at the expense of Indians, while remaining dependent on and subservient to scientific authorities in the colonial metropolis."

The analysis of cultural imperialism carried out by Edward Said drew principally from a study of the British Empire. According to Danilo Raponi, the cultural imperialism of the British in the 19th century had a much wider effect than only in the British Empire. He writes, "To paraphrase Said, I see cultural imperialism as a complex cultural hegemony of a country, Great Britain, that in the 19th century had no rivals in terms of its ability to project its power across the world and to influence the cultural, political and commercial affairs of most countries. It is the 'cultural hegemony' of a country whose power to export the most fundamental ideas and concepts at the basis of its understanding of 'civilisation' knew practically no bounds." In this, for example, Raponi includes Italy.

Other Pre-Second World War Examples

The New Cambridge Modern History writes about the cultural imperialism of Napoleonic France. Napoleon used the Institut de France "as an instrument for transmuting French universalism into cultural imperialism." Members of the Institute (who included Napoleon), descended upon Egypt in 1798. "Upon arrival they organised themselves into an Institute of Cairo. The Rosetta Stone is their most famous find. The science of Egyptology is their legacy."

After the First World War, Germans were worried about the extent of French influence in the annexed Rhineland, with the French occupation of the Ruhr Valley in 1923. An early use of the term appeared in an essay by Paul Ruhlmann (as "Peter Hartmann") at that date, entitled *French Cultural Imperialism on the Rhine*.

Nazi Colonialism

Cultural imperialism has also been used in connection with the expansion of German influence under the Nazis in the middle of the twentieth century. Alan Steinweis and Daniel Rogers note that even before the Nazis came to power, "Already in the Weimar Republic, German academic specialists on eastern Europe had contributed through their publications and teaching to the legitimization Of German territorial revanchism and cultural imperialism. These scholars operated primarily in the disciplines Of history, economics, geography, and literature."

In the area of music, Michael Kater writes that during the WWII German occupation of France, Hans Rosbaud, a German conductor based by the Nazi regime in Strasbourg, became "at least nominally, a servant of Nazi cultural imperialism directed against the French."

In Italy during the war, Germany pursued "a European cultural front that gravitates around German culture". The Nazi propaganda minister Joseph Goebbels set up the European Union of Writers, "one of Goebbels's most ambitious projects for Nazi cultural hegemony. Presumably a means of gathering authors from Germany, Italy, and the occupied countries to plan the literary life of the new Europe, the union soon emerged as a vehicle of German cultural imperialism."

For other parts of Europe, Robert Gerwarth, writing about cultural imperialism and Reinhard Heydrich, states that the "Nazis' Germanization project was based on a historically unprecedented programme of racial stock-taking, theft, expulsion and murder." Also, "The full integration of the Czech Protectorate into this New Order required the complete Germanization of the Protectorate's cultural life and the eradication of indigenous Czech and Jewish culture."

The actions by Nazi Germany reflect on the notion of race and culture playing a significant role in imperialism. The idea that there is a distinction between the Germans and the Jews has created the illusion of Germans believing they were superior to the Jewish inferiors, the notion of us/them and self/others.

Cultural Appropriation

Cultural appropriation is the adoption or use of the elements of one culture by members of another culture. Cultural appropriation, often framed as cultural misappropriation, is sometimes portrayed as harmful and is claimed to be a violation of the collective intellectual property rights of the originating culture. Often unavoidable when multiple cultures come together, cultural appropriation can include using other cultures' traditions, food, fashion, symbols, technology, language, and cultural songs without permission. According to critics of the practice, cultural misappropriation differs from acculturation, assimilation, or cultural exchange in that the "appropriation" or "misappropriation" refers to the adoption of these cultural elements in a colonial manner: elements are copied from a minority culture by members of a dominant culture, and these elements are used outside of their original cultural context—sometimes even against the expressly stated wishes of representatives of the originating culture.

Often, the original meaning of these cultural elements is lost or distorted, and such displays are often viewed as disrespectful by members of the originating culture, or even as a form of desecration. Cultural elements which may have deep meaning to the original culture may be reduced to "exotic" fashion or toys by those from the dominant culture. Kjerstin Johnson has written that, when this is done, the imitator, "who does not experience that oppression is able to 'play', temporarily, an 'exotic' other, without experiencing any of the daily discriminations faced by other cultures." The African-American academic, musician and journalist Greg Tate argues that appropriation and the "fetishizing" of cultures, in fact, alienates those whose culture is being appropriated. On the other hand some scholars argue that the concept is misunderstood by the general public. Cultural appropriation is often misapplied to situations that don't accurately fit.

Conversely, cultural appropriation or borrowing can be viewed as inevitable and a contribution to diversity and free expression. This view distinguishes outright theft of cultural artifacts or exotic stereotyping from more benign borrowing or appreciation. Cultural borrowing and cross-fertilization is seen by proponents as a generally positive thing, and as something which is usually done out of admiration of the cultures being imitated, with no intent to harm them.

Trans-cultural diffusion has occurred throughout history and is subject of study by a variety of academic disciplines, including folkloristics, cultural anthropology and cultural geography. For instance, most of the world have adopted the Hindu-Arabic numerals as the common, standard form of describing numbers, which can be interpreted as a form of cultural appropriation. Opposition to cultural appropriation is seen as controversial as it may clash with the right to participate in culture.

Overview

Cultural appropriation can involve the use of ideas, symbols, artifacts, or other aspects of human-made visual or non-visual culture. Anthropologists study the various processes of cultural borrowing, "appropriation," and cultural exchange (which includes art and urbanism), as part of cultural evolution and contact between different cultures.

As a concept that is controversial in its applications, the propriety of cultural appropriation has been the subject of much debate. Opponents of cultural appropriation view many instances as wrongful misappropriation when the subject culture is a minority culture or is subordinated in social, political, economic, or military status to the dominant culture or when there are other issues involved, such as a history of ethnic or racial conflict. This is often seen in cultural outsiders' use of an oppressed culture's symbols or other cultural elements, such as music, dance, spiritual ceremonies, modes of dress, speech, and social behaviour, notably when these elements are trivialized and used for fashion, rather than respected within their original cultural context. Opponents view the issues of colonialism, context, and the difference between appropriation and mutual exchange as central to analyzing cultural appropriation. They argue that mutual exchange happens on an "even playing field", whereas appropriation involves pieces of an oppressed culture being taken out of context by a people who have historically oppressed those they are taking from, and who lack the cultural context to properly understand, respect, or utilize these elements.

A different view of cultural appropriation characterizes critics of the practice as "engaged in a deeply conservative project: one which first seeks to preserve in formaldehyde the content of an established culture and second tries to prevent others from interacting with that culture." On the contrary, cultures as they exist now are themselves the products of previous instances of cultural appropriation. Appropriation can be wrongful under this view, but the wrongfulness is determined by the intent of the appropriator and not the perceived power dynamics between the cultures. Proponents of cultural appropriation view it as often benign or mutually beneficial, citing mutation, product diversity, technological diffusion, and cultural empathy as among its benefits. For example, the film *Star Wars* appropriated elements from Akira Kurosawa's *The Hidden Fortress*, which itself appropriated elements from Shakespeare; culture in the aggregate is arguably better off for each instance of appropriation. Fusion between cultures has produced such foods as American Chinese cuisine, modern Japanese sushi, and bánh mì, each of which is sometimes argued to reflect part of its respective culture's identity.

Academic Study

Cultural and racial theorist George Lipsitz used the term "strategic anti-essentialism" to refer to the calculated use of a cultural form, outside of your own, to define yourself or your group. Strategic anti-essentialism can be seen in both minority cultures and majority cultures, and is not confined only to the use of the other. However, Lipsitz argues, when the majority culture attempts to strategically anti-essentialize itself by appropriating a minority culture, it must take great care to recognize the specific socio-historical circumstances and significance of these cultural forms so as not to perpetuate the already existing majority vs. minority unequal power relations.

Examples

Art, Iconography, and Adornment

A common example of cultural appropriation is the adoption of the iconography of another culture, and using it for purposes that are unintended by the original culture or even offensive to that culture's mores. Examples include sports teams using Native American tribal names or images as mascots; wearing jewelry or fashion with religious symbols such as the war bonnet, medicine wheel, or cross without any belief in those religions; and mimicking iconography from another culture's history such as tattoos of Polynesian tribal iconography, Chinese characters, or Celtic art worn without regard to their original cultural significance. Critics of the practice of cultural appropriation contend that divorcing this iconography from its cultural context or treating it as kitsch risks offending people who venerate and wish to preserve their cultural traditions.

A war bonnet

In Australia, Aboriginal artists have discussed an "authenticity brand" to ensure consumers are aware of artworks claiming false Aboriginal significance. The movement for such a measure gained momentum after the 1999 conviction of John O'Loughlin for the fraudulent sale of works described as Aboriginal but painted by non-indigenous artists.

Historically, some of the most hotly debated cases of cultural appropriation have occurred in places where cultural exchange is the highest, such as along the trade routes in southwestern Asia and southeastern Europe. Some scholars of the Ottoman Empire and ancient Egypt argue that Ottoman and Egyptian architectural traditions have long been falsely claimed and praised as Persian or Arab.

Religion and Spirituality

Among critics, the misuse and misrepresentation of indigenous intellectual property is seen as an exploitative form of colonialism, and one step in the destruction of indigenous cultures.

The results of this use of indigenous knowledge have led some tribes, and the United Nations General Assembly, to issue several declarations on the subject. The *Declaration of War Against Exploiters of Lakota Spirituality* includes the passage:

We assert a posture of zero-tolerance for any "white man's shaman" who rises from within our own communities to "authorize" the expropriation of our ceremonial ways by non-Indians; all such "plastic medicine men" are enemies of the Lakota, Dakota and Nakota people.

Article 31 1 of the United Nations *Declaration on the Rights of Indigenous Peoples* states:

Indigenous peoples have the right to maintain, control, protect and develop their cultural heritage, traditional knowledge and traditional cultural expressions, as well as the manifestations of their sciences, technologies and cultures, including human and genetic resources, seeds, medicines, knowledge of the properties of fauna and flora, oral traditions, literatures, designs, sports and traditional games and visual and performing arts. They also have the right to maintain, control, protect and develop their intellectual property over such cultural heritage, traditional knowledge, and traditional cultural expressions.

Many Native Americans have criticized what they deem to be cultural appropriation of their sweat lodge and vision quest ceremonies by non-Natives, and even by tribes who have not traditionally had these ceremonies. They also contend that there are higher safety risks when the ceremonies are conducted by non-Natives, pointing to deaths or injuries in 1996, 2002, 2004, and several high-profile deaths in 2009.

In 2015, a group of Native American academics and writers issued a statement against the Rainbow Family members whose acts of "cultural exploitation... dehumanize us as an indigenous Nation because they imply our culture and humanity, like our land, is anyone's for the taking."

Fashion

Cultural appropriation is controversial in the fashion industry due to the belief that some trends commercialise and cheapen the ancient heritage of indigenous cultures. There is debate about whether designers and fashion houses understand the history behind the clothing they are taking from different cultures, besides the ethical issues of using these cultures' shared intellectual property without consent, acknowledgement, or compensation. In response to this criticism, many fashion experts claim that this occurrence is in fact "culture appreciation", rather than cultural appropriation. Companies and designers claim the use of unique cultural symbols is an effort to recognize and pay homage to that specific culture.

George IV of the United Kingdom wearing highland dress, 1822.

17th Century to Victorian Era

During the 17th century, the forerunner to the three piece suit was appropriated from the traditional dress of diverse Eastern European and Islamic countries. The Justacorps frock coat was copied from the long zupans worn in Poland and the Ukraine, the necktie or cravat was derived from a scarf worn by Croatian mercenaries fighting for Louis XIII, and the brightly colored silk waistcoats popularised by Charles II of England were inspired by exotic Turkish, Indian and Persian attire acquired by wealthy English travellers.

Less than a generation after the Highland Clearances, the British aristocracy appropriated traditional Scottish clothing. Tartan was given spurious association with specific Highland clans after publications such as James Logan's romanticised work *The Scottish Gael* (1831) led the Scottish tartan industry to invent clan tartans and tartan became a desirable material for dresses, waistcoats and cravats. In America, plaid flannel had become workwear by the time of Westward expansion, and was widely worn by Old West pioneers and cowboys who were not of Scottish descent. In the 21st century, tartan remains ubiquitous in mainstream fashion.

By the 19th century the fascination had shifted to Asian culture. English Regency era dandies adapted the Indian churidars into slim fitting pantaloons, and frequently wore turbans within their own houses. Later, Victorian gentlemen wore smoking caps based on the Islamic fez, and fashionable turn of the century ladies wore Orientalist Japanese inspired kimono dresses. During the tiki culture fad of the 1950s, white women frequently donned the qipao to give the impression that they had visited Hong Kong, although the dresses were frequently made by seamstresses in America using rayon rather than genuine silk. At the same time, teenage British Teddy Girls wore Chinese coolie hats due to their exotic connotations.

In Mexico, the sombrero associated with the mestizo peasant class was appropriated from an earlier hat introduced by the Spanish colonials during the 18th century. This, in turn, was adapted into the cowboy hat worn by white Americans after the US Civil War. In 2016, the University of East Anglia prohibited the wearing of sombreros to parties on campus, in the belief that these could offend Mexican students.

Modern Era

Blue denim jeans, originally traditional American clothing, have been appropriated by consumers throughout Europe and Asia.

During the 1920s and '30s, the British bowler hat was appropriated by Quechua and Aymara Indian women in Bolivia, and by various African tribal elders in the British Empire who associated the hat with authority. In Britain, the rough tweed cloth clothing of the Irish, English and Scottish peasantry, including the flat cap and Irish hat were appropriated by the upper classes as the British country clothing worn for sports such as hunting or fishing, in imitation of the then Prince of Wales. The country clothing, in turn, was appropriated by the wealthy American soc and later preppy subcultures during the 1950s and 1980s due to both its practicality and its association with the English elite.

In Britain, Germany and Japan during the 1950s, young boys began wearing traditional American clothing such as blue jeans and checked western shirts due to their association with the cowboys of the silver screen. The traditional cowboy shirts with pearl snaps would later be revived in Britain and America during the 1970s, 1980s and 2010s as unisex adult fashion. British Teddy Boys appropriated the bolo tie that had previously served as a folk costume in the Southwestern United States, and wore them with locally tailored imitations of the zoot suit. During their 2011 visit to Canada, Prince William and Kate Middleton appropriated cowboy hats and Western shirts, and posed for photographs which Charles, Prince of Wales criticised as tasteless.

When keffiyehs became popular in the late 2000s, experts made a clear distinction between the wearing of a genuine scarf, and a fake made in China. Palestinian independence activists and socialists denounced the wearing of scarves not made in Palestine as a form of cultural appropriation, but encouraged white indie kids and Muslim youths to buy shemaghs made in the Herbawi factory to demonstrate solidarity with the Palestinian people and improve the economy of the West Bank. In 2017, Topshop caused controversy by selling Chinese-made playsuits that imitated the pattern of the keffiyeh.

In 2012 during the annual Victoria's Secret fashion show, model Karlie Kloss was scrutinized for wearing a Native American headdress during her walk on the runaway. There was a mixed public response. People of mixed heritage were the most sensitive to headdress. USA Today ran a feature where they interviewed a woman of mixed heritage who said that the headdress is a symbol of leadership and honour, and also has a religious meaning behind it. This cultural meaning was not considered in Victoria's Secret's use of the headdress as an accessory. Victoria's Secret issued an apology stating that they had no intentions of offending anyone.

At the 2014 Coachella festival one of the most noted fashion trends was the bindi. The bindi is a traditional Hindu head mark and is a part of the religious culture of Hinduism. As pictures of the festival surfaced online there was public controversy over the casual wearing of the bindi. People were offended because they felt the people wearing the bindi do not understand the meaning behind it.

Hairstyles, Makeup and Body Modifications

- The leaders of ancient Israel strongly condemned the adoption of Egyptian and Canaanite practises, especially cutting the hair short or shaving the beard. At the same time, the Old Testament distinguishes the religious circumcision of the Hebrews, from cultures such as the Egyptians where the practise had aesthetic or practical purposes.

- During the early 16th century, European men imitated the short regular haircuts and beards on rediscovered Ancient Greek and Roman statues. The curled hair favoured by the Regency era dandy Beau Brummel was also inspired by the classical era.

- During the 17th century, Louis XIV began wearing powdered wigs to conceal his baldness. Like many other French fashions, these were quickly appropriated by baroque era courtiers in England and the rest of Europe to the extent that men often shaved their heads to ensure their wig fitted properly.

- American soldiers during World War II appropriated the Mohawk hairstyle of the Native American tribe of the same name to intimidate their enemies. These were later worn by 1950s jazz musicians like Sonny Rollins, and the 1980s punk subculture.

- During the early 2000s, it was popular for white people to get tribal tattoos appropriated from African and Polynesian culture. Others favoured stretched earlobe piercings known as flesh tunnels, in imitation of those worn by various Aboriginals, and by the Buddha.

Sports

The Washington Redskins logo in Maryland

While the history of colonization and marginalization is not unique to the Americas, the practice of non-Native sports teams deriving team names, imagery, and mascots from indigenous peoples is still common in the United States and Canada, and has persisted to some extent despite protests from Indigenous groups. Cornel Pewewardy, Professor and Director of Indigenous Nations Studies at Portland State University, cites indigenous mascots as an example of dysconscious racism which, by placing images of Native American or First Nations people into an invented media context, continues to maintain the superiority of the dominant culture. It is argued that such practices maintain the power relationship between the dominant culture and the indigenous culture, and can be seen as a form of cultural imperialism.

Such practices may be seen as particularly harmful in schools and universities which have a stated purpose of promoting ethnic diversity and inclusion. In recognition of the responsibility of higher education to eliminate behaviors that create a hostile environment for education, in 2005 the NCAA initiated a policy against "hostile and abusive" names and mascots that led to the change of many derived from Native American culture, with the exception of those that established an agreement with particular tribes for the use of their specific names. Other schools retain their names because they were founded for the education of Native Americans, and continue to have a significant number of indigenous students. The trend towards the elimination of indigenous names and mascots in local schools has been steady, with two thirds having been eliminated over the past 50 years according to the National Congress of American Indians (NCAI).

While nearly all Native Americans and their tribes object to depictions as sports mascots, only one tribe explicitly approves of such representations. The Florida State Seminoles, which uses the iconography of the Seminole tribe and whose mascots are Osceola and Renegade, a depiction of the Seminole chief Osceola and his Appaloosa horse. After the NCAA attempted to ban the use of Native American names and iconography in college sports in 2005, the Seminole Tribe of Florida passed a resolution offering explicit support for FSU's use of Seminole culture and Osceola as a mascot; the university was granted a waiver, citing the close relationship with and consultation between the team and the tribe. In 2013, the tribe's chairman objected to outsiders meddling in tribal approval, stating that the FSU mascot and use of Seminole iconography "represents the courage of the people who were here and are still here, known as the Unconquered Seminoles." Conversely, in 2013, the Seminole Nation of Oklahoma expressed disapproval of "the use of all American Indian sports-team mascots in the public school system, by college and university level and by professional sports teams", and not all members of the tribe's Florida branch are supportive of its stance.

In other former colonies in Asia, Africa, and South America, the adoption of indigenous names for majority indigenous teams is also found. There are also ethnicity-related team names derived from prominent immigrant populations in the area, such as the Boston Celtics, the Notre Dame Fighting Irish, and the Minnesota Vikings.

The All Blacks have performed a traditional haka dance (an element of Māori culture) at the start of most of their matches since at least 1905, though a very significant part of those matches (certainly the earlier ones) did not have any, let alone a majority, of indigenous players.

The 2018 Commonwealth Games to be held on the Gold Coast in Australia from 4 April 2018 has named its mascot Borobi, the local Yugambeh word for 'koala'. The Games organising committee used the word without proper consultation with the Yugambeh people, and to compound the cultural appropriation, has sought to trademark the word through IP Australia. The application is being opposed by a Yugambeh cultural heritage organisation.

African-American Culture

Example of hip hop fashion

The term wigger (common spelling "wigga") is a slang term for a white person who attempts to immitate the mannerisms, language, and fashions associated with African-American culture, particularly hip hop, and, in Britain, the grime scene, often implying a failed attempt at cultural appropriation by a white subject. Wigger is a portmanteau of *white* and *nigger* or *nigga,* and the related term wangsta is a mashup of *wannabe* or *white*, and *gangsta*. Among black hip-hop fans, nigga can sometimes be considered a friendly greeting, but when used by whites, it is usually viewed as offensive. "Wigger" may be derogatory, reflecting stereotypes of African-American, black British, and white culture (when used as synonym of white trash). The term is sometimes used in a racist manner, by other white people to belittle the person perceived as "acting black", but it is also widely used by African Americans like 50 Cent offended by the wigga or wanksta's demeaning of black people and culture.

The phenomenon of white people adopting stereotypical black mannerisms, speech, and apparel has appeared in several generations since slavery was abolished in the Western world. The concept has been documented in the United States, Canada, the United Kingdom, Australia, and other white-majority countries. An early form of this was the *white negro* in the jazz and swing music scenes of the 1920s and 1930s, as examined in the 1957 Norman Mailer essay "The White Negro". It was later seen in the zoot suiter of the 1930s and 1940s, the hipster of the 1940s, the beatnik of the 1950s–1960s, the blue-eyed soul of the 1970s, and the hip hop of the 1980s and 1990s. In 1993, an article in the UK newspaper *The Independent* described the phenomenon of white, middle-class kids who were "wannabe Blacks". 2005 saw the publication of *Why White Kids Love Hip Hop: Wangstas, Wiggers, Wannabes, and the New Reality of Race in America* by Bakari Kitwana, "a culture critic who's been tracking American hip hop for years".

Robert A. Clift's documentary *Blacking Up: Hip-Hop's Remix of Race and Identity* questions white enthusiasts of black hip-hop culture. Clift's documentary examines "racial and cultural ownership and authenticity – a path that begins with the stolen blackness seen in the success of Stephen Foster, Al Jolson, Benny Goodman, Elvis Presley, the Rolling Stones – all the way up to Vanilla Ice (popular music's ur-wigger...) and Eminem." A review of the documentary refers to the wiggers as "white poseurs", and states that the term *wigger* "is used both proudly and derisively to describe white enthusiasts of black hip-hop culture".

Language

Minority languages can also be appropriated, such as when non-speakers of Scottish Gaelic or Irish get tattoos in that language. Likewise, the use of incorrect Scottish Gaelic in a tokenistic fashion aimed at non-Gaelic speakers on signage and announcements has been criticized as disrespectful to fluent speakers of the language.

During the early 2000s, it was popular for young white people to get tattoos of Indian devanagari, Korean letters or Han characters (traditional, simplified or Japanese), often without knowing their true meanings. Asian tattooists responded to this cultural appropriation by tattooing offensive or amusing phrases onto their customers, including Golden Pig, Cheap Whore, Noodles, Hidden Criminal, and Dense Growth Of Bush.

Costumes

During Halloween, some people buy, wear, and sell Halloween costumes based on racial stereotypes. Costumes that depict blatant racial stereotypes, like "Indian Warrior" or "Kung Fool" are sometimes worn by people who do not belong to the respective corresponding racial or ethnic group. These costumes have been criticized as being in poor taste at best and, at worst, blatantly racist. In some cases, theme parties have been held where attendees are encouraged to dress up as stereotypes of a certain racial group. A number of these parties have been held at colleges, and at times other than Halloween, including Martin Luther King Jr. Day and Black History Month.

BSA Related Dance Teams

In chapter four of his book *Playing Indian*, Native American historian Philip J. Deloria refers to the Koshare Indian Museum and Dancers as an example of "object hobbyists" who adopt the material culture of indigenous peoples of the past ("the vanishing Indian") while failing to engage with contemporary native peoples or acknowledge the history of conquest and dispossession. Some Native Americans have stated that all such impersonations and performances are a form of cultural appropriation which place dance and costumes in an inappropriate context devoid of their true meaning, sometimes mixing elements from different tribes.

For 2015, the Koshare's Winter Night dances were canceled after a request was received from Cultural Preservation Office (CPO) of the Hopi Nation asking that the troop discontinue their interpretation of the dances of the Hopi and Pueblo Native Americans. Director of the CPO Leigh Kuwanwisiwma saw video of the performances online, and said the performers were "mimicking our dances, but they were insensitive, as far as I'm concerned." In the 1950s, the head councilman of the Zuni Pueblo saw a performance and said: "We know your hearts are good, but even with good hearts you have done a bad thing." In Zuni culture, religious object and practices are only for those that have earned the right to participate, following techniques and prayers that have been handed down for generations.

There are many other examples of groups associated with scout troops attempting to duplicate Native American dance with varying degrees of authenticity.

- Aabikta Indian Dancers, Slidell, Louisiana.

- Coyote Night Dancers, Northern California

- Kaniengehaga Dance Team

- Kootaga Indian Dancers, Parkersburg, West Virginia

- Kossa Indian Dancers, Sulphur, Louisiana

- Kwahadi Dancers, Amarillo, Texas

- Lakota Dancers, Belvidere, Illinois

- Mic-O-Say Dancers, St. Joseph, Missouri includes nine teams:
  - Crossed Arrows, Stewartsville, Missouri
  - Five Rivers, Jefferson City, Missouri
  - Kanza, Atchison, Kansas
  - Lone Star, Dallas, Texas
  - Ma-Has-Kah, Trenton, Missouri
  - Maha, Omaha, Nebraska
  - Otoe, Maryville, Missouri
  - Robidoux, St. Joseph, Missouri
  - White Shield, Kansas City, Missouri

- Paumanauke Dance Team, Amityville, New York

- Sahawe Indian Dancers, Uvalde, Texas

- Tsoyaha Indian Dancers & Mossy Creek Singers, Morristown, Tennessee

Other Uses

Costume of Saint Patrick (left)

In some cases, a culture usually viewed as the target of cultural appropriation can be accused of appropriation, particularly after colonization and an extensive period re-organization of that culture under the nation-state system. For example, the government of Ghana has been accused of cultural appropriation in adopting the Caribbean Emancipation Day and marketing it to African American tourists as an "African festival".

For some members of the South-Asian community, the wearing of a bindi dot as a decorative item, by a non-Hindu, or by a woman who is not South Asian, is considered cultural appropriation.

A common term among Irish people for someone who imitates or misrepresents Irish culture is *Plastic Paddy*.

Celebrity Controversies

In 2003, Prince Harry used Indigenous Australian art motifs in a painting for a school project. One Aboriginal group labelled it "misappropriation of our culture", claiming that to Aborigines, the motifs have symbolic meanings "indicative of our spiritualism", whereas when non-Aborigines use the motifs they are simply "painting a pretty picture".

In the Victoria's Secret Fashion Show 2012, former Victoria's Secret model Karlie Kloss donned a Native American-style feathered headdress with leather bra and panties and high-heeled moccasins. This was supposedly an example of cultural appropriation because the fashion show is showcasing the company's lingerie and image as a global fashion giant. The outfit was supposed to represent November, and thus "Thanksgiving", in the "Calendar Girls" segment. The outfit met with backlash and criticism as an appropriation of Native American culture and tradition. Victoria's Secret pulled it from the broadcast and apologized for its usage. Kloss also commented on the decision by tweeting "I am deeply sorry if what I wore during the VS Show offended anyone. I support VS's decision to remove the outfit from the broadcast."

Avril Lavigne with Hello Kitty outfit

Avril Lavigne has been cited as appropriating Japanese culture in her song "Hello Kitty". The song and music video depict Asian women dressed up in matching outfits and Lavigne eating Asian food while dressed in a pink tutu. Its depiction of Japanese culture was met with widespread criticism, which has included suggestions of racism. Lavigne responded by stating "I love Japanese culture and I spend half of my time in Japan. I flew to Tokyo to shoot this video ... specifically for my Japanese fans, *with* my Japanese label, Japanese choreographers *and* a Japanese director *in* Japan." A lot of the feedback Lavigne received on Twitter was favorable, and those who blamed her for racism were non-Japanese.

When Selena Gomez wore the bindi during a performance, there was debate on her reasoning behind wearing the culture specific piece. Some viewed this as "casting her vote for Team India" but it was also viewed as misuse of the symbol as Selena was seen as not supporting or relating the Bindi to its origin of Hinduism, but furthering her own self-expression. In 2014, Pharrell Williams posed in a Native American war bonnet on the cover of *Elle* UK magazine, after much controversy and media surrounding the photo Williams apologized.

Actress Amandla Stenberg made a school-related video called "Don't Cash Crop on My Cornrows" about the use of black hairstyles and black culture by non-black people, questioning celebrities like Katy Perry and Iggy Azalea for using "black culture as a way of being edgy and gaining attention". Stenberg later critiqued Kylie Jenner for embracing African-American aesthetic values without addressing the issues that affect the community. The African-American hip hop artist Azealia Banks has also criticized Iggy Azalea "for failing to comment on 'black issues' despite capitalising on the appropriation of African American culture in her music." Banks has called Azalea a "wigger" and there have been "accusations of racism against Azalea" focused on her "insensitivity to the complexities of race relations and cultural appropriation."

Rachel Dolezal made headlines in 2015 when it was discovered that she was not African-American, as she had claimed.

In 2017, Miley Cyrus talked to Billboard magazine regarding her new image. Cyrus discussed how Hip-Hop evoked the message "Come sit on my dick, suck my dick." This was met with backlash, with people calling her out for appropriating Hip-Hop culture.

Responses

Bindi

In 2011, a group of students at Ohio University started a poster campaign denouncing the use of cultural stereotypes as costumes. The campaign features people of color alongside their respective stereotypes with slogans such as "This is not who I am and this is not okay." The goal of the movement was to raise awareness around racism during Halloween in the university and the surrounding community, but the images also circulated online.

"Reclaim the Bindi" has become a hashtag used by people of South Asian descent who wear traditional garb. #CoachellaShutdown has been used in conjunction with #ReclaimtheBindi in order to combat the use of the bindi at music festivals, most notably the Coachella Valley Music and Arts Festival. Reclaim the Bindi Week seeks to promote the cultural significance of the bindi and combat its use as a fashion statement.

In 2016, author Lionel Shriver gave a speech at the Brisbane Writers Festival, asserting the right of authors to write from any point of view, including that of characters from cultural backgrounds other than their own – as writers "should be seeking to push beyond the constraining categories into which we have been arbitrarily dropped by birth. If we embrace narrow group-based identities too fiercely, we cling to the very cages in which others would seek to trap us." She also asserted the right of authors from a cultural majority to write in the voice of someone from a cultural minority, attacking the idea that this constitutes unethical "cultural appropriation". Referring to a case in which American college students were facing disciplinary action for wearing sombreros to a 'tequila party', she said "The moral of the sombrero scandals is clear: *you're not supposed to try on other people's hats*. Yet that's what we're paid to do, isn't it? Step into other people's shoes, and try on their hats." During the speech, Australian social activist Yassmin Abdel-Magied walked out. In a subsequent opinion piece published in *The Guardian*, Abdel-Magied called the speech "a poisoned package wrapped up in arrogance and delivered with condescension". She argued that "marginalised groups, even today, do not get the luxury of defining their own place in a norm that is profoundly white, straight and, often, patriarchal. And in demanding that the right to identity should be given up, Shriver epitomised the kind of attitude that led to the normalisation of imperialist, colonial rule: 'I want this, and therefore I shall take it.' The attitude drips of racial supremacy".

Cross-cultural Communication

Cross-cultural communication is a field of study that looks at how people from differing cultural backgrounds communicate, in similar and different ways among themselves, and how they endeavour to communicate across cultures. Intercultural communication is a related field of study.

Culture

During the Cold War, the economy of the United States was largely self-contained because the world was polarized into two separate and competing powers: the East and the West. However, changes and advancements in economic relationships, political systems, and technological options began to break down old cultural barriers. Business transformed from individual-country capitalism to global capitalism. Thus, the study of cross-cultural communication was originally found within businesses and government, both seeking to expand globally. Businesses began to offer language training to their employees and programs were developed to train employees to understand how to act when abroad. With this also came the development of the Foreign Service Institute, or FSI, through the Foreign Service Act of 1946, where government employees received trainings and prepared for overseas posts. There began also implementation of a "world view" perspective in the curriculum of higher education. In 1974, the International Progress Organization, with the support of UNESCO and under the auspices of Senegalese President Léopold Sédar Senghor, held an international conference on "The Cultural Self-comprehension of Nations" (Innsbruck, Austria, 27–29 July 1974) which called upon United Nations member states "to organize systematic and global comparative research on the different cultures of the world" and "to make all possible efforts for a more intensive training of diplomats in the field of international cultural co-operation and to develop the cultural aspects of their foreign policy."

There has become an increasing pressure for universities across the world to incorporate intercultural and international understanding and knowledge into the education of their students. International literacy and cross-cultural understanding have become critical to a country's cultural, technological, economic, and political health. It has become essential for universities to educate, or more importantly, "transform", to function effectively and comfortably in a world characterized by close, multi-faceted relationships and permeable borders. Students must possess a certain level of global competence to understand the world they live in and how they fit into this world. This level of global competence starts at ground level- the university and its faculty- with how they generate and transmit cross-cultural knowledge and information to students.

Interdisciplinary Orientation

Cross-cultural communication endeavours to bring together such relatively unrelated areas as cultural anthropology and established areas of communication. Its core is to establish and understand how people from different cultures communicate with each other. Its charge is to also produce some guidelines with which people from different cultures can better communicate with each other.

Cross-cultural communication, as with many scholarly fields, is a combination of many other fields. These fields include anthropology, cultural studies, psychology and communication. The field has also moved both toward the treatment of interethnic relations, and toward the study of communication strategies used by co-cultural populations, i.e., communication strategies used to deal with majority or mainstream populations.

The study of languages other than one's own can serve not only to help one understand what we as humans have in common, but also to assist in the understanding of the diversity which underlines our languages' methods of constructing and organizing knowledge. Such understanding has profound implications with respect to developing a critical awareness of social relationships. Understanding social relationships and the way other cultures work is the groundwork of successful globalization business affairs.

Language socialization can be broadly defined as "an investigation of how language both presupposes and creates anew, social relations in cultural context". It is imperative that the speaker understands the grammar of a language, as well as how elements of language are socially situated in order to reach communicative competence. Human experience is culturally relevant, so elements of language are also culturally relevant. One must carefully consider semiotics and the evaluation of sign systems to compare cross-cultural norms of communication. There are several potential problems that come with language socialization, however. Sometimes people can over-generalize or label cultures with stereotypical and subjective characterizations. Another primary concern with documenting alternative cultural norms revolves around the fact that no social actor uses language in ways that perfectly match normative characterizations. A methodology for investigating how an individual uses language and other semiotic activity to create and use new models of conduct and how this varies from the cultural norm should be incorporated into the study of language socialization.

Global Rise

However, with globalization, especially the increase of global trade, it is unavoidable that different cultures will meet, conflict, and blend together. People from different culture find it is difficult to communicate not only due to language barriers, but also are affected by culture styles. For instance, in individualistic cultures, such as in the United States, Canada, and Western Europe, an independent figure or self is dominant. This independent figure is characterized by a sense of self relatively distinct from others and the environment. In interdependent cultures, usually identified as Asian as well as many Latin American, African, and Southern European cultures, an interdependent figure of self is dominant. There is a much greater emphasis on the interrelatedness of the individual to others and the environment; the self is meaningful only (or primarily) in the context of social relationships, duties, and roles. In some degree, the effect brought by cultural difference override the language gap. This culture style difference contributes to one of the biggest challenges for cross-culture communication. Effective communication with people of different cultures is especially challenging. Cultures provide people with ways of thinking—ways of seeing, hearing, and interpreting the world. Thus the same words can mean different things to people from different cultures, even when they speak the "same" language. When the languages are different, and translation has to be used to communicate, the potential for misunderstandings increases.The study of cross-cultural communication is a global research area. As a result, cultural differences in the *study* of cross-cultural communication can already be found. For example, cross-cultural communication is generally considered to fall within the larger field of communication studies in the US, but it is emerging as a sub-field of applied linguistics in the UK.

As the application of cross-cultural communication theory to foreign language education is increasingly appreciated around the world, cross-cultural communication classes can be found within foreign language departments of some universities, while other schools are placing cross-cultural communication programs in their departments of education.

Incorporation into College Programs

With the increasing pressures and opportunities of globalization, the incorporation of international networking alliances has become an "essential mechanism for the internationalization of higher education". Many universities from around the world have taken great strides to increase intercultural understanding through processes of organizational change and innovations. In general, university processes revolve around four major dimensions which include: organizational change, curriculum innovation, staff development, and student mobility. Ellingboe emphasizes these four major dimensions with his own specifications for the internationalization process. His specifications include: (1) college leadership; (2) faculty members' international involvement in activities with colleagues, research sites, and institutions worldwide; (3) the availability, affordability, accessibility, and transferability of study abroad programs for students; (4) the presence and integration of international students, scholars, and visiting faculty into campus life; and (5) international co-curricular units (residence halls, conference planning centers, student unions, career centers, cultural immersion and language houses, student activities, and student organizations).

Above all, universities need to make sure that they are open and responsive to changes in the outside environment. In order for internationalization to be fully effective, the university (including all staff, students, curriculum, and activities) needs to be current with cultural changes, and willing to adapt to these changes. As stated by Ellingboe, internationalization "is an ongoing, future-oriented, multidimensional, interdisciplinary, leadership-driven vision that involves many stakeholders working to change the internal dynamics of an institution to respond and adapt appropriately to an increasingly diverse, globally focused, ever-changing external environment". New distance learning technologies, such as interactive teleconferencing, enable students located thousands of miles apart to communicate and interact in a virtual classroom.

Research has indicated that certain themes and images such as children, animals, life cycles, relationships, and sports can transcend cultural differences, and may be used in international settings such as traditional and online university classrooms to create common ground among diverse cultures (Van Hook, 2011).

The main theories for cross-cultural communication are based on the work done looking at value differences between different cultures, especially the works of Edward T. Hall, Richard D. Lewis, Geert Hofstede, and Fons Trompenaars. Clifford Geertz was also a contributor to this field. Also Jussi V. Koivisto's model on cultural crossing in internationally operating organizations elaborates from this base of research.

These theories have been applied to a variety of different communication theories and settings, including general business and management (Fons Trompenaars and Charles

Hampden-Turner) and marketing (Marieke de Mooij, Stephan Dahl). There have also been several successful educational projects which concentrate on the practical applications of these theories in cross-cultural situations.

These theories have also been criticized mainly by management scholars (e.g. Nigel Holden) for being based on the culture concept derived from 19th century cultural anthropology and emphasizing on culture-as-difference and culture-as-essence. Another criticism has been the uncritical way Hofstede's dimensions are served up in textbooks as facts (Peter W. Cardon). There is a move to focus on 'cross-cultural interdependence' instead of the traditional views of comparative differences and similarities between cultures. Cross-cultural management is increasingly seen as a form of knowledge management. Cross cultural communication gives opportunities to share ideas, experiences, and different perspectives and perception by interacting with local people.

International Educational Organizations

WYSE International

WYSE International is a worldwide educational charity specializing in education and development for emerging leaders established in 1989. It is a non-governmental organization associated with the Department of Public Information of the United Nations.

Over 3000 participants from 110 countries have attended their courses, they have run in 5 continents. Its flagship International Leadership Programme is a 12-day residential course for 30 people from on average 20 different countries (aged 18 – 35).

WYSE International's website states its aims are to:

"provide education independently of political, religious or social backgrounds and promote visionary leadership capable of responding to evolving world needs."

MEET - Middle East Education through Technology

MEET - Middle East Education through Technology is an innovative educational initiative aimed at creating a common professional language between Israeli and Palestinian young leaders. Israeli and Palestinian students are selected through an application process and work in small bi-national teams to develop technology and business projects for local impact. Through this process of cross-cultural communication, students build mutual respect, cultural competence and understanding of each others.

Aspects

There are several parameters that may be perceived differently by people of different cultures:

- High- and low-context cultures: context is the most important cultural dimension and also immensely difficult to define. The idea of context in culture was an idea put forth by an anthropologist by the name of Edward T Hall. He breaks up culture into two main groups: High and Low context cultures. He refers to context as the stimuli, environment or ambiance surrounding the environment. Depending on how a culture relies on the three points to communicate their meaning, will place them in either high or low- context cultures. For example, Hall goes on to explain that low-context cultures assume that the individuals know very little about what they are being told, and therefore must be given a lot of background information. High-context cultures assume the individual is knowledgeable about the subject and has to be given very little background information.

- Nonverbal, oral and written: the main goal behind improving intercultural audiences is to pay special attention to specific areas of communication to enhance the effectiveness of the intercultural messages. The specific areas are broken down into three sub categories: nonverbal, oral and written messages.

Nonverbal contact involves everything from something as obvious as eye contact and facial expressions to more discreet forms of expression such as the use of space. Experts have labeled the term kinesics to mean communicating through body movement. Huseman, author of *Business Communication*, explains that the two most prominent ways of communication through kinesics are eye contact and facial expressions.

Eye contact, Huseman goes on to explain, is the key factor in setting the tone between two individuals and greatly differs in meaning between cultures. In the Americas and Western Europe, eye contact is interpreted the same way, conveying interest and honesty. People who avoid eye contact when speaking are viewed in a negative light, withholding information and lacking in general confidence. However, in the Middle East, Africa, and especially Asia eye, contact is seen as disrespectful and even challenging of one's authority. People who make eye contact, but only briefly, are seen as respectful and courteous.

Facial expressions are their own language by comparison and universal throughout all cultures. Dale Leathers, for example, states that facial expression can communicate ten basic classes of meaning.

The final part to nonverbal communication lies in our gestures, and can be broken down into five subcategories:

- Emblems

Emblems refer to sign language (such as, thumbs up, one of the most recognized symbols in the world)

- Illustrators

Illustrators mimic what is spoken (such as gesturing how much time is left by holding up a certain number of fingers).

- Regulators

Regulators act as a way of conveying meaning through gestures (raising up a hand for instance indicates that one has a certain question about what was just said) and become more complicated since the same regulator can have different meanings across different cultures (making a circle with a hand, for instance, in the Americas means agreement, in Japan is symbolic for money, and in France conveys the notion of worthlessness).

- Affect displays

Affect displays reveal emotions such as happiness (through a smile) or sadness (mouth trembling, tears).

- Adaptors

Adaptors are more subtle such as a yawn or clenching fists in anger.

The last nonverbal type of communication deals with communication through the space around people, or proxemics. Huseman goes on to explain that Hall identifies three types of space:

1. Feature-fixed space: deals with how cultures arrange their space on a large scale, such as buildings and parks.

2. semifixed feature space: deals with how space is arranged inside buildings, such as the placement of desks, chairs and plants.

3. Informal space: the space and its importance, such as talking distance, how close people sit to one another and office space are all examples. A production line worker often has to make an appointment to see a supervisor, but the supervisor is free to visit the production line workers at will.

Oral and written communication is generally easier to learn, adapt and deal with in the business world for the simple fact that each language is unique. The one difficulty that comes into play is paralanguage, how something is said.

Differences Between Western Communication and Traditional Indigenous Communication

According to Michael Walsh and Ghil'ad Zuckermann, Western conversational interaction is typically "dyadic", between two particular people, where eye contact is important and the speaker controls the interaction; and "contained" in a relatively short, defined time frame. However, traditional Australian Aboriginal conversational interaction is "communal", broadcast to many people, eye contact is not important, the listener controls the interaction; and "continuous", spread over a longer, indefinite time frame.

Interculturalism

Interculturalism refers to support for cross-cultural dialogue and challenging self-segregation tendencies within cultures. Interculturalism involves moving beyond mere passive acceptance of a multicultural fact of multiple cultures effectively existing in a society and instead promotes dialogue and interaction between cultures.

Interculturalism has arisen in response to criticisms of existing policies of multiculturalism, such as criticisms that such policies had failed to create inclusion of different cultures within society, but instead have divided society by legitimizing segregated separate communities that have isolated themselves and accentuated their specificity. It is based on the recognition of both differences and similarities between cultures. It has addressed the risk of the creation of absolute relativism within postmodernity and in multiculturalism.

Philosopher Martha Nussbaum in her work *Cultivating Humanity*, describes interculturalism as involving "the recognition of common human needs across cultures and of dissonance and critical dialogue within cultures" and that interculturalists "reject the claim of identity politics that only members of a particular group have the ability to understand the perspective of that group". Ali Rattansi, in his book *Multiculturalism: A Very Short Introduction* (2011) argues that Interculturalism offers a more fruitful way than conventional multiculturalism for different ethnic groups to co-exist in an atmosphere that encourages both better inter-ethnic understanding and civility; he provides useful examples of how interculturalist projects in the UK have shown in practice a constructive way forward for promoting multi-ethnic civility. Based on a considerable body of research, he also sets out the outlines of a new interpretation of global history which shows that concepts of tolerance are not restricted to the West, and that what is usually regarded as a unique Western cultural achievement should more appropriately be regarded as a Eurasian achievement. He thus offers a more interculturalist view of global history which undermines notions of 'a clash of civilisations'.

Interculturalism has both supporters and opponents amongst people who endorse multiculturalism. Gerald Delanty views interculturalism as capable of incorporating multiculturalism within it. In contrast, Nussbaum views interculturalism as distinct from multiculturalism and notes that several humanities professors have preferred interculturalism over multiculturalism because they view multiculturalism as being "associated with relativism and identity politics".

The United Nations' agency UNESCO adopted the Convention on the Protection and Promotion of the Diversity of Cultural Expressions in 2005 that declares support for interculturality. In Germany, all universities are required to have a section on inter-cultural competence in their social work programs, that involves students being able to be open to listen and communicate with people of different cultural backgrounds, have knowledge of the backgrounds of cultural groups, knowledge of existing stereo-types and prejudices involving cultural groups, and other criteria. Salman Cheema, the Head of Marketing and Communications of the British Council, in an article ti-tled "From Multiculturalism to Interculturalism – A British perspective", spoke of an event co-hosted by the British Council and Canada's Institute for Research on Public Policy (IRPP) in Montreal, Quebec, Canada on April 11, 2013, interculturalist advocate Phil Wood declared that multiculturalism has faced serious problems that need to be resolved through interculturalism, and rejected those opponents of multiculturalism who seek to restore a pre-multiculturalist monoculturalist society. Several days later in Montreal, the New Democratic Party of Canada (NDP) declared support for inter-culturalism in the preamble of its constitution adopted its federal convention held in Montreal on April 14, 2013.

Multiculturalism

The *Monument to Multiculturalism* by Francesco Perilli in Toronto, Ontario, Canada.
Four identical sculptures are located in Buffalo City, South Africa;
Changchun, China; Sarajevo, Bosnia and Sydney, Australia.

Multiculturalism is a term used in both sociology and political philosophy and can be confused with one another. It is an ambiguous term : it can mean a cultural pluralism in which the various ethnic groups collaborate and dialog with one another without having to sacrifice their particular identities.

In sociology and everyday usage it is a synonym for pluralism with the two terms often used interchangeably and refers to either specific mixed ethnic community areas where multiple cultural traditions exist or a single country within which they do. Groups associated with an aboriginal ethnic group and foreigner ethnic groups are most often the focus.

In reference to sociology, multiculturalism is the end state of either a natural or artificial process (e.g. legally controlled immigration) and occurs on either a large national scale or a smaller scale within a nations communities. On a smaller scale this can occur artificially when a jurisdiction is created or expanded by amalgamating areas with two or more different cultures (e.g. French Canada and English Canada). On a large scale, it can occur as a result of either legal or illegal immigration from different jurisdictions around the world (e.g. United States, Australia, Canada, Brazil, United Kingdom, New Zealand, Argentina and many other countries).

Multiculturalism as a political philosophy involves ideologies and policies which vary widely, ranging from the advocacy of equal respect to the various cultures in a society, to policies of promoting the maintenance of cultural diversity, to policies in which people of various ethnic and religious groups are addressed by the authorities as defined by the group to which they belong.

Multiculturalism that promotes maintaining the distinctiveness of multiple cultures is often contrasted to other settlement policies such as social integration, cultural assimilation and racial segregation. Multiculturalism has been described as a "salad bowl" and "cultural mosaic".

Two different and seemingly inconsistent strategies have developed through different government policies and strategies. The first focuses on interaction and communication between different cultures; this approach is also often known as interculturalism. The second centers on diversity and cultural uniqueness which can sometimes result in intercultural competition over jobs among other things and may lead to ethnic conflict. Controversy surrounding the issue of cultural isolation includes the ghettoization of a culture within a nation and the protection of the cultural attributes of an area or nation. Proponents of government policies often claim that artificial, government guided protections also contribute to global cultural diversity. The second approach to multiculturalist policy making maintains that they avoid presenting any specific ethnic, religious, or cultural community values as central.

It can also mean a kind of Esperantic Disney World, a tutti frutti cocktail of cultures, languages and art forms in which 'everything becomes everything else'.

Prevalence

In the political philosophy of multiculturalism, ideas are focused on the ways in which societies are either believed to, or should, respond to cultural and religious differences. It is often associated with "identity politics", "the politics of difference", and "the politics of recognition". It is also a matter of economic interests and political power.

(Stanford Encyclopedia of Philosophy). In more recent times political multicultural-ist ideologies have been expanding in their use to include and define disadvantaged groups such as African Americans, LGBT, with arguments often focussing on ethnic and religious minorities, minority nations, indigenous peoples and even the disabled. It is within this context which the term is most commonly understood and the broad-ness and scope of the definition, as well as its practical use, has been the subject of serious debate.

Most debates over multiculturalism center around whether or not multiculturalism is the appropriate way to deal with diversity and immigrant integration. The arguments regarding the perceived rights to a multicultural education include the proposition that it acts as a way to demand recognition of aspects of a group's culture osubordination and its entire experience.

The term multiculturalism is most often used in reference to Western nation-states, which had seemingly achieved a de facto single national identity during the 18th and/or 19th centuries. Multiculturalism has been official policy in several Western nations since the 1970s, for reasons that varied from country to country, including the fact that many of the great cities of the Western world are increasingly made of a mosaic of cul-tures.

The Canadian government has often been described as the instigator of multicultural ideology because of its public emphasis on the social importance of immigration. The Canadian Royal Commission on Bilingualism and Biculturalism is often referred to as the origins of modern political awareness of multiculturalism. In the Western En-glish-speaking countries, multiculturalism as an official national policy started in Can-ada in 1971, followed by Australia in 1973 where it is maintained today. It was quickly adopted as official policy by most member-states of the European Union. Recently, right-of-center governments in several European states – notably the Netherlands and Denmark – have reversed the national policy and returned to an official monoculcural-ism. A similar reversal is the subject of debate in the United Kingdom, among others, due to evidence of incipient segregation and anxieties over "home-grown" terrorism. Several heads-of-state have expressed doubts about the success of multicultural pol-icies: The United Kingdom's ex-Prime Minister David Cameron, German Chancellor Angela Merkel, Australia's ex-prime minister John Howard, Spanish ex-prime minister Jose Maria Aznar and French ex-president Nicolas Sarkozy have voiced concerns about the effectiveness of their multicultural policies for integrating immigrants.

Many nation-states in Africa, Asia, and the Americas are culturally diverse, and are 'multicultural' in a descriptive sense. In some, communalism is a major political issue. The policies adopted by these states often have parallels with multiculturalist policies in the Western world, but the historical background is different, and the goal may be a mono-cultural or mono-ethnic nation-building – for instance in the Malaysian govern-ment's attempt to create a 'Malaysian race' by 2020.

Australia

The next country to adopt an official policy of multiculturalism after Canada was Australia, a country with similar immigration situations and similar policies, for example the formation of the Special Broadcasting Service. The Australian government retains multiculturalism in policy, and as a defining aspect of Australia today.

Sydney's Chinatown

The White Australia Policy was quietly dismantled after World War II by various changes to immigration policy, although the official policy of multiculturalism was not formally introduced until 1972. The election of John Howard's Liberal-National Coalition government in 1996 was a major watershed for Australian multiculturalism. Howard had long been a critic of multiculturalism, releasing his One Australia policy in the late 1980s. A Practical Reference to Religious Diversity for Operational Police and Emergency Services was a publication of the Australasian Police Multicultural Advisory Bureau designed to offer guidance to police and emergency services personnel on how religious affiliation can affect their contact with the public. The first edition was published in 1999. The first edition covered Buddhist, Hindu, Islamic, Jewish and Sikh faiths with participation of representatives of the various religions. The second edition added Christian, Australian Aboriginal and Torres Strait Islander religions and the Bahá'í Faith to the list of religions was published in 2002.

Contact between people of different cultures in Australia has been characterised by tolerance and engagement, but have also occasionally resulted in conflict and rifts.

Australia's diverse migrant communities have brought with them food, lifestyle and cultural practices, which have been absorbed into mainstream Australian culture.

Mauritius

Multiculturalism has been a characteristic feature of the island of Mauritius. Mauritian society includes people from many different ethnic and religious groups: Hindu,

Muslim and Indo-Mauritians, Mauritian Creoles (of African and Malagasy descent), Buddhist and Roman Catholic Sino-Mauritians and Franco-Mauritians (descendants of the original French colonists).

Europe

Ethno-linguistic map of Austria–Hungary, 1910.

Ethno-linguistic map of the Second Polish Republic, 1937.

The European Union is facing unprecedented demographic changes (an ageing population, low birth rates, changing family structures and migration). According to the European Commission, it is important, both at EU and national level, to review and adapt existing policies. Following a public debate, a 2006 EU policy paper identified five key policy responses to manage demographic change, among them receiving and integrating migrants into Europe.

Historically, Europe has always been a mixture of Latin, Slavic, Germanic, Uralic, Celtic, Hellenic, Illyrian, Thracian and other cultures influenced by the importation of Jewish, Christian, Muslim and other belief systems; although the continent was supposedly unified by the super-position of Imperial Roman Christianity, it is accepted that geographic and cultural differences continued from antiquity into the modern age.

In the 19th century, the ideology of nationalism transformed the way Europeans thought about the state. Existing states were broken up and new ones created; the new nation-states were founded on the principle that each nation is entitled to its own sovereignty and to engender, protect, and preserve its own unique culture and history. Unity, under this ideology, is seen as an essential feature of the nation and the nation-state – unity of descent, unity of culture, unity of language, and often unity of religion. The nation-state constitutes a culturally homogeneous society, although some national movements recognized regional differences.

Where cultural unity was insufficient, it was encouraged and enforced by the state. The 19th-century nation-states developed an array of policies – the most important was compulsory primary education in the national language. The language itself was often standardized by a linguistic academy, and regional languages were ignored or suppressed. Some nation-states pursued violent policies of cultural assimilation and even ethnic cleansing.

Some European Union countries have introduced policies for "social cohesion", "integration", and (sometimes) "assimilation". The policies include:

- compulsory courses and/or tests on national history, on the constitution and the legal system (e.g., the computer-based test for individuals seeking naturalization in the UK named Life in the United Kingdom test)

- introduction of an official national history, such as the national canon defined for the Netherlands by the van Oostrom Commission, and promotion of that history (e.g., by exhibitions about national heroes)

- tests designed to elicit "unacceptable" values. In Baden-Württemberg immigrants are asked what they would do if their son says he is a homosexual (the desired answer is that they would accept it).

Other countries have instituted policies which encourage cultural separation. The concept of "Cultural exception" proposed by France in the General Agreement on Tariffs and Trade (GATT) negotiations in 1993 was an example of a measure aimed at protecting local cultures.

Bulgaria

Since its establishment in 7th century Bulgaria has hosted many religions, ethnic groups and nations. The capital Sofia is the only European city that has peacefully functioning, within walking distance of 300 meters, four Places of worship of the major religions: Eastern Orthodox (St Nedelya Church), Islam (Banya Bashi Mosque), Roman Catholicism (St Joseph Cathedral), and Orthodox Judaism (Sofia Synagogue, the third largest synagogue in Europe).

This unique arrangement has been called by historians a "multicultural cliche". It has also become known as "The Square of Religious Tolerance" and has initiated the construction of a 100-square-meter scale model of the site that is to become a symbol of the capital.

Sofia Synagogue

Banya Bashi Mosque in Sofia

Furthermore, unlike some other Nazi Germany allies or German-occupied countries excluding Denmark, Bulgaria managed to save its entire 48,000-strong Jewish population during World War II from deportation to Nazi concentration camps. According to Dr Marinova-Christidi the main reason for the efforts of Bulgarian people to save the Bulgarian Jews during WWII is that within the region they "co-existed for centuries with other religions" – giving it a unique multicultural and multiethnic history.

Consequently, within the Balkan region Bulgaria has become an example for multiculturalism in terms of variety of religions, artistic creativity and ethnicity. Its largest ethnic minorities, Turks and Roma, enjoy wide political representation. In 1984, following a campaign by the communist regime for a forcible change of the Islamic names of the Turkish minority, an underground organization called "National Liberation Movement of the Turks in Bulgaria" was formed which headed the Turkish community's opposition movement. On January 4, 1990 the activists of the movement registered an organization with the legal name "Movement for Rights and Freedom" (MRF) in the Bulgarian city of Varna. At the moment of registration it had 33 members, at present, according to the organization's website, 68,000 members plus 24,000 in the organization's youth wing . In 2012 Bulgarian Turks were represented at every level of government: local, with MRF having mayors in 35 municipalities, at parliamentary level with MRF having 38 deputies (14% of the votes in Parliamentary elections for 2009–13) and at executive level, where there is one Turkish minister, Vezhdi Rashidov. Twenty-one Roma political organizations were founded between 1997 and 2003 in Bulgaria.

Germany

In October 2010, Angela Merkel told a meeting of younger members of her centrist Christian Democratic Union (CDU) party at Potsdam, near Berlin, that attempts to build a multicultural society in Germany had "utterly failed", stating: "The concept that we are now living side by side and are happy about it does not work". She continued to say that immigrants should integrate and adopt Germany's culture and values. This has added to a growing debate within Germany on the levels of immigration, its effect on Germany and the degree to which Muslim immigrants have integrated into German society. The Ahmadiyya Muslim Community of Germany is the first Muslim group to have been granted "corporation under public law status", putting the Community on par with the major Christian churches and Jewish communities of Germany.

Netherlands

Süleymanìye Mosque in Tilburg built in 2001.

Multiculturalism in the Netherlands began with major increases in immigration during the mid-1950s and 1960s. As a consequence, an official national policy of multiculturalism was adopted in the early 1980s. This policy subsequently gave way to more assimilationist policies in the 1990s. Following the murders of Pim Fortuyn (in 2002) and Theo van Gogh (in 2004) there was increased political debate on the role of multiculturalism in the Netherlands.

Lord Sacks, Chief Rabbi of the United Hebrew Congregations of the Commonwealth, made a distinction between tolerance and multiculturalism, citing the Netherlands as a tolerant, rather than multicultural, society. In June 2011 the First Rutte cabinet said the Netherlands would turn away from multiculturalism: "Dutch culture, norms and values must be dominant" Minister Donner said.

Serbia

Csárdás traditional Hungarian folk dance in Doroslovo.

In Serbia there are 19 officially recognised ethnical groups with a status of national minorities. Vojvodina is an autonomous province of Serbia, located in the northern part of the country. It has a multi-ethnic and multi-cultural identity; there are more than 26 ethnic groups in the province, which has six official languages. Largest ethnic groups in Vojvodina are Serbs (67%), Hungarians (13%), Slovaks, Croats, Romani, Romanians, Montenegrins, Bunjevci, Rusyns.

Radio Television of Vojvodina broadcasts program in 10 local languages. The project by the Government of AP Vojvodina titled "Promotion of Multiculturalism and Tolerance in Vojvodina", whose primary goal is to foster the cultural diversity and develop the atmosphere of interethnic tolerance among the citizens of Vojvodina, has been successfully implemented since 2005. Serbia is continually working on improving its relationship and inclusion of minorities in its effort to gain full accession to the European Union. Serbia has initiated talks through Stabilisation and Association Agreement on 7 November 2007.

Sweden

Sweden was the first country to adopt an official policy of multiculturalism in Europe. In May 1975, a unanimous Swedish parliament passed an act on a new multiculturalist immigrant and minority policy put forward by the social democratic government, that explicitly rejected the ideal ethnic homogeneity and the policy of assimilation. The three main principles of the new policy were equality, partnership and freedom of choice. The explicit policy aim of the freedom of choice principle was to create the opportunity for minority groups in Sweden to retain their own languages and cultures. From the mid-1970s, the goal of enabling the preservation of minorities and creating a positive attitude towards the new officially endorsed multicultural society among the majority population became incorporated into the Swedish constitution as well as cultural, educational and media policies. Despite the anti-multiculturalist protestations of the Sweden Democrats, multiculturalism remains official policy in Sweden.

United Kingdom

Multicultural policies were adopted by local administrations from the 1970s and 1980s onwards. In 1997 the New Labour government committed to a multiculturalist approach at a national level, but after 2001 there was something of a backlash, led by centre-left commentators such as David Goodhart and Trevor Phillips. The government then embraced a policy of community cohesion instead. In 2011 Prime Minister and Conservative Party leader David Cameron said in a speech that "state multiculturalism has failed".

Asia

India

Jama Masjid, Delhi, one of the largest mosques in India

According to the 1961 Census of India, there are 1652 indigenous languages in the country. The culture of India has been shaped by its long history, unique geography and diverse demography. India's languages, religions, dance, music, architecture and customs differ from place to place within the country, but nevertheless possess a commonality. The culture of India is an amalgamation of these diverse sub-cultures spread all over the Indian subcontinent and traditions that are several millennia old. The previously prevalent Indian caste system describes the social stratification and social restrictions in the Indian subcontinent, in which social classes are defined by thousands of endogamous hereditary groups, often termed *jātis* or castes.

Religiously, Hindus form the majority, followed by Muslims. The statistics are: Hindu (80.5%), Muslim (13.4%), Christian (2.3%), Sikh (2.1%), Buddhist, Bahá'í, Jain, Jew and Parsi populations. Linguistically, the two main language families in India are Indo-Aryan (a branch of Indo-European) and Dravidian. In India's northeast, people speaking Sino-Tibetan group of languages such as Meitei (Meitei-lon) recognized by the Indian constitution and Austroasiatic languages are commonly found. India (officially) follows a three-language policy. Hindi (spoken in the form of Hindustani) is the official federal language, English has the federal status of associate/subsidiary official language and each state has its own state official language (in the Hindi *sprachraum*, this reduces to bilingualism). Further, India does not have any national language. The Republic of India's state boundaries are largely drawn based on linguistic groups; this decision led to the preservation and continuation of local ethno-linguistic sub-cultures, except for the Hindi *sprachraum* which is itself divided into many states. Thus, most states differ from one another in language, culture, cuisine, clothing, literary style, architecture, music and festivities.

India has encountered religiously motivated violence, such as the Moplah Riots, the Bombay riots, the 1984 anti-Sikh riots, the 2002 Gujarat riots, the 2012 Assam violence, and the 2013 Muzaffarnagar riots. This has resulted from traditionally disadvantaged communities in public employment such as the policing of the same locality, apprehension of owners in giving properties for sale or rent and of society in accepting inter-marriages.

India has the world's largest population of some non-Indian origin religions, such as Bahá'í Faith and Zoroastrianism. Indians have more than 200 languages.

Indonesia

Pluralism, diversity and multiculturalism is a daily fact of life in Indonesia. There are over 300 ethnic groups in Indonesia. 95% of those are of Native Indonesian ancestry. The Javanese are the largest ethnic group in Indonesia who make up nearly 42% of the total population. The Sundanese, Malay, and Madurese are the next largest groups in the country. There are also more than 700 living languages spoken in Indonesia and although predominantly Muslim the country also has large Christian and Hindu populations.

Indonesia's national motto, *Bhinneka Tunggal Ika* ("Unity in Diversity" lit. "many, yet one") enshrined in Pancasila national ideology, articulates the diversity that shapes the country. The government nurture and promote the diversity of Indonesian local culture and adopting a pluralist approach.

Due to migration within Indonesia (as part of government transmigration programs or otherwise), there are significant populations of ethnic groups who reside outside of their traditional regions. The Javanese for example, moved from their traditional homeland in Java to the other parts of the archipelago. The expansion of Javanese and their influence throughout Indonesia has raised the issue of Javanization, although Minangkabau, Malay, Madurese, Bugis and Makassar people, as a result of their *merantau* (migrating) culture are also quite widely distributed throughout Indonesian archipelago, while Chinese Indonesians can be found in most of urban areas. Because of urbanization, major Indonesian cities such as Greater Jakarta, Surabaya, Bandung, Palembang, Medan and Makassar has attracted large numbers of Indonesians from various ethnics, cultural and religious background. Jakarta in particular, has almost all of Indonesian ethnic groups represented.

However, this transmigration program and close interactions between people of different cultural backgrounds might caused socio-cultural problems, as the inter-ethnics interactions might not always conducted harmoniously. After the fall of Suharto in 1998 into the 2000s, there were numbers of inter-ethnic and inter-religious clashes erupted in Indonesia. Such as clashes between native Dayak tribes against Madurese transmigrants in Kalimantan during Sambas riots in 1999 and the Sampit conflict in 2001. There were also clashes between Muslims and Christians, such as violence erupted in Poso between 1998 and into 2000, and violences in Maluku between 1999 and into 2002. Nevertheless, Indonesia today still struggle and has managed to maintain unity and inter-cultural harmony, through national adherence of pro-pluralism policy of Pancasila promoted and enforced by the government and its people.

Chinese Indonesians are the largest foreign-origin minority that has been residing in Indonesia for generations. Despite centuries of acculturation with native Indonesians, because of their disproportionate influence on Indonesian economy, and alleged question of national loyalty, Chinese Indonesian have suffered discrimination. The Suharto *Orde Baru* or New Order adopted a forced assimilation policy; which indicated that Chinese cultural elements were unacceptable. Chinese Indonesians were forced to adopt Indonesian-sounding names, and the use of Chinese culture and language was banned. The violence targeting Chinese Indonesians erupted during riots in 1998 as the looting and destructions took place, numbers of Chinese Indonesians as well as looters were died. The Chinese Indonesians were treated as the scapegoat of 1997 Asian Financial Crisis, and it was the result of ongoing discrimination and segregation policy enforced during Suharto's New Order regime. Soon after the fourth Indonesian President, Abdurrahman Wahid came into power in 1999, he quickly abolished some of the discriminatory laws in efforts to promote acceptance and to improve inter-racial relationships, such as abolishing the ban on Chinese culture and allowed Chinese traditions to be practised freely. Two years later President Megawati Sukarnoputri declared that the Chinese New Year (*Imlek*) would be marked as a national holiday from 2003. Today, Chinese Indonesians enjoy the same rights as other Indonesians.

Japan

An Ainu man, circa 1930

Japanese society, with its ideology of homogeneity, has traditionally rejected any need to recognize ethnic differences in Japan, even as such claims have been rejected by such ethnic minorities as the Ainu and Ryukyuan people. In 2005, former Japanese Prime Minister and current Japanese Deputy Prime Minister Taro Aso described Japan as a "one civilization, one language, one culture and one race" nation. However, there are "International Society" NPOs funded by local governments throughout Japan.

According to Harvard University professor Theodore Bestor, Japan does look very homogeneous from a distant perspective, but in fact there are a number of very significant minority groups – ethnically different minority groups – in Japan today. Such as the already mentioned Ainu and Ryukyuan people.

Kazakhstan

Kazakhstan is among the most multicultural countries in Eurasia, with sizeable populations of ethnic Kazakhs, Russians, Uzbeks, Ukrainians, Uighurs, Tatars, Germans and more. Kazakhstan is one of a few countries in post-Soviet territories that managed to avoid interethnic clashes and conflicts in the period of USSR's final crisis and its eventual breakup. In 1995, Kazakhstan created the Assembly of People of Kazakhstan, an advisory body designed to represent the country's ethnic minorities.

Malaysia

Malaysia is a multiethnic country, with Malays making up the majority, close to 58% of the population. About 25% of the population are Malaysians of Chinese descent. Malaysians of Indian descent comprise about 7% of the population. The remaining 10% comprises:

- Native East Malaysians, namely Bajau, Bruneian, Bidayuh, Dusun, Iban, Kadazan, Kedayan, Melanau, Orang Ulu, Sarawakian Malays, etc.

- Other native tribes of Peninsular Malaysia, such as the Orang Asli and Siamese people, and

- Non-native tribes of Peninsular Malaysia such as the Chettiars, the Peranakan and the Portuguese.

The Malaysian New Economic Policy or NEP serves as a form of racial equalization. It promotes structural changes in various aspects of life from education to economic to social integration. Established after the 13 May racial riots of 1969, it sought to address the significant imbalance in the economic sphere where the minority Chinese population had substantial control over commercial activity in the country.

The Malay Peninsula has a long history of international trade contacts, influencing its ethnic and religious composition. Predominantly Malays before the 18th century, the ethnic composition changed dramatically when the British introduced new industries, and imported Chinese and Indian labor. Several regions in the then British Malaya such as Penang, Malacca and Singapore became Chinese dominated. Until the riots 1969, co-existence between the three ethnicities (and other minor groups) was largely peaceful, although the three main racial groups for the most part lived in separate communities – the Malays in the villages, the Chinese in the urban areas, and the Indians in the towns and plantation. More Malays however have moved into the cities since the 1970s, and the proportion of the non-Malays have been decreasing continually, especially the Chinese, due in large part to lower birth-rate and emigration as a result of institutionalized discrimination.

Preceding independence of the Federation of Malaya, a social contract was negotiated as the basis of a new society. The contract as reflected in the 1957 Malayan Constitution and the 1963 Malaysian Constitution states that the immigrant groups are granted citizenship, and Malays' special rights are guaranteed. This is often referred to the Bumiputra policy.

These pluralist policies have come under pressure from racialist Malay parties, who oppose perceived subversion of Malay rights. The issue is sometimes related to the controversial status of religious freedom in Malaysia.

Philippines

The Philippines ranks 8th among 240 countries in terms of ethnic diversity. Among its several ethnic groups, the country has 10 major distinct groups, mainly the Visayans, Tagalogs, Ilocanos, Bicolanos, Moros, Kapampangans, Pangasinans, Sambals and Ibanags. The Philippines also has several aboriginal stocks such as the Aetas, Igorots, Lumads, Mangyans and the Sama-Bajau. The country also has huge Spanish and Chinese communities, as well as a substantial number of American, Korean, Japanese and Indian communities. The Philippine government has various programs supporting and preserving the nation's ethnic diversity.

Although there had been no ethnic-based incidents of armed conflict between many Christian and animist groups, the same cannot be said about relations between them on one hand and their Muslim compatriots on the other. The enduring war in Muslim Mindanao is one of the most prominent examples of religious conflicts pestering the economically frail southwestern Philippines. Since the 1899 Moro Rebellion, Muslim groups across Mindanao have bolstered armed offensives against foreign colonizers due to aspirations of self-determination. However, these efforts have failed resulting to the annexation of the Islamic regions, particularly the Sultanate of Sulu to the Philippines.

Singapore

Because of immigration, Singapore has a Chinese majority population with significant minority populations of Malays and Indians (predominantly Tamils). Other prominent smaller groups include Peranakans and Eurasians. Besides English, Singapore recognizes three other languages – Malay, Mandarin Chinese and Tamil. English was established as the medium of instruction in schools during the 1960s and 1970s and is the language of trade and government while the other three languages are taught as second languages ("mother tongues"). Besides being a multilingual country, Singapore also acknowledges festivals celebrated by the three main ethnic communities.

During British colonial rule, ethnic enclaves such as Geylang, Chinatown, and Little India were enforced. Presently, remnants of colonial ethnic concentration still exist but housing in Singapore is governed by the Ethnic Integration Policy, which ensures an even ethnic distribution throughout Singapore. A similar policy exists in politics as all Group Representation Constituencies are required to field at least one candidate from an ethnic minority.

South Korea

South Korea remains a relatively homogenous country ethnically, linguistically, and culturally. Foreigners, expatriates, and immigrants are often rejected by the mainstream South Korean society and face discrimination.

However, the word "multiculturalism" is increasingly heard in South Korea. In 2007, Han Geon-Soo, Professor of Cultural Anthropology at Kangwon National University, published an article entitled "Multicultural Korea: Celebration or Challenge of Multiethnic Shift in Contemporary Korea?", noting: "As the increase of foreign migrants in [South] Korea transforms a single-ethnic homogeneous [South] Korean society into multiethnic and multicultural one, [the South] Korean government and the civil society pay close attention to multiculturalism as an alternative value to their policy and social movement."

He argued, however, that "the current discourses and concerns on multiculturalism in [South] Korea" lacked "the constructive and analytical concepts for transforming a society".

The same year, Stephen Castles of the International Migration Institute argued:

> "Korea no longer has to decide whether it wants to become a multicultural society. It made that decision years ago – perhaps unconsciously – when it decided to be a full participant in the emerging global economy. It confirmed that decision when it decided to actively recruit foreign migrants to meet the economic and demographic needs of a fast-growing society. Korea is faced by a different decision today: what type of multicultural society does it want to be?"

The *Korea Times* suggested in 2009 that South Korea was likely to become a multicultural society. In 2010, an opinion editorial written by Peter Underwood for the *JoongAng Ilbo* stated: "Media in [South] Korea is abuzz with the new era of multiculturalism. With more than one million foreigners in [South] Korea, 2 percent of the population comes from other cultures." He further opined:

> "If you stay too long, Koreans become uncomfortable with you. [...] Having a 2 percent foreign population unquestionably causes ripples, but having one million temporary foreign residents does not make Korea a multicultural society. [...] In many ways, this homogeneity is one of Korea's greatest strengths. Shared values create harmony. Sacrifice for the nation is a given. Difficult and painful political and economic initiatives are endured without discussion or debate. It is easy to anticipate the needs and behavior of others. It is the cornerstone that has helped Korea survive adversity. But there is a downside, too. [...] Koreans are immersed in their culture and are thus blind to its characteristics and quirks. Examples of group think are everywhere. Because Koreans share values and views, they support decisions even when they are obviously bad. Multiculturalism will introduce contrasting views and challenge existing assumptions. While it will undermine the homogeneity, it will enrich Koreans with a better understanding of themselves."

Although many debates still take place as to whether South Korea really is a multicultural society or not, it is generally agreed that South Korea has probably entered a stage of multiculturalism and has moved away from its homogeneous identity. Around 35–40% of South Korean men in the rural area outside Seoul are engaged with wives from different countries. According to the *Dongponews*, an online media that connects migrants and immigrants of South Korea, the number of foreigners residing in South Korea reached 1.43 million by 2012, and is likely to increase more and more, reaching to the scale that cannot be undermined. More than that, South Korea is going through a serious stage of low birthrate, leading to an aging society in shortage of labor forces. Another big changing factor is that Korea already has multi-ethnic, multi-cultural families appearing in great numbers, as one in every ten marriage is between a South Korean and a foreigner, and in the rural side this portion is greater. As such change takes place in such short period of time, it can be understood that many conflicts arise among different groups of people; the immigrants, government, and the rest of Korean society. Recently a lot of media attention is given to these people; documentaries on the lives of wives and their children are often shown, as well as talk shows that portray struggles and conflicts these people go through such as Love in Asia; a talk show hosting foreign wives, sharing their experience of marriage and family life, broadcast by the national broadcasting channel, KBS. Many South Koreans recently have recognized that the change that South Korean society is going through due to this media attention. Government policies have also changed very recently; a lot of welfare programs and extracurricular activities are launched under the name of "multicultural policy." The policy is quite recent phenomenon.

United Arab Emirates

Although Arabic is the official language of the United Arab Emirates, English, Malayalam, Hindi, Urdu, Tagalog, Bengali, Indonesian, Persian and many other languages are widely spoken and understood, particularly in the main cities of Dubai and Abu Dhabi. The UAE hosts expatriate workers from 200 countries, with a majority coming from the Indian subcontinent. The UAE has widely accepted all other religions, granting permission for the construction of temples or churches. Foreigners make up about 85% of the population. However, the UAE does not have an open immigration policy and Emirati citizens form a largely homogeneous Arab society; all foreigners reside in the country as temporary workers and visitors.

Americas

Argentina

Russian Orthodox Cathedral of the Most Holy Trinity in Buenos Aires.

Though not called *Multiculturalism* as such, the preamble of Argentina's constitution explicitly promotes immigration, and recognizes the individual's multiple citizenship from other countries. Though 97% of Argentina's population self-identify as of European descent to this day a high level of multiculturalism remains a feature of Argentina's culture, allowing foreign festivals and holidays (e.g. Saint Patrick's Day), supporting all kinds of art or cultural expression from ethnic groups, as well as their diffusion through an important multicultural presence in the media; for instance it is not uncommon to find newspapers or radio programs in English, German, Italian or French in Argentina.

Canada

Sikhs celebrating the Sikh new year in Toronto, Canada

Canadian society is often depicted as being "very progressive, diverse, and multicultural". Multiculturalism (a Just Society) was adopted as the official policy of the Canadian government during the premiership of Pierre Elliott Trudeau in the 1970s and 1980s. Multiculturalism is reflected in the law through the Canadian Multiculturalism Act and section 27 of the Canadian Charter of Rights and Freedoms. The Broadcasting Act of 1991 asserts the Canadian broadcasting system should reflect the diversity of cultures in the country. Canadian multiculturalism is looked upon with admiration outside the country, resulting in the Canadian public dismissing most critics of the concept. Multiculturalism in Canada is often looked at as one of Canada's significant accomplishments, and a key distinguishing element of Canadian identity.

In a 2002 interview with the *Globe and Mail*, Karīm al-Hussainī the 49th Aga Khan of the Ismaili Muslims described Canada as "the most successful pluralist society on the face of our globe", citing it as "a model for the world". He explained that the experience of Canadian governance – its commitment to pluralism and its support for the rich multicultural diversity of its peoples – is something that must be shared and would be of benefit to all societies in other parts of the world. *The Economist* ran a cover story in 2016 praising Canada as the most successful multicultural society in the West. *The*

Economist argued that Canada's multiculturalism was a source of strength that united the diverse population and by attracting immigrants from around the world was also an engine of economic growth as well.

Mexico

Mexico has historically always been a multicultural country, with people of ethnic groups including those of indigenous background, various European backgrounds, Africans, and a small Asian community. Mexico City has recently been integrating rapidly, doing much better than many cities in a sample conducted by the Intercultural Cities Index (being the only non-European city, alongside Montreal, on the index).

United States

Little Italy (top, ca. 1900) in New York City abuts Manhattan's Chinatown.

In the United States, multiculturalism is not clearly established in policy at the federal level, but ethnic diversity is common in both rural and urban areas.

Continuous mass immigration was a feature of the United States economy and society since the first half of the 19th century. The absorption of the stream of immigrants became, in itself, a prominent feature of America's national myth. The idea of the melting pot is a metaphor that implies that all the immigrant cultures are mixed and amalgamated without state intervention. The melting pot theory implied that each individual immigrant, and each group of immigrants, assimilated into American society at their own pace. This is different than multiculturalism as defined above, which does not include complete assimilation and integration. An Americanized (and often stereotypical) version of the original nation's cuisine, and its holidays, survived. The melting pot tradition co-exists with a belief in national unity, dating from the American founding fathers:

> Providence has been pleased to give this one connected country to one united people – a people descended from the same ancestors, speaking the same language, professing the same religion, attached to the same principles of government, very similar in their manners and customs... This country and this people seem to have been made for each other, and it appears as if it was the design of Providence, that an inheritance so proper and convenient for a band of brethren, united to each other by the strongest ties, should never be split into a number of unsocial, jealous, and alien sovereignties.

Staff of President Clinton's One America Initiative. The President's Initiative on Race was a critical element in President Clinton's effort to prepare the country to embrace diversity.

As a philosophy, multiculturalism began as part of the pragmatism movement at the end of the nineteenth century in Europe and the United States, then as political and cultural pluralism at the turn of the twentieth. It was partly in response to a new wave of European imperialism in sub-Saharan Africa and the massive immigration of Southern and Eastern Europeans to the United States and Latin America. Philosophers, psychologists and historians and early sociologists such as Charles Sanders Peirce, William James, George Santayana, Horace Kallen, John Dewey, W. E. B. Du Bois and Alain Locke developed concepts of cultural pluralism, from which emerged what we understand today as multiculturalism. In *Pluralistic Universe* (1909), William James espoused the idea of a "plural society." James saw pluralism as "crucial to the formation of philosophical and social humanism to help build a better, more egalitarian society.

The educational approach to multiculturalism has since spread to the grade school system, as school systems try to rework their curricula to introduce students to diversity earlier – often on the grounds that it is important for minority students to see themselves represented in the classroom. Studies estimated 46 million Americans ages 14 to 24 to be the most diverse generation in American society. In 2009 and 2010, controversy erupted in Texas as the state's curriculum committee made several changes to the state's requirements, often at the expense of minorities. They chose to juxtapose Abraham Lincoln's inaugural address with that of Confederate president Jefferson Davis; they debated removing Supreme Court Justice Thurgood Marshall and labor-leader Cesar Chavez and rejected calls to include more Hispanic figures, in spite of the high Hispanic population in the state.

Support

Multiculturalism is seen by its supporters as a fairer system that allows people to truly express who they are within a society, that is more tolerant and that adapts better to social issues. They argue that culture is not one definable thing based on one race or religion, but rather the result of multiple factors that change as the world changes.

Historically, support for modern multiculturalism stems from the changes in Western societies after World War II, in what Susanne Wessendorf calls the "human rights revolution", in which the horrors of institutionalized racism and ethnic cleansing became almost impossible to ignore in the wake of the Holocaust; with the collapse of the European colonial system, as colonized nations in Africa and Asia successfully fought for their independence and pointed out the discriminatory underpinnings of the colonial system; and, in the United States in particular, with the rise of the Civil Rights Movement, which criticized ideals of assimilation that often led to prejudices against those who did not act according to Anglo-American standards and which led to the development of academic ethnic studies programs as a way to counteract the neglect of contributions by racial minorities in classrooms. As this history shows, multiculturalism in Western countries was seen to combat racism, to protect minority communities of all types, and to undo policies that had prevented minorities from having full access to the opportunities for freedom and equality promised by the liberalism that has been the hallmark of Western societies since the Age of Enlightenment. The contact hypothesis in sociology is a well documented phenomenon in which cooperative interactions with those from a different group than one's own reduce prejudice and inter-group hostility.

C. James Trotman argues that multiculturalism is valuable because it "uses several disciplines to highlight neglected aspects of our social history, particularly the histories of women and minorities [...and] promotes respect for the dignity of the lives and voices of the forgotten. By closing gaps, by raising consciousness about the past, multiculturalism tries to restore a sense of wholeness in a postmodern era that fragments human life and thought."

Tariq Modood argues that in the early years of the 21st century, multiculturalism "is most timely and necessary, and [...] we need more not less", since it is "the form of integration" that (1) best fits the ideal of egalitarianism, (2) has "the best chance of succeeding" in the "post-9/11, post 7/7" world, and (3) has remained "moderate [and] pragmatic".

Bhikhu Parekh counters what he sees as the tendencies to equate multiculturalism with racial minorities "demanding special rights" and to see it as promoting a "thinly veiled racis[m]". Instead, he argues that multiculturalism is in fact "not about minorities" but "is about the proper terms of relationship between different cultural communities", which means that the standards by which the communities resolve their differences, e.g., "the principles of justice" must not come from only one of the cultures but must come "through an open and equal dialogue between them."

Balibar characterizes criticisms of multiculturalism as "differentialist racism", which he describes as a covert form of racism that does not purport ethnic superiority as much as it asserts stereotypes of perceived "incompatibility of life-styles and traditions".

While there is research that suggests that ethnic diversity increases chances of war, lower public goods provision and decreases democratization, there is also research that shows that ethnic diversity in itself is not detrimental to peace, public goods provision or democracy. Rather, it was found that promoting diversity actually helps in advancing disadvantaged students.

Criticism

Critics of multiculturalism often debate whether the multicultural ideal of benignly co-existing cultures that interrelate and influence one another, and yet remain distinct, is sustainable, paradoxical, or even desirable. It is argued that nation states, who would previously have been synonymous with a distinctive cultural identity of their own, lose out to enforced multiculturalism and that this ultimately erodes the host nations' distinct culture.

Harvard professor of political science Robert D. Putnam conducted a nearly decade-long study on how multiculturalism affects social trust. He surveyed 26,200 people in 40 American communities, finding that when the data were adjusted for class, income and other factors, the more racially diverse a community is, the greater the loss of trust. People in diverse communities "don't trust the local mayor, they don't trust the local paper, they don't trust other people and they don't trust institutions," writes Putnam. In the presence of such ethnic diversity, Putnam maintains that

We hunker down. We act like turtles. The effect of diversity is worse than had been imagined. And it's not just that we don't trust people who are not like us. In diverse communities, we don't trust people who do look like us.

Ethnologist Frank Salter writes: Relatively homogeneous societies invest more in public goods, indicating a higher level of public altruism. For example, the degree of ethnic homogeneity correlates with the government's share of gross domestic product as well as the average wealth of citizens. Case studies of the United States, Africa and

South-East Asia find that multi-ethnic societies are less charitable and less able to co-operate to develop public infrastructure. Moscow beggars receive more gifts from fellow ethnics than from other ethnies [*sic*]. A recent multi-city study of municipal spending on public goods in the United States found that ethnically or racially diverse cities spend a smaller portion of their budgets and less per capita on public services than do the more homogeneous cities.

Dick Lamm, former three-term Democratic governor of the US state of Colorado, wrote in his essay "I have a plan to destroy America":

> "Diverse peoples worldwide are mostly engaged in hating each other—that is, when they are not killing each other. A diverse, peaceful, or stable society is against most historical precedent."

A number of conservative historians used the religion of the Mexica, better known as the Aztecs as an example of what they see as the flaws of multiculturalism. The Australian historian Keith Windschuttle cited the accounts of his fellow Australian historian Inga Clendinnen of the festival of Ochpaniztli where to honor the Maize Lord a young woman was sacrificed by ripping out heart her so the crops might grow:

> "Then, still in darkness, silence, and urgent haste, her body was flayed, and a naked priest, a 'very strong man, very powerful, very tall', struggled into the wet skin, with its slack breasts and pouched genitalia: a double nakedness of layered, ambiguous sexuality. The skin of one thigh was reserved to be fashioned into a face-mask for the man impersonating Centeotl, Young Lord Maize Cob, the son of Toci".

Windschuttle argued that the gruesome religion of the Aztecs that required that dozens of young people be sacrificed and eaten every day so that the sun might rise the next day and hundreds of people sacrificed for major holidays as proving that multiculturalism is a facile doctrine that requires Westerners to respect Aztec religion as equal to any other religion. Along the same lines, the American classist Victor Davis Hanson denounced Aztec culture as fundamentally barbarous and irrational, which he compared unfavorably with the "rationalism" of the Spanish who conquered Mexico in 1519–21. Hanson argued that Hernán Cortés conquered Mexico because he was a product of the rational culture of the West, unlike Moctezuma II who Hanson noted dismissively at first believed the Spanish were gods and who consulted "sorcerers and necromancers" instead using his reason. Hanson used the differences between Moctezuma and Cortés to argue that Western culture was superior to every culture in the entire world, which thus led him to reject multiculturalism as a false doctrine that placed all cultures on an equal footing.

In New Zealand (Aotearoa), which is officially bi-cultural, multiculturalism has been seen as a threat to the Maori, and possibly an attempt by the New Zealand Government to undermine Maori demands for self determination.

References

- Ousterhout, Robert. "Ethnic Identity and Cultural Appropriation in Early Ottoman Architecture." Archived June 13, 2006, at the Wayback Machine. Muqarnas Volume XII: An Annual on Islamic Art and Architecture. Leiden: E.J. Brill. 1995. Retrieved January 3, 2010

- Ghosh, Biswajit (2011). "Cultural changes in the era of globalisation". Journal of Developing Societies. 27 (2): 153–175. doi:10.1177/0169796x1102700203

- Salvatore Babones (15 April 2008). "Studying Globalization: Methodological Issues". In George Ritzer. The Blackwell Companion to Globalization. John Wiley & Sons. p. 146. ISBN 978-0-470-76642-2

- Berg, Chris (December 21, 2015). "Is cultural appropriation the bogeyman it's made out to be?". The Drum. Retrieved April 19, 2016

- White, Livingston A. (Spring–Summer 2001). "Reconsidering cultural imperialism theory". Transnational Broadcasting Studies. The Center for Electronic Journalism at the American University in Cairo and the Centre for Middle East Studies, St. Antony's College, Oxford (6)

- Barber, Benjamin R., Jihad vs. McWorld", Hardcover: Crown, 1995, ISBN 0-8129-2350-2; Paperback: Ballantine Books, 1996, ISBN 0-345-38304-4

- "The Aboriginal Arts 'fake' controversy." Archived April 20, 2012, at the Wayback Machine. European Network for Indigenous Australian Rights. July 29, 2000. Retrieved January 3, 2010

- Alcoff, Linda Martin (1998). "What Should White People Do?". Hypatia. 13 (3): 6–26. doi:10.1111/j.1527-2001.1998.tb01367.x. Retrieved November 22, 2014

- Pewewardy, Cornel (1999). "From enemy to mascot: The deculturation of Indian mascots in sports culture". Canadian Journal of Native Education. 23 (2): 176–189. ISSN 0710-1481. Retrieved 2014-11-22

- George Ritzer (15 April 2008). The Blackwell Companion to Globalization. John Wiley & Sons. pp. 140–141. ISBN 978-0-470-76642-2. Retrieved 4 February 2013

- Byard, RW (2005-09-26). "Dehydration and heat-related death: sweat lodge syndrome". Forensic Science SA. Retrieved 2006-09-26

- Wayland, Shara (1997). "Immigration, Multiculturalism and National Identity in Canada". International Journal of Group Rights. 5 (1). pp. 33–58. doi:10.1163/15718119720907408

- Tomlinson, John (1991). Cultural imperialism: a critical introduction (illustrated, reprint ed.). Continuum International Publishing Group. ISBN 978-0-8264-5013-5

- Byard, RW (2005-09-26). "Dehydration and heat-related death: sweat lodge syndrome". Forensic Science SA. Retrieved 2006-09-26

- Arrowsmith, Aidan (April 1, 2000). "Plastic Paddy: Negotiating Identity in Second-generation 'Irish-English' Writing". Irish Studies Review. Routledge. 8 (1): 35–43. doi:10.1080/09670880050005093

- Han Geon-Soo, "Multicultural Korea: Celebration or Challenge of Multiethnic Shift in Contemporary Korea?", Korea Journal, Vol. 47 No. 4, Winter 2007, pp. 32–63

- Elizabeth J. Meyer (30 August 2010). Gender and sexual diversity in schools: an introduction. Springer. p. 16. ISBN 978-90-481-8558-0

- Culpepper, Chuck (December 29, 2014). "Florida State's Unusual Bond with Seminole Tribe Puts Mascot Debate in a Different Light". The Washington Post. Retrieved December 6, 2015

- Reysen, S.; Katzarska-Miller, I. (2013). "A model of global citizenship: Antecedents and outcomes". International Journal of Psychology. 48: 858–870. doi:10.1080/00207594.2012.701749

- Brian Galligan; John Ravenhill (15 June 1997). New developments in Australian politics. Macmillan Education AU. p. 13. ISBN 978-0-7329-4304-2

- Herel, Suzanne (2002-06-27). "2 seeking spiritual enlightenment die in new-age sweat lodge". San Francisco Chronicle. Hearst Communications. Retrieved 2006-09-26

- Fearon, James D.; Laitin, David D. (2003-02-01). "Ethnicity, Insurgency, and Civil War". American Political Science Review. null (01): 75–90. ISSN 1537-5943. doi:10.1017/S0003055403000534

- Reysen, Stephen; Katzarska-Miller, Iva (2013). "Intentional worlds and global citizenship". Journal of Global Citizenship and Equity Education. 3 (1): 34–52

- "Aboriginal art under fraud threat." Archived April 11, 2016, at the Wayback Machine. BBC News. November 28, 2003. Retrieved January 3, 2010

- Susanne Wessendorf (2010). The multiculturalism backlash: European discourses, policies and practices. Taylor & Francis. pp. 73–75. ISBN 978-0-415-55649-1

Political Impact of Globalization

Political globalization studies the worldwide political system in correspondence with new agents of political change. Political globalization along with economic globalization and cultural globalization forms the basics of globalization. Global politics, global civics, global commons and transnationalism are topics that have been explained in this section.

Political Globalization

Political globalization refers to the growth of the worldwide political system, both in size and complexity. That system includes national governments, their governmental and intergovernmental organizations as well as government-independent elements of global civil society such as international non-governmental organizations and social movement organizations. One of the key aspects of the political globalization is the declining importance of the nation-state and the rise of other actors on the political scene. The creation and existence of the United Nations has been called one of the classic examples of political globalization.

Political globalization is one of the three main dimensions of globalization commonly found in academic literature, with the two other being economic globalization and cultural globalization.

Definitions

The Flag of the United Nations flying at United Nations Plaza in the Civic Center, San Francisco, California. The UN is one of the key organizations in the process of the political globalization.

William R. Thompson has defined it as "the expansion of a global political system, and its institutions, in which inter-regional transactions (including, but certainly not limited to trade) are managed". Valentine M. Moghadam defined it as "an increasing trend toward multilateralism (in which the United Nations plays a key role), toward an emerging 'transnational state apparatus,' and toward the emergence of national and international nongovernmental organizations that act as watchdogs over governments and have increased their activities and influence". Manfred B. Steger in turn wrote that it "refers to the intensification and expansion of political interrelations across the globe". The longer definition by Colin Crouch goes as follows: "Political globalization refers to the growing power of institutions of global governance such as the World Bank, the International Monetary Fund (IMF) and the World Trade Organization (WTO). But it also refers to the spread and influence of international non-governmental organizations, social movement organizations and transnational advocacy networks operating across borders and constituting a kind of global civil society." Finally, Gerard Delanty and Chris Rumford define it as "a tension between three processes which interact to produce the complex field of global politics: global geopolitics, global normative culture and polycentric networks."

Methodology

Salvatore Babones discussing sources used by scholars for studying political globalizations noted the usefulness of Europa World Year Book for data on diplomatic relationships between countries, publications of International Institute for Strategic Studies such as *The Military Balance* for matters of military, and US government publication *Patterns of Global Terrorism* for matters of terrorism.

Political globalization is measured by aggregating and weighting data on the number of embassies and high commissioners in a country, the number of the country's membership in international organization, its participation in the UN peacekeeping missions, and the number of international treaties signed by said country. This measure has been used by Axel Dreher, Noel Gaston, Pim Martens Jeffrey Haynes and is available from the KOF institute at ETH Zurich.

Aspects

Like globalization itself, political globalization has several dimensions and lends itself to a number of interpretations. It has been discussed in the context of new emancipatory possibilities, as well as in the context of loss of autonomy and fragmentation of the social world. Political globalization can be seen in changes such as democratization of the world, creation of the global civil society, and moving beyond the centrality of the nation-state, particularly as the sole actor in the field of politics. Some of the questions central to the discussion of the political globalization are related to the future of the nation-state, whether its importance is diminishing and what are the causes for those changes; and understanding the emergence of the concept of global governance. The creation and existence of the United Nations has been called one of the classic examples of political globalization. Political actions by non-governmental organizations and social movements, concerned about various topics such as environmental protection, is another example.

David Held has proposed that continuing political globalization may lead to the creation of a world government-like cosmopolitan democracy, through this vision has also been criticized as too idealistic.

Global Politics

Global politics names both the discipline that studies the political and economical patterns of the world and the field that is being studied. At the centre of that field are the different processes of political globalization in relation to questions of social power.

The discipline studies the relationships between cities, nation-states, shell-states, multinational corporations, non-governmental organizations and international organizations. Current areas of discussion include national and ethnic conflict regulation, democracy and the politics of national self-determination, globalization and its relationship to democracy, conflict and peace studies, comparative politics, political economy, and the international political economy of the environment. One important area of global politics is contestation in the global political sphere over legitimacy.

It can be argued that global politics should be distinguished from the field of international politics, which seeks to understand political relations between nation-states, and thus has a narrower scope. Similarly, international relations, which seeks to understand general economic and political relations between nation-states, is a narrower field than global politics.

Defining the Field

Beginning in the late nineteenth century, several groups extended the definition of the political community beyond nation-states to include much, if not all, of humanity. These "internationalists" include Marxists, human rights advocates, environmentalists, peace activists, feminists, and dalits. This was the general direction of thinking on global politics, though the term was not used as such.

Today, the practices of global politics are defined by values: norms of human rights, ideas of human development, and beliefs such as Internationalism or cosmopolitanism about how we should relate to each. Over the last couple of decades cosmopolitanism has become one of the key contested ideologies of global politics:

"Cosmopolitanism can be defined as a global politics that, firstly, projects a sociality of common political engagement among all human beings across the globe, and, secondly, suggests that this sociality should be either ethically or organizationally privileged over other forms of sociality".

Debates

The intensification of globalization led some writers to suggest that states were no longer relevant to global politics. This view has been subject to debate:

"On the other hand, other commentators have been arguing that states have remained essential to global politics. They have facilitated globalizing processes and projects; not been eclipsed by them. They have been rejuvenated because, among other reasons, they are still the primary providers of (military) security in the global arena; they are still the paramount loci for articulating the voices of (procedurally democratic) national communities, and for ordering their interactions with similar polities; and finally, they are indispensable to relations of (unequal) economic exchange insofar as they legitimize and enforce the global legal frameworks that enable globalization in the first place".

Global Civics

Global civics suggests to understand civics in a global sense as a social contract among all world citizens in an age of interdependence and interaction. The disseminators of the concept define it as the notion that we have certain rights and responsibilities towards each other by the mere fact of being human on Earth.

The advocates of the notion attempt to demonstrate that it is possible to imagine global civics. According to this notion, in an increasingly interdependent world, the world citizens need a compass that would frame mindsets on a global scale, and create a shared consciousness and sense of global responsibility related to specific world issues such as environmental problems and nuclear proliferation.

History of the Concept

The term global civics was first coined by Hakan Altinay, a nonresident senior fellow with the Global Economy and Development program at the Brookings Institution, in a working paper published in March 2010. The concept builds upon the basic tenets behind global ethics, global justice and world citizenship, inviting everyone to question their increasingly important role in a highly interdependent world. In early 2011, Altinay published *Global Civics: Responsibilities and Rights in an Interdependent World,* a book of articles on global civics put forth by academics and intellectuals all around the world.

Objections to the Concept

Opponents of the global civics concept argue that even a modest level of exercising responsibility towards all the people living in the world is so overwhelming and nearly impossible to achieve. These arguments also posit that civics assumes an effective state and enforcement. The claim goes that since there is no such thing as a world government, global civics implementation is not feasible. Also, it has been suggested that superpowers of the world are selfish and dangerous nations, and that they do not feel constrained by international legitimacy and laws. Finally, the critics claim that any experience of pan-global solidarity among human beings cannot form the basis of constellation of rights and responsibilities as it is nascent at best and the experience of being a global citizen is a privilege restricted to international elites and a few activists.

The Role of Universities

The proponents of global civics also suggest that university campuses play a vital role in spreading a thorough understanding of how today's global world functions and contributes toward preparation of future generations for life in an interdependent world. This view calls for visionary universities that could successfully "provide their students with the forums and the tools to discuss and figure out what their responsibilities are to their fellow human beings."

Global Commons

Global commons is a term typically used to describe international, supranational, and global resource domains in which common-pool resources are found. Global commons include the earth's shared natural resources, such as the high oceans, the atmosphere, outer space and the Antarctic in particular. Cyberspace may also meet the definition of a global commons.

Definition and Usage

Global commons is a term typically used to describe international, supranational, and global resource domains in which common-pool resources are found. In economics, common goods are rivalrous and non-excludable, constituting one of the four main types of goods. A common-pool resource, also called a common property resource, is a special case of a common good (or public good) whose size or characteristics makes it costly, but not impossible, to exclude potential users. Examples include both natural or human-made resource domains (e.g., a "fishing hole" or an irrigation system). Unlike global public goods, global common-pool resources face problems of congestion, over-use, or degradation because they are subtractable (which makes them rivalrous).

The term "commons" originates from the term common land in the British Isles. "Commoners rights" referred to traditional rights held by commoners, such as mowing meadows for hay or grazing livestock on common land held in the open field system of old English common law. Enclosure was the process that ended those traditional rights, converting open fields to private property. Today, many commons still exist in England, Wales, Scotland, and the United States, although their extent is much reduced from the millions of acres that existed until the 17th century. There are still over 7,000 registered commons in England alone.

The term "global commons" is typically used to indicate the earth's shared natural resources, such as the deep oceans, the atmosphere, outer space and the Northern and Southern polar regions, the Antarctic in particular.

According to the *World Conservation Strategy*, a report on conservation published by the International Union for Conservation of Nature and Natural Resources (IUCN) in collaboration with UNESCO and with the support of the United Nations Environment Programme (UNEP) and the World Wildlife Fund (WWF):

> A commons is a tract of land or water owned or used jointly by the members of a community. The global commons includes those parts of the Earth's surface beyond national jurisdictions — notably the open ocean and the living resources found there — or held in common — notably the atmosphere. The only landmass that may be regarded as part of the global commons is Antarctica.

Today, the Internet, World Wide Web and resulting cyberspace are often referred to as global commons. Other usages sometimes include references to open access information of all kinds, including arts and culture, language and science, though these are more formally referred to as the common heritage of mankind.

Management of the Global Commons

The key challenge of the global commons is the design of governance structures and management systems capable of addressing the complexity of multiple public and private interests, subject to often unpredictable changes, ranging from the local to the global level. As with global public goods, management of the global commons requires pluralistic legal entities, usually international and supranational, public and private, structured to match the diversity of interests and the type of resource to be managed, and stringent enough with adequate incentives to ensure compliance. Such management systems are necessary to avoid, at the global level, the classic tragedy of the commons, in which common resources become overexploited.

There are several key differences in management of resources in the global commons from those of the commons, in general. There are obvious differences in scale of both the resources and the number of users at the local versus the global level. Also, there are differences in the shared culture and expectations of resource users; more localized commons users tend to be more homogeneous and global users more heterogeneous. This contributes to differences in the possibility and time it takes for new learning about resource usage to occur at the different levels. Moreover, global resource pools are less likely to be relatively stable and the dynamics are less easily understood. Many of the global commons are non-renewable on human time scales. Thus, resource degradation is more likely to be the result of unintended consequences that are unforeseen, not immediately observable, or not easily understood. For example, the carbon dioxide emissions that drive climate change continue to do so for at least a millennium after they enter the atmosphere and species extinctions last forever. Importantly, because there are significant differences in the benefits, costs, and interests at the global level, there are significant differences in externalities between more local resource uses and uses of global-level resources.

Several environmental protocols have been established as a type of international law, "an intergovernmental document intended as legally binding with a primary stated purpose of preventing or managing human impacts on natural resources." International environmental protocols came to feature in environmental governance after trans-boundary environmental problems became widely perceived in the 1960s. Following the Stockholm Intergovernmental Conference in 1972, creation of international environmental agreements proliferated. Due to the barriers already discussed, environmental protocols are not a panacea for global commons issues. Often, they are slow to produce the desired effects, tend to the lowest common denominator, and lack monitoring and enforcement. They also take an incremental approach to solutions where sustainable development principles suggest that environmental concerns should be mainstream political issues.

The Global Ocean

The global or world ocean, as the interconnected system of the Earth's oceanic (or marine) waters that comprise the bulk of the hydrosphere, is a classic global commons. It is divided into a number of principal oceanic areas that are delimited by the continents and various oceanographic features. In turn, oceanic waters are interspersed by many smaller seas, gulfs, and bays. Further, most freshwater bodies ultimately empty into the ocean and are derived through the Earth's water cycle from ocean waters. The Law of the Sea is a body of public international law governing relationships between nations in respect to navigational rights, mineral rights, and jurisdiction over coastal waters. Maritime law, also called Admiralty law, is a body of both domestic law governing maritime activities and private international law governing the relationships between private entities which operate vessels on the oceans. It deals with matters including marine commerce, marine navigation, shipping, sailors, and the transportation of passengers and goods by sea. However, these bodies of law do little to nothing to protect deep oceans from human threats.

In addition to providing significant means of transportation, a large proportion of all life on Earth exists in its ocean, which contains about 300 times the habitable volume of terrestrial habitats. Specific marine habitats include coral reefs, kelp forests, seagrass meadows, tidepools, muddy, sandy and rocky bottoms, and the open ocean (pelagic) zone, where solid objects are rare and the surface of the water is the only visible boundary. The organisms studied range from microscopic phytoplankton and zooplankton to huge cetaceans (whales) 30 meters (98 feet) in length.

At a fundamental level, marine life helps determine the very nature of our planet. Marine life resources provide food (especially food fish), medicines, and raw materials. It is also becoming understood that the well-being of marine organisms and other organisms are linked in very fundamental ways. The human body of knowledge regarding the relationship between life in the sea and important cycles is rapidly growing, with new discoveries being made nearly every day. These cycles include those of matter (such as the carbon cycle) and of air (such as Earth's respiration, and movement of energy through ecosystems including the ocean). Marine organisms contribute significantly to the oxygen cycle, and are involved in the regulation of the Earth's climate. Shorelines are in part shaped and protected by marine life, and some marine organisms even help create new land.

The United Nations Environment Programme (UNEP) has identified several areas of need in managing the global ocean: strengthen national capacities for action, especially in developing countries; improve fisheries management; reinforce cooperation in semi-enclosed and regional seas; strengthen controls over ocean disposal of hazardous and nuclear wastes; and advance the Law of the Sea. Specific problems identified as in need of attention include rising sea levels; contamination by hazardours chemicals (including oil spills); microbiological contamination; ocean acidification; harmful algal blooms; and over-fishing and other overexploitation. Further, the Pew Charitable Trusts Environmental Initiative program has identified a need for a worldwide system of very large, highly protected marine reserves where fishing and other extractive activities are prohibited.

Atmosphere

The atmosphere is a complex dynamic natural gaseous system that is essential to support life on planet Earth. A primary concern for management of the global atmosphere is air pollution, the introduction into the atmosphere of chemicals, particulates, or biological materials that cause discomfort, disease, or death to humans, damage other living organisms such as food crops, or damage the natural environment or built environment. Stratospheric ozone depletion due to air pollution has long been recognized as a threat to human health as well as to the Earth's ecosystems.

Pollution of breathable air is a central problem in the management of the global commons. Pollutants can be in the form of solid particles, liquid droplets, or gases and may be natural or man-made. Although controversial and limited in scope by methods of enforcement, in several parts of the world the polluter pays principle, which makes the party responsible for producing pollution responsible for paying for the damage done to the natural environment, is accepted. It has strong support in most Organisation for Economic Co-operation and Development (OECD) and European Community (EC) countries. It is also known as extended producer responsibility (EPR). EPR seeks to shift the responsibility dealing with waste from governments (and thus, taxpayers and society at large) to the entities producing it. In effect, it attempts to internalise the cost of waste disposal into the cost of the product, theoretically resulting in producers improving the waste profile of their products, decreasing waste and increasing possibilities for reuse and recycling.

The 1979 Convention on Long-Range Transboundary Air Pollution, or CLRTAP, is an early international effort to protect and gradually reduce and prevent air pollution. It is implemented by the European Monitoring and Evaluation Programme (EMEP), directed by the United Nations Economic Commission for Europe (UNECE). The Montreal Protocol on Substances that Deplete the Ozone Layer, or Montreal Protocol (a protocol to the Vienna Convention for the Protection of the Ozone Layer), is an international treaty designed to protect the ozone layer by phasing out the production of numerous substances believed to be responsible for ozone depletion. The treaty was opened for signature on 16 September 1987, and entered into force on 1 January 1989.

Global dimming is the gradual reduction in the amount of global direct irradiance at the Earth's surface, which has been observed for several decades after the start of systematic measurements in the 1950s. Global dimming is thought to have been caused by an increase in particulates such as sulfate aerosols in the atmosphere due to human action. It has interfered with the hydrological cycle by reducing evaporation and may have reduced rainfall in some areas. Global dimming also creates a cooling effect that may have partially masked the effect of greenhouse gases on global warming.

Along with global warming, generalized climate change is an ongoing global commons concern. Although global warming is now a generally accepted scientific observation, the precise causes of global warming are still a matter of research and debate. The Kyoto Protocol to the United Nations Framework Convention on Climate Change (UN-FCCC) is an international environmental treaty that sets binding obligations on industrialised countries to reduce emissions of greenhouse gases and prevent potentially harmful anthropogenic (i.e., human-induced) interference in the climate system. There are 192 parties to the convention, including 191 states and the European Union, but not all have ratified and implemented the protocol.

Polar Regions

The eight Arctic nations Canada, Denmark (Greenland and the Faroe Islands), Norway, the United States (Alaska), Sweden, Finland, Iceland, and Russia, are all members of the treaty organization, the Arctic Council, as are organizations representing six indigenous populations. The Council operates on consensus basis, mostly dealing with environmental treaties and not addressing boundary or resource disputes. Currently, the Antarctic Treaty and related agreements, collectively called the Antarctic Treaty System or ATS, regulate international relations with respect to Antarctica, Earth's only continent without a native human population. The treaty, entering into force in 1961 and currently having 50 signatory nations, sets aside Antarctica as a scientific preserve, establishes freedom of scientific investigation and bans military activity on that continent.

Climate change in the Arctic region is leading to widespread ecosystem restructuring. The distribution of species is changing along with the structure of food webs. Changes in ocean circulation appear responsible for the first exchanges of zooplankton between the North Pacific and North Atlantic regions in perhaps 800,000 years. These changes can allow the transmission of diseases from subarctic animals to Arctic ones, and vice versa, posing an additional threat to species already stressed by habitat loss and other impacts. Where these changes lead is not yet clear, but are likely to have far-reaching impacts on Arctic marine ecosystems.

Climate models tend to reinforce that temperature trends due to global warming will be much smaller in Antarctica than in the Arctic, but ongoing research may show otherwise.

Outer Space

Management of outer space global commons has been contentious since the successful launch of the Sputnik satellite by the former Soviet Union on 4 October 1957. There is no clear boundary between Earth's atmosphere and space, although there are several standard boundary designations: one that deals with orbital velocity (the Kármán line), one that depends on the velocity of charged particles in space, and some that are determined by human factors such as the height at which human blood begins to boil without a pressurized environment (the Armstrong line).

Space policy regarding a country's civilian space program, as well as its policy on both military use and commercial use of outer space, intersects with science policy, since national space programs often perform or fund research in space science, and also with defense policy, for applications such as spy satellites and anti-satellite weapons. It also encompasses government regulation of third-party activities such as commercial communications satellites and private spaceflight as well as the creation and application of space law and space advocacy organizations that exist to support the cause of space exploration.

The Outer Space Treaty provides a basic framework for international space law. It covers the legal use of outer space by nation states. The treaty states that outer space is free for all nation states to explore and is not subject to claims of national sovereignty. It also prohibits the deployment of nuclear weapons in outer space. The treaty was passed by the United Nations General Assembly in 1963 and signed in 1967 by the USSR, the United States of America and the United Kingdom. As of mid-year, 2013 the treaty has been ratified by 102 states and signed by an additional 27 states.

Beginning in 1958, outer space has been the subject of multiple resolutions by the United Nations General Assembly. Of these, more than 50 have concerned the international co-operation in the peaceful uses of outer space and preventing an arms race in space. Four additional space law treaties have been negotiated and drafted by the UN's Committee on the Peaceful Uses of Outer Space. Still, there remain no legal prohibitions against deploying conventional weapons in space and anti-satellite weapons have been successfully tested by the US, USSR and China. The 1979 Moon Treaty turned the jurisdiction of all heavenly bodies (including the orbits around such bodies) over to the international community. However, this treaty has not been ratified by any nation that currently practices manned spaceflight.

In 1976 eight equatorial states (Ecuador, Colombia, Brazil, Congo, Zaire, Uganda, Kenya, and Indonesia) met in Bogotá, Colombia to make the "Declaration of the First Meeting of Equatorial Countries," also known as "the Bogotá Declaration", a claim to control the segment of the geosynchronous orbital path corresponding to each country. These claims are not internationally accepted.

The International Space Station programme is a joint project among five participating space agencies: NASA, the Russian Federal Space Agency (RSA), Japan Aerospace Exploration Agency (JAXA), European Space Agency (ESA), and Canadian Space Agency (CSA). National budget constraints led to the merger of three space station projects into the International Space Station. In 1993 the partially built components for a Soviet/Russian space station Mir-2, the proposed American Freedom, and the proposed European Columbus merged into this multinational programme. The ownership and use of the space station is established by intergovernmental treaties and agreements. The ISS is arguably the most expensive single item ever constructed, and may be one of the most significant instances of international cooperation in modern history.

According to the original Memorandum of Understanding between NASA and the RSA, the International Space Station was intended to be a laboratory, observatory and factory in space. It was also planned to provide transportation, maintenance, and act as a staging base for possible future missions to the Moon, Mars and asteroids. In the 2010 United States National Space Policy, it was given additional roles of serving commercial, diplomatic and educational purposes.

Internet

As a global system of computers interconnected by telecommunication technologies consisting of millions of private, public, academic, business, and government resources, it is difficult to argue that the Internet is a global commons. These computing resources are largely privately owned and subject to private property law, although many are government owned and subject to public law. The World Wide Web, as a system of interlinked hypertext documents, either public domain or subject to copyright law, is, at best, a mixed good.

The resultant virtual space or cyberspace, however, is often viewed as an electronic global commons that allows for as much or more freedom of expression as any public space. Access to those digital commons and the actual freedom of expression allowed does vary widely by geographical area. Management of the electronic global commons presents as many issues as do other commons. In addition to issues related to inequity in access, issues such as net neutrality, Internet censorship, Internet privacy, and electronic surveillance arise.

Transnationalism

Transnationalism is a social phenomenon and scholarly research agenda grown out of the heightened interconnectivity between people and the receding economic and social significance of boundaries among nation states.

The term was popularized in the early 20th century by writer Randolph Bourne to describe "a new way of thinking about relationships between cultures".However, the term itself was coined by a colleague in college.

Transnationalism as an economic process involves the global reorganization of the production process, in which various stages of the production of any product can occur in various countries, typically with the aim of minimizing costs. Economic transnationalism, commonly known as Globalization, was spurred in the latter half of the 20th century by the development of the internet and wireless communication, as well as the reduction in global transportation costs caused by containerization. Multinational corporations could be seen as a form of transnationalism, in that they seek to minimize costs, and hence maximize profits, by organizing their operations in the most efficient means possible irrespective of political boundaries.

Proponents of capitalists transnationalism seek to facilitate the flow of people, ideas, and goods among regions. They believe that it has increasing relevance with the rapid growth of capitalist globalization. They contend that it does not make sense to link specific nation-state boundaries with for instance migratory workforces, globalized corporations, global money flow, global information flow, and global scientific cooperation.

However, critical theories of transnationalism have argued that transnational capitalism has occurred through the increasing monopolization and centralization of capital by leading dominant groups in the global economy and various power blocs. Scholars critical of global capitalism (and its global ecological and inequality crises) have argued instead for a transnationalism from below between workers and co-operatives as well as popular social and political movements.

Transnationalism as concept, theory and experience has nourished an important literature in social sciences. In practice transnationalism refers to increasing functional integration of processes that cross-borders or according to others trans bordered relations of individuals, groups, firms and to mobilizations beyond state boundaries. Individuals, groups, institutions and states interact with each other in a new global space where cultural and political characteristic of national societies are combined with emerging multilevel and multinational activities. Transnationalism is a part of the process of capitalist globalization. The concept of transnationalism refers to multiple links and interactions linking people and institutions across the borders of nation-states. Although much of the more recent literature has focused on popular protest as a form of transnational activism, some research has also drawn attention to clandestine and criminal networks, as well as foreign fighters, as examples of a wider form of transnationalism.

Some have argued that Diasporas, such as the overseas Chinese, are a historical precursor to modern transnationalism. However, unlike some people with transnationalist lives, most diasporas have not been voluntary. The field of diaspora politics does consider modern diasporas as having the potential to be transnational political actors and be influenced by transnational political forces. While the term transnationalism emphasizes the ways in which nations are no longer able to contain or control the disputes and negotiations through which social groups annex a global dimension to their meaningful practices, the notion of diaspora brings to the fore the racial dynamics underlying the international division of labor and the economic turmoil of global capital. In an article published in 2006, Asale Angel-Ajani claimed that "there is the possibility within diaspora studies to move away from the politically sanitized discourse that surrounds transnational studies." Since African diaspora studies have focused on racial formation, racism, and white supremacy, diaspora theory has the potential to bring to transnationalism "a varied political, if not radical political, perspective to the study of transnational processes and —globalization".

What Drives Transnationalism

Different approaches have attempted to explain this. Some argue that the main driver of transnationalism has been the development of technologies that have made transportation and communication more accessible and affordable, thus dramatically changing the relationship between people and places. It is now possible for immigrants to maintain closer and more frequent contact with their home societies than ever before. However, the integration of international migrations to the demographic future of many developed countries is another important driver for transnationalism. Beyond simply filling a demand for low-wage workers, migration also fills the demographic gaps created by declining natural populations in most industrialized countries. Today, migration accounts for 3/5 of population growth on western countries as a whole. And this trend shows no sign of slowing down. Moreover, global political transformations and new international legal regimes have weakened the state as the only legitimate source of rights. Decolonization, coupled with the fall of communism and the ascendance of human rights, have forced states to take account of persons qua persons, rather than persons qua citizens. As a result, individuals have rights regardless of their citizenship status within a country. Others, from a neo-marxist approach, argue that transnational class relations have come about which have occurred concomitant with novel organizational and technological advancements and the spread of transnational chains of production and finance.

Immigrant Transnational Activities

When immigrants engage in transnational activities, they create "social fields" that link their original country with their new country or countries of residence. "We have defined transnationalism as the process by which immigrants build social fields that link together their country of origin and their country of settlement". These social fields are the product of a series of interconnected and overlapping economic, political, and socio-cultural activities:

Economic Transnational Activities

Economic transnational activities such as business investments in home countries and monetary remittances are both pervasive and well documented. The Inter-American Development Bank (IDB) estimates that in 2006 immigrants living in developed countries sent home the equivalent of $300 billion in remittances, an amount more than double the level of international aid. This intense influx of resources may mean that for some nations development prospects become inextricably linked- if not dependent upon_ the economic activities of their respective diasporas.

Political Transnational Activities

Political transnational activities can range from retained membership in political parties in one's country of origin and voting in its elections to even running for political office. Less formal but still significant roles include the transfer or dissemination of political ideas and norms, such as publishing an op-ed in a home country newspaper, writing a blog, or lobbying a local elected official. There is also the more extreme example of individuals such as Jesus Galvis, a travel agent in New Jersey who in 1997 ran for a Senate seat in his native Colombia. He was elected and intended to hold office simultaneously in Bogota and Hackensack, New Jersey where he served as a city councilor.

Political Economy and Transnationalism

The rise of global capitalism has occurred through a novel and increasingly functional integration of capitalist chains of production and finance across borders which is tied to the formation of a transnational capitalist class. This approach has led to a broader study of corporate networks, the global working class and the transnationalization of state apparatuses and elites.

Socio-cultural Transnational Activities

Transnationalism is an analytic lens used to understand immigrant and minority populations as a meeting of multiple simultaneous histories. Socio-cultural transnational activities cover a wide array of social and cultural transactions through which ideas and meanings are exchanged. Recent research has established the concept and importance of social remittances which provide a distinct form of social capital between migrants living abroad and those who remain at home. These transfers of socio-cultural meanings and practices occur either during the increased number of visits that immigrants take back to their home countries or visits made by non-migrants to friends and families living in the receiving countries or through the dramatically increased forms of correspondence such as emails, online chat sessions, telephone calls, CDs/ VDOs, and traditional letters.

In the late 1980s, ethnic studies scholars would largely move towards models of diaspora to understand immigrant communities in relation to area studies, although lone patterns of international flow would become accompanied by the multiple flows of transnationalism. However, to say that immigrants build social fields that link those abroad with those back home is not to say that their lives are not firmly rooted in a particular place and time. Indeed, they are as much residents of their new community as anyone else.

Transnationalism is criticized for being too far removed from ethnic studies' efforts to empower solidarity in minority communities. Asian American Studies provides a counterargument in that its inception was based in comparative analysis of the racial discrimination against Asian Americans and Vietnamese during the Vietnam War.

Transnationalism and Migration

Transnationalism has significant implications for the way we conceptualize immigration. Traditionally, immigration has been seen as an autonomous process, driven by conditions such as poverty and overpopulation in the country of origin and unrelated to conditions (such as foreign policy and economic needs) in the receiving country. Even though overpopulation, economic stagnation, and poverty all continue to create pressures for migration, they alone are not enough to produce large international migration flows. There are many countries, for example, which lack significant emigration history despite longstanding poverty. Also, most international immigration flows from the global South to the global North are not made up by the poorest of the poor, but, generally by professionals. In addition, there are countries with high levels of job creation that continue to witness emigration on a large scale.

The reasons and promoters for migration are not only embodied within the country of origin. Instead, they are rooted within the broader geopolitical and global dynamics. Significant evidence of geographic migration patterns suggests that receiving countries become home to immigrants from the receiving country's zone of influence. Then, immigration is but a fundamental component of the process of capitalist expansion, market penetration, and globalization. There are systematic and structural relations between globalization and immigration.

The emergence of a global economy has contributed both to the creation of potential emigrants abroad and to the formation of economic, cultural, and ideological links between industrialized and developing countries that later serve as bridges for the international migration. For example, the same set of circumstances and processes that have promoted the location of factories and offices abroad have also contributed to the creation of large supply of low-wage jobs for which immigrant workers constitute a desirable labor supply. Moreover, the decline of manufacturing jobs and the growth of the service sector, key drivers of the globalization of production, have transformed western economies' occupational and income structure.

Unlike the manufacturing sector, which traditionally supplied middle-income jobs and competitive benefits, the majority of service jobs are either extremely well-paid or extremely poorly paid, with relatively few jobs in the middle-income range. Many of the jobs lack key benefits such as health insurance. Sales representatives, restaurant wait staff, administrative assistants, and custodial workers are among the growth occupations.

Finally, the fact that the major growth sectors rather than declining sectors are generating the most low-wage jobs shows that the supply of such jobs will continue to increase for the predictable future. The entry of migrant workers will similarly continue to meet the demand. In turn, this inflow provides the raw material out of which transnational communities emerge.

References

- Loader, Brian D (2004). The Governance of Cyberspace: Politics, Technology and Global Restructuring. Routledge. ISBN 978-0415147248

- Shaffer, Gregory (August 2012). "International Law and Global Public Goods in a Legal Pluralist World". European Journal of International Law. 23 (3): 669–693. doi:10.1093/ejil/chs036

- Salvatore Babones (15 April 2008). "Studying Globalization: Methodological Issues". In George Ritzer. The Blackwell Companion to Globalization. John Wiley & Sons. p. 146. ISBN 978-0-470-76642-2

- Keneth L. Denman; Guy Brasseur; et al. (2007). "Couplings between changes in Climate System and the Biogeochemistry, 7.5.3" (PDF). IPCC. Retrieved 2008-04-09

- Stern, Paul C. "Design principles for global commons: natural resources and emerging technologies". International Journal of the Commons

- George Modelski; Tessaleno Devezas; William R. Thompson (20 December 2007). Globalization as Evolutionary Process: Modeling Global Change. Routledge. p. 59. ISBN 978-1-135-97764-1

- "7.c Doha Amendment to the Kyoto Protocol". United Nations. Archived from the original on 14 November 2013. Retrieved 21 January 2013

- Wassmann, P.; et al. (2011). "Footprints of climate change in the Arctic marine ecosystem.". Global Change Biology. 17 (2): 1235–1249. doi:10.1111/j.1365-2486.2010.02311.x

- Arif Dirlik (1996) Asian on the Rim: Transnational Capital and Local Community in the Making of Contemporary Asian America. Amerasia Journal: 1996, Vol. 22, No. 3, pp. 1-24

- Ostrom, Elinor (1990). Governing the Commons: The Evolution of Institutions for Collective Action. Cambridge, UK: Cambridge University Press. ISBN 0 521 40599 8

- "Chronological lists of ratifications of, accessions and successions to the Convention and the related Agreements". United Nations Division for Ocean Affairs and the Law of the Sea. April 22, 2009. Archived from the original on 14 April 2009. Retrieved April 30, 2009

- Jonathan Okamura (2003) Asian American Studies in the Age of Transnationalism: Diaspora, Race, Community. Amerasia Journal: 2003, Vol. 29, No. 2, pp. 171-194

- Neeson, Jeanette M. (1996). Commoners: Common Right, Enclosure and Social Change in England, 1700—1820. Cambridge, UK: Cambridge University Press. ISBN 978-0521567749

- "Information about the Antarctic Treaty and how Antarctica is governed.". Polar Conservation Organisation. December 28, 2005. Retrieved February 6, 2011

- Alice Yang Murray (2000) Oral History Research, Theory, and Asian American Studies. Amerasia Journal: 2000, Vol. 26, No. 1, pp. 105-118

- Baslar, Kemal (1998). The Concept of the Common Heritage of Mankind in International Law. Martinus Nijhoff Pubs. ISBN 978-90-411-0505-9

- "National Space Policy of the United States of America" (PDF). White House; USA Federal government. Retrieved 20 July 2011

- Brousseau, Eric; et al. (2012). Global Environmental Commons: Analytical and Political Challenges in Building Governance Mechanisms. Cambridge, UK: Oxford University Press. ISBN 978-0199656202

- Steig, Eric J.; Anais J. Orsi (2013). "Climate science: The heat is on in Antarctica". Nature Geoscience. 6 (2): 87–88. Bibcode:2013NatGe...6...87S. doi:10.1038/ngeo1717

Globalization: Issues and Challenges

This chapter studies the challenges and issues that globalization faces. Critics cite political, environmental, social, cultural and psychological factors to curb globalization. The topics discussed in the chapter are of great importance to broaden the existing knowledge on issues and challenges of globalization.

Criticisms of Globalization

Criticism of globalization is skepticism of the claimed benefits of globalization. Many of these views are held by the anti-globalization movement. Globalization has created much global and internal unrest in many countries. While the dynamics of capitalism is changing and each country is unique in its political makeup, globalization is a set-in-stone "program" that is difficult to implement without political unrest. Globalization can be partly responsible for the current global economic crisis. Case studies of Thailand and the Arab nations' view of globalization show that globalization is a threat to culture and religion, and it harms indigenous people groups while multinational corporations profit from it. Although globalization has promised an improved standard of living and economic development, it has been heavily criticized for its production of negative effects. Globalization is not simply an economic project, but it also heavily influences the country environmentally, politically, and socially as well.

Economic Impacts

Limitations on Growth

The founder of Local Futures (formerly the International Society for Ecology and Culture), Helena Norberg-Hodge, has suggested that globalization does not work for all the economies that it affects, and that it does not always deliver the economic growth that is expected of it.

Globalization has been described as an "uneven process" in Africa due to the global integration of some groups happening alongside the marginalization or exclusion of others. Therefore, the worldwide trade will have the restrictions on the growth of economy.

Global Economic Crisis

The Global Economic Crisis, the worst financial crisis since the Great Depression, can be partially attributed to neoliberal globalization. Although globalization promised an improved standard of living, it has actually worsened the financial situation of many homes and has made the financial crisis global through the influences of international financial institutions such as the World Bank. Globalization limits development and civilization to a path that only leads to a Western and capitalistic system. Because of the political and structural differences in countries, the implementation of globalization has been detrimental for many countries.

Political Impacts

Globalization as American Hegemony

John Gray described globalization as a post-Cold War American triumphalism, and stated "global laissez faire is an American project." Globalization is a project in which American ideals and values are executed and implemented into other countries. However, this effort has been criticized, mainly by the examination of America today. In America, there are high levels of economic and social inequalities as the gap between the rich and poor are great. Furthermore, America has the highest rates of incarceration, and anxiety due to economic uncertainty is great. The criticism that follows is that the implementation of the American system into other countries may reproduce these negative effects.

Power of Transnational Corporations

Globalization has fueled the rise of transnational corporations, and their power has vaulted to the point where they can now rival many nation states. Of the world's one hundred largest economies, forty-two of them are corporations. Many of these transnational corporations now hold sway over many nation states, as their fates are intertwined with the nations that they are located in.

Also, transnational corporations could offer massive influence regarding the Third World, and bring about more pressure to help increase worker salaries and working conditions in sweatshops. On account of doing the business globally, transnational corporations have the huge influence in many nation states.

In the process of implementing globalization in developing countries, the creation of winners and losers are often predetermined. Multinational corporations often benefit from globalization while poor, indigenous locals are negatively affected. Globalization can be seen as a new form of colonization, as economic inequality and the rise in unemployment have followed with its implementation. Globalization has been criticized for benefitting those who are already large and in power at the risk and growing vulnerability of the countries' indigenous population. Furthermore, globalization is non-democratic, as it is enforced through top-down methods.

Sovereignty

Globalization requires a country to give up its sovereignty for the sake of executing Western ideals in its country. As a result, sovereignty only belongs to a select few: those whose views and ideals are being implemented. In the name of free markets and with the promise of an improved standard of living, countries give up their political and social powers to international organizations. Thus, globalization causes the greater empowerment of these international organizations and the diminishing influence of local state institutions.

Environmental Impacts

Damage from Transnational Corporations

International trade in petroleum products has expanded significantly over the past decades through globalization so that the environmental problems in Nigeria have been deteriorated. As the international trade in petroleum products keeps increasing, there is also corresponding increase in activities in the petroleum industry to meet the requirement of the ever increasing demand for petroleum products. As a result, it gives rise to the environmental pollution. The petroleum is toxic to almost all forms of life and its extraction fuels climate change including air pollution, water pollution, noise pollution, land degradation and erosion.

Infectious Diseases

Infection is the invasion of an organism's body tissues by disease-causing agents, their multiplication, and the reaction of host tissues to these organisms and the toxins they produce. Infectious diseases, also known as transmissible diseases or communicable diseases, kill more people worldwide than any other single cause. Infectious diseases are caused by germs, such as bacteria, viruses, parasites or fungi. Germs are tiny living things that are found everywhere in air, soil and water. You can get infected by touching, eating, drinking or breathing something that contains germs. Infectious diseases, such as SARS and Ebola, have traveled across the world due to increased world trade and tourism.

Invasive Organisms

As International commerce develops new trade routes, markets and products Globalization facilitates the spread of invasive species. The modern technology offer the opportunity that human and commodities can move around the world. On account of the development of new source, larger and faster ships and increased air transport, the commercial trade propels rising annual and cumulative rates of invasion.

Case study of Thailand's Pak Mun River

In the late 1970s and 1980s, hydropower dam projects were conducted in order to recreate Thailand's economy into an export-oriented economy. The projects were funded by loans from the World Bank and was part of globalization efforts. The local villagers whom the project would directly affect were not notified, and the World Bank disregarded their concerns. As a result of the building of the dams, villages that heavily depended on the river lost their livelihood and their means of economic gains (i.e., fishing). The projects contaminated the river, which made the river unfit for villagers to drink, bathe, and do laundry without experiencing negative health conditions such as rashes. Furthermore, the projects resulted in the extinction of 40 edible plant species, 45 mushroom species, and 10 bamboo species, all of which the income of the local markets were dependent on, some of which were important for medical usage. Furthermore, the decline in fish population exterminated fishermen's ways of life, as 169 different fish species were affected and 56 species became extinct. The globalization efforts in Thailand resulted in environmental impacts that affected the social and economic welfare of indigenous populations.

Social Impacts

Growing Inequality

The Governor of the Bank of England, Mark Carney, put forward globalization as a factor of an increase in the inequality of outcomes in societies.

Globalization has been one of the main causes of the increase in inequality in many countries in the Organization of Economic Cooperation and Development. These countries, including the United States, Canada, and Argentina, have faced an increase in inequality by between one-half to one-third between the 1970s and the late 1990s.

Loss of Languages

Acceleration in language death has been attributed to globalization, and is predicted to continue.

Prejudice

Professor Conor Gearty, of the London School of Economics, has suggested that global freedom of movement, brought on by globalization, has increased the scope for prejudice within societies.

Psychological Impacts

Identity

The collision between global and local cultures have created challenges in adapting to and reconciling the two. Globalization and the introduction of the Western culture in different countries have shown to produce bicultural identities, identity confusion, and self-selected cultures.

Bicultural identity is defined as one adapting to the global culture while simultaneously being familiar with local traditions. As a result, two identities are formed: global identity and local identity. One's global identity allows for him/her to participate and succeed globally by being able to relate to those outside of his/her local sphere. One's local identity allows him/her to still be relevant to family and friends nearby. Often, those experiencing globalization in their country are seen to develop a *hybrid identity*, an identity in which merges their global and local identities. This can also be seen with immigrants.

However, adapting to both cultures may be difficult, especially if the distance between the two cultures is great. In these cases, globalization may cause identity confusion, preventing the proper development of identity and self (Erikson's theory of identity formation). Similarly, globalization may create a crisis in which John Berry calls "marginalization," in which one is unable to identify with local culture due to the heavy exposure of globalization and Western influences; however he/she is also excluded from the global culture as well.

The implementation of globalization requires a certain degree of culture shedding, as global culture alters and disrupts the preexisting local culture. This also leads to identity confusion, primarily in adolescents.

Cultural impacts

Urban and Adolescent Issues

Many times, in countries where globalization is introduced, problems that arise among adolescents are often blamed to the intrusion of Western culture and ideals through globalization. Adolescents are most vulnerable and receptive to the introduction of new cultures. Developing countries where Western values and technology have been introduced are more aware of current events taking place in other countries, and adolescents and youths can be seen copying American fashion and music styles. Therefore, Western media is blamed for the rise in premarital sex and teenage pregnancies that follow when globalization is introduced.

Globalization claims to have improved countries' global status. However, companies attempting to compete globally have exploited workers, and global competition has been achieved through poor working conditions. Furthermore, due to global influences, juvenile crimes have increased because of the disruption of traditional norms.

Arab and Muslim Countries

The Arab and Islamic countries see globalization as an attempt to instill Western superiority and a threat to the preservation of their cultural identity. Although differing views of globalization exist among Arab nations, a large percentage of Muslims see it to be imperialistic and a cultural invasion that attempts to destroy their heritage and cultural beliefs.

Despite the differing opinions of globalization, almost all acknowledge and believe that globalization is simply Americanism— the implementation of American cultures and ideals into other countries.

Globalization is especially threatening to Arab nations because Islam is not simply a religious practice, but it dominates laws and social norms such as marriages and spending habits. Since globalization is seen to be a way of secularizing a nation, Muslims also see it as a cultural and religious invasion, requiring the separation of religion and daily life. Radicalists see it as a perversion of pure Islamic doctrine, as globalization is seen to merge the domain of Islam (Dar al-Islam) and the domain of infidelity (Dar-al-Kufr).

The Western influence on media is also unwelcome. The Western control of media is viewed as a way to brainwash young Muslims to strip them of their nationality and cultural heritage. They also oppose the creation of a new, global, hegemonic culture, referencing the Quran (49:13) which states that God has purposefully divided mankind into different nations and tribes. Arab intellects have stated that globalization rids the earth of human cultural diversity and civilizations' peculiarities, which many see as barbaric. Authors and publishers have expressed fear of Western ideals penetrating their nations.

Anti-globalization Movement

The anti-globalization movement, or counter-globalisation movement, is a social movement critical of economic globalization. The movement is also commonly referred to as the global justice movement, alter-globalization movement, anti-globalist movement, anti-corporate globalization movement, or movement against neoliberal globalization.

Participants base their criticisms on a number of related ideas. What is shared is that participants oppose large, multinational corporations having unregulated political power, exercised through trade agreements and deregulated financial markets. Specifically, corporations are accused of seeking to maximize profit at the expense of work safety conditions and standards, labor hiring and compensation standards, environmental conservation principles, and the integrity of national legislative authority, independence and sovereignty. As of January 2012, some commentators have characterized changes in the global economy as "turbo-capitalism" (Edward Luttwak), "market fundamentalism" (George Soros), "casino capitalism" (Susan Strange), and as "McWorld" (Benjamin Barber).

Thousands of people gathered for a demonstration in Warsaw, the capital of Poland,
as the country prepared to enter the European Union in 2004.

Many anti-globalization activists do not oppose globalization in general and call for forms of global integration that better provide democratic representation, advancement of human rights, fair trade and sustainable development and therefore feel the term "anti-globalization" is misleading.

Ideology and Causes

Supporters believe that by the late 20th century those they characterized as "ruling elites" sought to harness the expansion of world markets for their own interests; this combination of the Bretton Woods institutions, states, and multinational corporations has been called "globalization" or "globalization from above." In reaction, various social movements emerged to challenge their influence; these movements have been called "anti-globalization" or "globalization from below."

Opposition to International Financial Institutions and Transnational Corporations

People opposing globalization believe that international agreements and global financial institutions, such as the International Monetary Fund (IMF) and the World Trade Organization, undermine local decision-making. Corporations that use these institutions to support their own corporate and financial interests, can exercise privileges that individuals and small businesses cannot, including the ability to:

1. move freely across borders.

2. extract desired natural resources.

3. use a wide variety of human resources.

The movement aims for an end to the legal status of "corporate personhood" and the dissolution of free market fundamentalism and the radical economic privatization measures of the World Bank, the IMF, and the World Trade Organization.

Protest against the G8-meeting in Heiligendamm, 2007.

Activists are especially opposed to the various abuses which they think are perpetuated by globalization and the international institutions that, they say, promote neoliberalism without regard to ethical standards or environmental protection. Common targets include the World Bank (WB), International Monetary Fund (IMF), the Organisation for Economic Co-operation and Development (OECD) and the World Trade Organization (WTO) and free trade treaties like the North American Free Trade Agreement (NAFTA), Free Trade Area of the Americas (FTAA), the Trans Pacific Trade Agreement (TPPA), the Multilateral Agreement on Investment (MAI) and the General Agreement on Trade in Services (GATS). In light of the economic gap between rich and poor countries, adherents of the movement claim that free trade without measures to protect the environment and the health and wellbeing of workers will merely increase the power of industrialized nations (often termed the "North" in opposition to the developing world's "South"). Proponents of this line of thought refer to the process as polarization and argue that current neo-liberal economic policies have given wealthier states an advantage over developing nations, enabling their exploitation and leading to a widening of the global wealth gap.

A report by Jean Ziegler, UN Special Rapporteur on the right to food, notes that "millions of farmers are losing their livelihoods in the developing countries, but small farmers in the northern countries are also suffering" and concludes that "the current inequities of the global trading system are being perpetuated rather than resolved under the WTO, given the unequal balance of power between member countries." Activists point to the unequal footing and power between developed and developing nations within the WTO and with respect to global trade, most specifically in relation to the protectionist policies towards agriculture enacted in many developed countries. These activists also point out that heavy subsidization of developed nations' agriculture and the aggressive use of export subsidies by some developed nations to make their agricultural products more attractive on the international market are major causes of declines in the agricultural sectors of many developing nations.

World Bank/IMF protesters smashed the windows of this PNC Bank branch located in the Logan Circle neighborhood of Washington, D.C.

Global Opposition to Neoliberalism

Through the Internet, a movement began to develop in opposition to the doctrines of neoliberalism which were widely manifested in the 1990s when the Organisation for Economic Co-operation and Development (OECD) proposed liberalization of cross-border investment and trade restrictions through its Multilateral Agreement on Investment (MAI). This treaty was prematurely exposed to public scrutiny and subsequently abandoned in November 1998 in the face of strenuous protest and criticism by national and international civil society representatives.

Neoliberal doctrine argued that untrammeled free trade and reduction of public-sector regulation would bring benefits to poor countries and to disadvantaged people in rich countries. Anti-globalization advocates urge that preservation of the natural environment, human rights (especially workplace rights and conditions) and democratic institutions are likely to be placed at undue risk by globalization unless mandatory standards are attached to liberalization. Noam Chomsky stated in 2002 that:

> The term "globalization" has been appropriated by the powerful to refer to a specific form of international economic integration, one based on investor rights, with the interests of people incidental. That is why the business press, in its more honest moments, refers to the "free trade agreements" as "free investment agreements" (Wall St. Journal). Accordingly, advocates of other forms of globalization are described as "anti-globalization"; and some, unfortunately, even accept this term, though it is a term of propaganda that should be dismissed with ridicule. No sane person is opposed to globalization, that is, international integration. Surely not the left and the workers movements, which were founded on the principle of international solidarity—that is, globalization in a form that attends to the rights of people, not private power systems.

Anti-War Movement

By 2002, many parts of the movement showed wide opposition to the impending invasion of Iraq. Many participants were among those 11 million or more protesters that on the weekend of February 15, 2003, participated in global protests against the imminent Iraq war. Other anti-war demonstrations were organized by the antiglobalization movement: see for example the large demonstration, organized against the impending war in Iraq, which closed the first European Social Forum in November 2002 in Florence, Italy.

Anti-globalization militants worried for a proper functioning of democratic institutions as the leaders of many democratic countries (Spain, Italy, Poland and the United Kingdom) were acting against the wishes of the majorities of their populations in supporting the war. Chomsky asserted that these leaders "showed their contempt for democracy". Critics of this type of argument have tended to point out that this is just a standard criticism of representative democracy — a democratically elected government will not always act in the direction of greatest current public support — and that, therefore, there is no inconsistency in the leaders' positions given that these countries are parliamentary democracies.

The economic and military issues are closely linked in the eyes of many within the movement.

Appropriateness of the Term

Many participants consider the term "anti-globalization" to be a misnomer. The term suggests that its followers support protectionism and/or nationalism, which is not always the case - in fact, some supporters of anti-globalization are strong opponents of both nationalism and protectionism: for example, the No Border network argues for unrestricted migration and the abolition of all national border controls. S. A. Hamed Hosseini (an Australian sociologist and expert in global social movement studies), argues that the term anti-globalization can be ideal-typically used only to refer to only one ideological vision he detects alongside three other visions (the anti-globalist, the alter-globalist and the alter-globalization). He argues that the three latter ideal-typical visions can be categorized under the title of global justice movement. According to him, while the first two visions (the alter-globalism and the anti-globalism) represent the reconstructed forms of old and new left ideologies, respectively, in the context of current globalization, only the third one has shown the capacity to respond more effectively to the intellectual requirements of today's global complexities. Underlying this vision is a new conception of justice, coined accommodative justice by Hosseini, a new approach towards cosmopolitanism (transversal cosmopolitanism), a new mode of activist knowledge (accommodative consciousness), and a new format of solidarity, interactive solidarity.

Some activists, notably David Graeber, see the movement as opposed instead to neoliberalism or "corporate globalization". He argues that the term "anti-globalization" is a term coined by the media, and that radical activists are actually more in favor of globalization, in the sense of "effacement of borders and the free movement of people, possessions and ideas" than are the IMF or WTO. He also notes that activists use the terms "globalization movement" and "anti-globalization movement" interchangeably, indicating the confusion of the terminology. The term "alter-globalization" has been used to make this distinction clear.

While the term "anti-globalization" arose from the movement's opposition to free-trade agreements (which have often been considered part of something called "globalization"), various participants contend they are opposed to only certain aspects of globalization and instead describe themselves, at least in French-speaking organizations, as "anti-capitalist", "anti-plutocracy," or "anti-corporate." *Le Monde Diplomatique* 's editor, Ignacio Ramonet's, expression of "the one-way thought" (*pensée unique*) became slang against neoliberal policies and the Washington consensus.

Nationalist Opposition Against Globalization

Donald Trump was elected President of the United States on November 8, 2016.

The term "anti-globalization" does not distinguish the international leftist anti-globalization position from a strictly nationalist anti-globalization position. Many nationalist movements, such as the French National Front, Austrian Freedom Party, the Italian Lega Nord, the Greek Golden Dawn or the National Democratic Party of Germany are opposed to globalization, but argue that the alternative to globalization is the protection of the nation-state. Other groups, influenced by the Third Position, are also classifiable as anti-globalization. However, their overall world view is rejected by groups such as Peoples Global Action and anti-fascist groups such as ANTIFA. In response, the nationalist movements against globalization, argue that the leftist anti-globalization position is actually a support to alter-globalization.

Influences

Several influential critical works have inspired the anti-globalization movement. *No Logo*, the book by the Canadian journalist Naomi Klein who criticized the production practices of multinational corporations and the omnipresence of brand-driven marketing in popular culture, has become "manifesto" of the movement, presenting in a simple way themes more accurately developed in other works. In India some intellectual references of the movement can be found in the works of Vandana Shiva, an ecologist and feminist, who in her book *Biopiracy* documents the way that the natural capital of indigenous peoples and ecoregions is converted into forms of intellectual capital, which are then recognized as exclusive commercial property without sharing the private utility thus derived. The writer Arundhati Roy is famous for her anti-nuclear position and her activism against India's massive hydroelectric dam project, sponsored by the World Bank. In France the well-known monthly paper *Le Monde Diplomatique* has advocated the antiglobalization cause and an editorial of its director Ignacio Ramonet brought about the foundation of the association ATTAC. Susan George of the Transnational Institute has also been a long-term influence on the movement, as the writer of books since 1986 on hunger, debt, international financial institutions and capitalism. The works of Jean Ziegler, Christopher Chase-Dunn, and Immanuel Wallerstein have detailed underdevelopment and dependence in a world ruled by the capitalist system. Pacifist and anti-imperialist traditions have strongly influenced the movement. Critics of United States foreign policy such as Noam Chomsky, Susan Sontag, and anti-globalist pranksters The Yes Men are widely accepted inside the movement.

Arundhati Roy

Anti-WEF graffiti in Lausanne. The writing reads:
La croissance est une folie ("Growth is madness").

Although they may not recognize themselves as antiglobalists and are pro-capitalism, some economists who don't share the neoliberal approach of international economic institutions have strongly influenced the movement. Amartya Sen's *Development as Freedom* (Nobel Prize in Economics, 1999), argues that third world development must be understood as the expansion of human capability, not simply the increase in national income per capita, and thus requires policies attuned to health and education, not simply GDP. James Tobin's (winner of the Nobel Prize in Economics) proposal for a tax on financial transactions (called, after him, the Tobin tax) has become part of the agenda of the movement. Also, George Soros, Joseph E. Stiglitz (another Economic Sciences Nobel prize winner, formerly of the World Bank, author of Globalization and Its Discontents) and David Korten have made arguments for drastically improving transparency, for debt relief, land reform, and restructuring corporate accountability systems. Korten and Stiglitz's contribution to the movement include involvement in direct actions and street protest.

In some Roman Catholic countries such as Italy there have been religious influences, especially from missionaries who have spent a long time in the Third World (the most famous being Alex Zanotelli).

Internet sources and free-information websites, such as Indymedia, are a means of diffusion of the movement's ideas. The vast array of material on spiritual movements, anarchism, libertarian socialism and the Green Movement that is now available on the Internet has been perhaps more influential than any printed book.

Organization

Anti-globalization protests in Edinburgh during the start of the 31st G8 summit.

Although over the past years more emphasis has been given to the construction of grassroots alternatives to (capitalist) globalization, the movement's largest and most visible mode of organizing remains mass decentralized campaigns of direct action and civil disobedience. This mode of organizing, sometimes under the banner of the Peoples' Global Action network, tries to tie the many disparate causes together into one global struggle. In many ways the process of organizing matters overall can be more important to activists than the avowed goals or achievements of any component of the movement.

At corporate summits, the stated goal of most demonstrations is to stop the proceedings. Although the demonstrations rarely succeed in more than delaying or inconveniencing the actual summits, this motivates the mobilizations and gives them a visible, short-term purpose. This form of publicity is expensive in police time and the public purse. Rioting has occurred at some protests, for instance in Genoa, Seattle and London - and extensive damage was done to the area, especially targeting corporations, including McDonald's and Starbucks restaurants.

Despite, or perhaps because of, the lack of formal coordinating bodies, the movement manages to successfully organize large protests on a global basis, using information technology to spread information and organize. Protesters organize themselves into "affinity groups," typically non-hierarchical groups of people who live close together and share a common political goal. Affinity groups will then send representatives to planning meetings. However, because these groups can be infiltrated by law enforcement intelligence, important plans of the protests are often not made until the last minute. One common tactic of the protests is to split up based on willingness to break the law. This is designed, with varying success, to protect the risk-averse from the physical and legal dangers posed by confrontations with law enforcement. For example, in Prague during the anti-IMF and World Bank protests in September 2000 demonstrators split into three distinct groups, approaching the conference center from three directions: one engaging in various forms of civil disobedience (the Yellow march), one (the Pink/Silver march) advancing through "tactical frivolity" (costume, dance, theatre, music, and artwork), and one (the Blue march) engaging in violent conflicts with the baton-armed police, with the protesters throwing cobblestones lifted from the street. These demonstrations come to resemble small societies in themselves. Many protesters take training in first aid and act as medics to other injured protesters. In the USA, some organizations like the National Lawyer's Guild and, to a lesser extent, the American Civil Liberties Union, provide legal witnesses in case of law enforcement confrontation. Protesters often claim that major media outlets do not properly report on them; therefore, some of them created the Independent Media Center, a collective of protesters reporting on the actions as they happen.

Key Grassroots Organizations

- Abahlali base M Jondolo in South Africa

- The EZLN in Mexico

- Fanmi Lavalas in Haiti

- The Homeless Workers' Movement in Brazil

- The Landless Peoples Movement in South Africa

- The Landless Workers' Movement in Brazil

- Movement for Justice en el Barrio in the United States of America

- Narmada Bachao Andolan in India

- The Western Cape Anti-Eviction Campaign in South Africa

Demonstrations and Appointments

Berlin88

The Annual Meetings osf the International Monetary Fund (IMF) and the World Bank, that took place in West Berlin in 1988, saw strong protests that can be categorized as a precursor of the anti-globalization movement. One of the main and failed objectives (as it was to be so many times in the future) was to derail the meetings.

Paris89

A counter summit against G7 was organized in Paris in July 1989. The event was called "ça suffit comme ça" ("we had enough")and principally aimed at cancelling the debt contracted by southern countries. A demonstration gathered 10,000 people and an important concert was held in la Bastille square with 200 000 people. It was the first anti-G7 event, fourteen years before that of Washington. The main political consequence was that France took position to favor debt cancellation.

Madrid94

The 50th anniversary of the IMF and the World Bank, which was celebrated in Madrid in October 1994, was the scene of a protest by an ad-hoc coalition of what would later be called anti-globalization movements. Starting from the mid-1990s, Annual Meetings of the IMF and the World Bank Group have become center points for anti-globalization movement protests. They tried to drown the bankers' parties in noise from outside and held other public forms of protest under the motto "50 Years is Enough". While Spanish King Juan Carlos was addressing the participants in a huge exhibition hall, two Greenpeace activists climbed to the top and showered the attendants with fake dollar bills carrying the slogan "No $s for Ozone Layer Destruction". A number of the demonstrators were sent to the notorious Carabanchel prison.

J18

One of the first international anti-globalization protests was organized in dozens of cities around the world on June 18, 1999, with those in London and Eugene, Oregon most often noted. The drive was called the Carnival Against Capital, or J18 for short. The day coincided with the 25th G8 Summit in Cologne, Germany. The protest in Eugene turned into a riot where local anarchists drove police out of a small park. One anarchist, Robert Thaxton, was arrested and convicted of throwing a rock at a police officer.

Seattle/N30

The second major mobilization of the movement, known as N30, occurred on November 30, 1999, when protesters blocked delegates' entrance to WTO meetings in Seattle, Washington, USA. The protests forced the cancellation of the opening ceremonies and lasted the length of the meeting until December 3. There was a large, permitted march by members of the AFL-CIO, and other unauthorized marches by assorted affinity groups who converged around the Convention Center. The protesters and Seattle riot police clashed in the streets after police fired tear gas at demonstrators who blocked the streets and refused to disperse. Over 600 protesters were arrested and thousands were injured. Three policemen were injured by friendly fire, and one by a thrown rock. Some protesters destroyed the windows of storefronts of businesses owned or franchised by targeted corporations such as a large Nike shop and many Starbucks windows. The mayor put the city under the municipal equivalent of martial law and declared a curfew. As of 2002, the city of Seattle had paid over $200,000 in settlements of lawsuits filed against the Seattle Police Department for assault and wrongful arrest, with a class action lawsuit still pending.

Washington A16

On April 2000, around 10,000 to 15,000 protesters demonstrated at the IMF, and World Bank meeting (official numbers are not tallied). International Forum on Globalization (IFG) held training at Foundry United Methodist Church. Police raided the Convergence Center, which was the staging warehouse and activists' meeting hall on Florida Avenue on April 15. The day before the larger protest scheduled on April 16, a smaller group of protesters demonstration against the Prison-Industrial Complex in the District of Columbia. Mass arrests were conducted; 678 people were arrested on April 15. Three-time Pulitzer Prize winning, *Washington Post* photographer Carol Guzy was detained by police and arrested on April 15, and two journalists for the Associated Press also reported being struck by police with batons. On April 16 and 17 the demonstrations and street actions around the IMF that followed, the number of those arrested grew to 1,300 people. A class action lawsuit was filed for false arrest. In June 2010, the class action suit for the April 15th events called '*Becker, et al. v. District of Columbia, et al.*' were settled, with $13.7 million damages awarded.

Washington D.C. 2002

In September 2002, estimated number of 1,500 to 2,000 people gathered to demonstrate against the Annual Meetings of IMF and World Bank in the streets of Washington D.C. Protesting groups included the Anti-Capitalist Convergence, the Mobilization for Global Justice. 649 people were reported arrested, five were charged with destruction of property, while the others were charged with parading without a permit, or failing to obey police orders to disperse. At least 17 reporters were in the round-up. Protestors sued in Federal Court about the arrests. The D.C. Attorney General had outside counsel investigate apparent destruction of evidence, and forensic investigations continue, and the testimony of the Chief of Police. In 2009, the city agreed to pay $8.25 million to almost 400 protesters and bystanders to end a class-action lawsuit over kettling and mass arrests in Pershing Park during 2002 World Bank protests

Law Enforcement Reaction

Although local police were surprised by the size of N30, law enforcement agencies have since reacted worldwide to prevent the disruption of future events by a variety of tactics, including sheer weight of numbers, infiltrating the groups to determine their plans, and preparations for the use of force to remove protesters.

At the site of some of the protests, police have used tear gas, pepper spray, concussion grenades, rubber and wooden bullets, night sticks, water cannons, dogs, and horses to repel the protesters. After the November 2000 G20 protest in Montreal, at which many protesters were beaten, trampled, and arrested in what was intended to be a festive protest, the tactic of dividing protests into "green" (permitted), "yellow" (not officially permitted but with little confrontation and low risk of arrest), and "red" (involving direct confrontation) zones was introduced.

In Quebec City, municipal officials built a 3 metre (10 ft) high wall around the portion of the city where the Summit of the Americas was being held, which only residents, delegates to the summit, and certain accredited journalists were allowed to pass through.

Gothenburg

Attack of police during the riots in Gothenburg, 15 June 2001

On June 15 and 16, 2001, a strong demonstration took place in Göteborg during the meeting of the European Council in the Swedish town. Clashes between police and protesters were exacerbated by the numerous vandalism of the extreme fringes of the demonstrators, the so-called black-blocs. Images of devastation bounced through the mass media, putting a negative shadow on the movement, and increasing a sense of fear through commons people.

Genoa

The Genoa Group of Eight Summit protest from July 18 to July 22, 2001 was one of the bloodiest protests in Western Europe's recent history, as evidenced by the wounding of hundreds of policemen and civilians forced to lock themselves inside of their homes and the death of a young Genoese anarchist named Carlo Giuliani—who was shot while trying to throw a fire extinguisher on a policeman—during two days of violence and rioting by groups supported by the nonchalance of more consistent and peaceful masses of protesters, and the hospitalization of several of those peaceful demonstrators just mentioned. Police have subsequently been accused of brutality, torture and interference with the non-violent protests as a collateral damage provoked by the clash between the law enforcement ranks themselves and the more violent and brutal fringes of protesters, who repeatedly hid themselves amongst peaceful protesters of all ages and backgrounds. Several hundred peaceful demonstrators, rioters, and police were injured and hundreds were arrested during the days surrounding the G8 meeting; most of those arrested have been charged with some form of "criminal association" under Italy's anti-mafia and anti-terrorist laws.

International Social Forums

The first World Social Forum (WSF) in 2001 was an initiative of Oded Grajew, Chico Whitaker, and Bernard Cassen. It was supported by the city of Porto Alegre (where it took place) and the Brazilian Worker's Party. The motivation was to constitute a counter-event to the World Economic Forum held in Davos at the same time. The slogan of the WSF is "Another World Is Possible". An *International Council* (IC) was set up to discuss and decide major issues regarding the WSF, while the local organizing committee in the host city is responsible for the practical preparations of the event. In June 2001, the IC adopted the World Social Forum Charter of Principles, which provides a framework for international, national, and local Social Forums worldwide.

The WSF became a periodic meeting: in 2002 and 2003 it was held again in Porto Alegre and became a rallying point for worldwide protest against the American invasion of Iraq. In 2004 it was moved to Mumbai, India), to make it more accessible to the populations of Asia and Africa. This Forum had 75,000 delegates. In 2006 it was held in three cities: Caracas, Venezuela, Bamako, Mali, and Karachi, Pakistan. In 2007, the Forum was hosted in Nairobi, Kenya, in 2009 it was in Belém, Brazil, and in 2011 it was in Dakar, Senegal. In 2012, the WSF returned to Porto Alegre.

The idea of creating a meeting place for organizations and individuals opposed to Neoliberalism was soon replicated elsewhere. The first European Social Forum (ESF) was held in November 2002 in Florence. The slogan was "Against the war, against racism and against neo-liberalism". It saw the participation of 60,000 delegates and ended with a huge demonstration against the war (1,000,000 people according to the organizers). The following ESFs took place in Paris (2003), London (2004), Athens (2006), Malmö (2008), and the latest ESF in Istanbul (2010).

In many countries Social Forums of national and local scope where also held.

Recently there has been some discussion behind the movement about the role of the social forums. Some see them as a "popular university", an occasion to make many people aware of the problems of globalization. Others would prefer that delegates concentrate their efforts on the coordination and organization of the movement and on the planning of new campaigns. However it has often been argued that in the dominated countries (most of the world) the WSF is little more than an 'NGO fair' driven by Northern NGOs and donors most of which are hostile to popular movements of the poor.

Criticisms

The anti-globalization movement has been criticized by politicians, members of conservative think tanks, and many mainstream economists.

Lack of Evidence

Critics assert that the empirical evidence does not support the views of the anti-globalization movement. These critics point to statistical trends which are interpreted to be results of globalization, capitalism, and the economic growth they encourage.

- There has been an absolute decrease in the percentage of people in developing countries living below $1 per day in east Asia (adjusted for inflation and purchasing power). Sub Saharan Africa, as an area that felt the consequences of poor governance and was less responsive to globalization, has seen an increase in poverty while all other areas of the world have seen no change in rates.

- The world income per head has increased by more over period 2002–2007 than during any other period on the record.

- The increase in universal suffrage, from no nations in 1900 to 62.5% of all nations in 2000.

- There are similar trends for electric power, cars, radios, and telephones per capita as well as the percentage of the population with access to clean water. However 1.4 billion people still live without clean drinking water and 2.6 billion of the world's population lack access to proper sanitation. Access to clean water has actually decreased in the world's poorest nations, often those that have not been as involved in globalization.

Members of the anti-globalization movement argue that positive data from countries which largely ignored neoliberal prescriptions, notably China, discredits the evidence that pro-globalists present. For example, concerning the parameter of per capita income growth, development economist Ha-Joon Chang writes that considering the record of the last two decades the argument for continuing neo-liberal policy prescriptions are "simply untenable." Noting that "It depends on the data we use, but roughly speaking, per capita income in developing countries grew at 3% per year between 1960 and 1980, but has grown only at about 1.5% between 1980 and 2000. And even this 1.5% will be reduced to 1%, if we take out India and China, which have not pursued liberal trade and industrial policies recommended by the developed countries." Jagdish Bhagwati argues that reforms that opened up the economies of China and India contributed to their higher growth in 1980s and 1990s. From 1980 to 2000 their GDP grew at average rate of 10 and 6 percent respectively. This was accompanied by reduction of poverty from 28 percent in 1978 to 9 percent in 1998 in China, and from 51 percent in 1978 to 26 percent in 2000 in India. Likewise, Joseph E. Stiglitz, speaking not only on China but East Asia in general, comments "The countries that have managed globalization...such as those in East Asia, have, by and large, ensured that they reaped huge benefits..." According to The Heritage Foundation, development in China was anticipated by Milton Friedman, who predicted that even a small progress towards economic liberalization would produce dramatic and positive effects. China's economy had grown together with its economic freedom. Critics of corporate-led globalization have expressed concern about the methodology used in arriving at the World Bank's statistics and argue that more detailed variables measuring poverty should be studied. According to the Center for Economic and Policy Research (CEPR), the period from 1980–2005 has seen diminished progress in terms of economic growth, life expectancy, infant and child mortality, and to a lesser extent education.

Disorganization

One of the most common criticisms of the movement, which does not necessarily come from its opponents, is simply that the anti-globalization movement lacks coherent goals, and that the views of different protesters are often in opposition to each other. Many members of the movement are also aware of this, and argue that, as long as they have a common opponent, they should march together - even if they don't share exactly the same political vision. Writers Michael Hardt & Antonio Negri have together in their books (*Empire* & *Multitude*) expanded on this idea of a disunified multitude: humans coming together for shared causes, but lacking the complete sameness of the notion of 'the people'.

Lack of Effectiveness

One argument often made by the opponents of the anti-globalization movement (especially by *The Economist*), is that one of the major causes of poverty amongst third-world farmers are the trade barriers put up by rich nations and poor nations alike. The WTO is an organization set up to work towards removing those trade barriers. Therefore, it is argued, people really concerned about the plight of the third world should actually be encouraging free trade, rather than attempting to fight it. Specifically, commodities such as sugar are heavily distorted by subsidies on behalf of powerful economies (the United States, Europe, and Japan), who have a disproportionate influence in the WTO. As a result, producers in these countries often receive 2-3x the world market price. As Amani Elobeid and John Beghin note, the world price might decline by as much as 48% (by 2011 / 2012 baselines) were these distortions to be removed.

Many supporters of globalization think that policies different from those of today should be pursued, although not necessarily those advocated by the anti-globalization movement. For example, some see the World Bank and the IMF as corrupt bureaucracies which have given repeated loans to dictators who never do any reforms. Some, like Hernando De Soto, argue that much of the poverty in the Third World countries is caused by the lack of Western systems of laws and well-defined and universally recognized property rights. De Soto argues that because of the legal barriers poor people in those countries can not utilize their assets to produce more wealth.

Lack of Widespread "Third World" Support

Critics have asserted that people from poor (the Developing countries) have been relatively accepting and supportive of globalization while the strongest opposition to globalization has come from wealthy "First World" activists, unions and NGOs. Alan Shipman, author of "The Globalization Myth" accuses the anti-globalization movement of "defusing the Western class war by shifting alienation and exploitation to developing-country sweatshops." He later goes on to claim that the anti-globalization movement has failed to attract widespread support from poor and working people from the developing nations, and that its "strongest and most uncomprehending critics had always been the workers whose liberation from employment they were trying to secure."

These critics assert that people from the Third World see the anti-globalization movement as a threat to their jobs, wages, consuming options and livelihoods, and that a cessation or reversal of globalization would result in many people in poor countries being left in greater poverty. Jesús F. Reyes Heroles the former Mexican Ambassador to the US, stated that "in a poor country like ours, the alternative to low-paid jobs isn't well-paid ones, it's no jobs at all."

Egypt's Ambassador to the UN has also stated "The question is why all of a sudden, when third world labor has proved to be competitive, why do industrial countries start feeling concerned about our workers? When all of a sudden there is a concern about the welfare of our workers, it is suspicious."

On the other hand, there have been notable protests against certain globalization policies by workers in developing nations as in the cause of Indian farmers protesting against patenting seeds.

In the last few years, many developing countries (esp. in Latin America and Caribbean) created alter-globalization organizations as economic blocs Mercosur and Unasur, political community CELAC or Bank of the South which are supporting development of low income countries without involvement from IMF or World Bank.

Alter-globalization

Alter-globalization slogans during the protests in Le Havre against the
37th G8 summit in Deauville, France

Alter-globalization (also known as alternative globalization, alter-mundialization—from the French "alter-mondialisation"—or the global justice movement) is the name of a social movement whose proponents support global cooperation and interaction, but oppose what they describe as the negative effects of economic globalization, considering that it often works to the detriment of, or does not adequately promote, human values such as environmental and climate protection, economic justice, labor protection, protection of indigenous cultures, peace, and civil liberties.

The name may have been derived from a popular slogan of the movement: 'Another world is possible', which came out of the World Social Forum. "The alter-globalization movement is a cooperative movement designed to protest the direction and perceived negative economic, political, social, cultural and ecological consequences of neoliberal globalization". Many alter-globalists seek to avoid the "disestablishment of local economies and disastrous humanitarian consequences". Most members of this movement shun the label "anti-globalization" as pejorative and incorrect since they actively support human activity on a global scale and do not oppose economic globalization *per se*.

Instead they see their movement as an alternative to what they term neo-liberal globalization in which international institutions (World Trade Organisation, World Bank, International Monetary Fund etc.) and major corporations devote themselves to enriching the developed world while giving little or no attention to the detrimental effects of their actions on the people and environments of less developed countries, countries whose governments are often too weak or too corrupt to resist or regulate them. It is different than proletarian internationalism as put forth by communists in that alter-globalists do not necessarily oppose the free market, but a subset of free-market practices characterized by certain business attitudes and political policies that often lead to violations of human rights.

Etymology

The term was coined against accusations of nationalism by neoliberal proponents of globalization, meaning a support of both humanism and universal values but a rejection of the Washington consensus and similar neoliberal policies. ("Alter" is Latin for "other", as in "alternative" and French "autre".) The "alter-globalization" French movement was thus opposed to the "Treaty establishing a Constitution for Europe" on the grounds that it only advanced neoliberalism and an Anglo-Saxon economic model.

Originally developed in French as *altermondialisme*, it has been borrowed into English in the form of altermondialism or altermondialization. It defines the stance of movements opposed to a neoliberal globalization, but favorable to a globalization respectful of human rights, the environment, national sovereignty, and cultural diversity.

Following the French usage of the word *altermondialist*, the English counterpart *alter-globalist* may have been coined.

The term *alter-globalization* is derived from the term *anti-globalization*, which journalists and others have used to describe the movement. Many French journalists, in particular, have since ceased using the term *anti-globalization* in favor of *alter-globalization*. It is supposed to distinguish proponents of alter-globalization from different "anti-globalization" activists (those who are against *any* kind of globalization: nationalists, protectionists, communitarians, etc.).

History

Economic integration via trade, financial flows, and investments had been occurring for many years, but the World Trade Organization Ministerial Conference of 1999 brought significant attention to the outcry for such integration through vast media outlets, support groups, and activists. Though this opposition first became highly popularized in the 1999 Seattle WTO protests, it can be traced back prior to the 1980s when the Washington Consensus became a dominant development in thinking and policy-making.

Factors Historically Provoking Economic Integration and Resistance

- The Great Depression

- The period of European colonialism

- The early post World War II period

- The 1970s, when Southern governments banded together to pose alternative rules and institutions and when popular resistance to different aspects of economic integration spread in many nations

The Period of European Colonialism

During the late 15th century most regions of the world were self-sufficient; although this led to much starvation and famine. As nations grew in power, sought to expand, and increased their wealth they forged on a mission to gain new lands. The central driving force of these nations was colonialism. Once in power in these new territories, colonists began to change the face of the economy in the area which provided them with motivation to sustain their efforts. Since they no longer had to solely rely on their own lands to produce goods, some nations began global commerce after establishing colonies in continents like Africa, Asia, the Pacific and the Middle East, the Americas and the Caribbean.

Once lands were conquered the native inhabitants or others brought along as slaves grew rebellious towards their captors. This is evident in a number of slave rebellions, such as Harper's Ferry, Stono, and the New York Burning, and Native American attacks on European colonists on the North American continent. Over time these skirmishes gave way to social movements aimed at eliminating international trade in goods and labor, an example of which is the attempt to abolish the slave trade and the establishment of the First International Workingmen's Association (IWA).

The Post World War II Era

The global economic state of post-World War II led to the creation of the International Monetary Fund (IMF), the World Bank (the International Bank for Reconstruction and Development) and the General Agreement on Tariffs and Trade (GATT). The International Monetary Fund's purpose was to supervise the exchange rate system and provide immediate loans for financial supplement of countries whereas the World Bank's goals were aimed at creating long term/low interest loans that aided in the 'reconstruction' of Europe and the 'development' of independent Third World countries. GATT originated from a perceived need to "oversee the reduction of tariff barriers to trade in manufactured goods".

These financial institutions allowed for the development of global private corporations as administration over trade fell. Free market systems began to grow in popularity as developing countries were required to globalize their economies instead of concentrating on creating jobs and stimulating economic growth. As such, poor countries that are struggling under debts are more familiar to the neoliberal opposition to "handouts" or "short cuts," but at the same time winning only minimal relief and receiving cuts to various programs. This allowed for private corporations to expand globally, without regard to central issues facing the home country like the environment, social structure or culture.

The 1970s and Southern Resistance

The 1970s saw resistance to global expansion by both government and non-government parties. Senator Frank Church was concerned with the role multinational corporations were beginning to play and created a subcommittee that reviewed corporate practices to see if they were advancing U.S. interests or not (i.e. exporting jobs that could be kept within the United States). It was through these public revelations that Southern nations around the world wanted rules to govern the global economy. More specifically, these Southern nations (ranging from Tanzania to the Philippines) wanted to raise/stabilize raw material prices, and to increase Southern exports. These nations began their movement not only with central goals but with codes of conduct as well (though non-enforceable). Thus two manifestations, one individual, and the other collective, amongst Southern nation-states, existed in their attempts to generate reform.

Preconditions for Alter-globalization

It is suggested by some scholars, such as Lagin Russia, that the effects and growth of alter-globalization can be felt worldwide due to progress made as a result of the Internet. The Internet can provide easy, free-flowing and mobile information/network organization that is in its very nature democratic; knowledge is for everyone and is perceived to be needed for further development of our modern world. Furthermore, Internet access makes possible the rapid spread of various groups' principles, progress, growth, opposition and development. The Internet has provided a means of communication that stretches beyond the limits of distance, time and space so ideas may not only be generated but implemented as well.

Alter-globalization as a Social Movement

Alter-globalization can be characterized as a social movement based on Charles Tilly's WUNC displays. WUNC is an acronym for Worthiness, Unity, Numbers and Commitment. Alter-globalization is seen as a worthy cause because its goals aim to sustain those being afflicted by the selfish acts of global corporations and their negative effect on human value, the environment, and social justices. It also serves to unite various people around the world for a good cause: to fight for better treatment of Third World countries and their economies, workers rights, fair/equal human rights. Many are committed to the goals set forth by alter-globalization groups because of the perceived negative effects globalization is creating around the world. Examples include: the exploitation of labor, outsourcing of jobs to foreign nations (though some argue this is a nationalistic rather than alter-globalist motive), pollution of local environments, and harm to foreign cultures to which jobs are outsourced.

Alter-globalization can be viewed as being purposeful and creating solidarity, which are two of the three incentives posited by the rational choice theory proposed by Dennis Chong. Rational choice theory focuses on the incentives of activism, stating that activism follows when the benefits to protesting outweigh the costs. Alter-globalization allows one the opportunity to see the difference they are working towards by eliminating the negative side effects already affecting our world (e.g., environmental pollution). It also calls for solidarity amongst peer/community relations that can only be experienced by being a part of the system that causes change.

Another type of social movement that applies to alter-globalization and our understanding of how it relates is found in collective action frames. Collective action frames provide a schemata of interpretation that allows for organization of experience into guided action. Action frames are perceived as powerful because they draw from people's emotions, re-enforce the collective identity of the group, and create a statement from the groups' collective beliefs. Frame analysis is helpful to alter-globalization because it calls for activists to learn through their socialization and interactions with others. One of the key tasks of action frames is generating agency, or a plausible story that indicates the ability of the activists to create change. With alter-globalization every aspect of the movement suggests this ability because the goals affect the economies, environments and human relations of various countries around the world.

Examples of Alter-globalization as A Movement

1. Attempts at an alter-globalization movement to reform policies and processes of the WTO include: "alternative principles of public accountability, the rights of people and the protection of the environment" through the theoretical framework of Robert Cox.

2. Labor movement and trade union initiatives have begun to respond to economic and political globalisation by extending their cooperation and initiatives to the transnational level.

3. Fair trade initiatives, corporate codes of conduct, and social clauses as well as a return to local markets instead of relying too heavily on global markets.

4. "Alter-globalization activists have promoted alternative water governance models through North-South red-green alliances between organized labor, environmental groups, women's groups, and indigenous groups..." (spoken in response to the increase in privatization of the global water supply).

5. "The first current of the alter-globalization movement considers that instead of getting involved in a global movement and international forums, the path to social change lies through giving life to horizontal, participatory, convivial and sustainable values in daily practices, personal life and local spaces. Many urban activists cite the way that, for example, the Zapatistas in Mexico and other Latin American indigenous movements now focus on developing communities' local autonomy via participatory self-government, autonomous education systems

and improving the quality of life. They appreciate too, the convivial aspect of local initiatives and their promise of small but real alternatives to corporate globalization and mass consumption."

Groups

Advocates of alter-globalization have set up an online global news network, the Independent Media Center, to report on developments pertinent to the movement. Groups in favor of alter-globalization include ATTAC, an international trade reform network headquartered in France.

World Social Forum

Opening walk of 2002 World Social Forum, held by participants in the movement

The largest forum for alter-globalization activity is the annual World Social Forum. The World Social Forum is intended as a democratic space organized in terms of the movement's values.

Counter-hegemonic Globalization

Counter-hegemonic globalization is a social movement based in a perspective of globalization that challenges the contemporary view of globalization; neoliberal globalization. Counter-hegemonic globalization confronts the implicit idea of neoliberal globalization that the system of domination, as a consequence of the development of transnational networks, transportation and communication, is a natural and inevitable course for globalization. It maintains that transnational connections can instead be harnessed as the means to bring about more equitable distribution of wealth, power, and sustainable communities. Counter-hegemonic globalization, unlike neoliberal globalization, uses the assets of globalization to stand against any form of domination by hegemony, operating from a bottom-up process that stresses the empowerment of the local.

Peter Evans, a political sociologist renowned for his contributions to the development of this theory, defined counter-hegemonic globalization as "a globally organized effort to replace the neoliberal global regime with one that maximizes democratic political control and makes the equitable development of human capabilities and environment stewardship its priorities."

In defense to the arbitrary exploitation by neo-liberal globalization, the number of advocates of counter-hegemonic globalization seems to have increased. There are already sets of transnational networks and ideological frames imposed by many activists pursuing the perspectives of counter-hegemonic globalization; collectively called the "global justice movement". The number of transnational Non-governmental organizations (NGOs) supporting counter-hegemonic globalization have doubled between 1973 and 1983 and doubled again between 1983 and 1993. Furthermore, with the cultural and ideological diffusion of counter-hegemonic globalization proven significant in the recent Wall Street Protest, the movement is beginning to be regarded as an effective and promising political antidote to the current domination-oriented globalization by many activists and theorists.

While Peter Evans and Boaventura de Sousa Santos remain two prominent theorists who have contributed to the counter-hegemonic globalization theory, classic Marxist socialist ideas are implicated in the theory. For example, Antonio Gramsci asserted that any struggle over globalization must be conducted at the level of the superstructure (culture, institutions, political power structures, roles, rituals, and state), the revolutionary bloc is no longer determined solely by objective and economic factors of class but through subjective factors related to shared perceptions that cut across class lines to include all those individuals and social groups experiencing difficulty in the economic globalization.

History

The project of counter-hegemonic globalization emerged mainly as a result of neoliberal policies and Structural Adjustment Programs in Latin America in the 1980s. The fundamental base for counter-hegemonic globalization movement has been the long history of labor unions struggle for better work environments and equitable distribution of welfare against the dominating authority. Currently, local and transnational trade unions play majors parts in the counter-hegemonic globalization movement.

For example, the South-based World Social Forum (WSF) was organized as a joint venture between ATTAC and the Brazilian Workers Party to counter the World Economic Forum. It first began with the mission of rescuing classic social democratic agendas of social protection in danger of disappearing under neoliberal globalization and is now the representative organization that supports counter-hegemonic globalization.

A Global Social Movement

Originated from the worker's movement, the counter-hegemonic globalization movement has expanded to various different fields of social movements. Three primary pillars constitute counter-hegemonic globalization: the labor, women's, and environmental movements, respectively. The success of each of these three global social movements depends on being able to complement each other and generate broad alliances among them.

Labor Movement

Under the influence of neo-liberal globalization, labor was systematically reconstructed into a spot market rather than a social contract between employer and employee. Employment was outsourced and informalized throughout different countries and labor was bought and sold with minimum expectations regarding employment contract. Such security-threatening phenomenon triggered powerful global labor solidarity; various NGOs and activists unified to fight for labor security against abrupt and powerful hegemonies sweeping across the globe.

Teamsters UPS Strike

The 1997 UPS strike by the International Brotherhood of Teamsters (IBT) is recognized as one of the most triumphant moments in the history of counter-hegemonic globalization movements; for it has perfectly demonstrated the nature of counter-hegemonic globalization. The Teamsters Union went on strike against the UPS because UPS was "seen as representing the intrusion of the "American Model" of aggressive anti-union behavior, coupled with the expansion of part-time and temporary jobs with low pay and benefits and the use of subcontracting".

The first victory was in how IBT took advantage of a previously underexploited global organization — The International Transport Workers Federation (ITF). Through ITF, a World Council of UPS union was created. It started a "World Action Day" which mounted 150 jobs actions and demonstrators around the world. This action taken by ITF helped the workers win the strike, and also showed how international organizations, a product of hegemonic globalization, could be successfully used as a tool to fight against hegemonic globalization. The second victory came when numbers of European union's took action in support of US strikers.

Women's Movement

Due to this new form of globalization, the transnational women's movement has been brought to the forefront of transnational social movement. Until the emergence of such revolutionary transformation of gender roles came into places, the disadvantages of inequitably allocation of resources derived from neo-liberal globalism fell heavily on women. According to Peter Evans, the "structural adjustment" and many of neo-liberal strategies for global governance of feminism is embedded in gender bias. Consequently, transnational women's movements now account for many of the leading roles in counter-hegemonic movements.

While the women's movement has been quite like the labor movement, in working with the issue of human rights, it also has more difficulty with the "contradictions of building politics around the universalistic language of rights." Evans points out that feminists have the advantage of universal recognition of "women's rights are human rights," and have been benefiting from globalization in helping and empowering oppressed women across the world. However, he also suggests that feminist movements are still confronted with the challenge of "one size fits all" global feminist agendas implemented by neo-liberal globalization. For example, the critics of the 1995 Beijing World Conference on Women argue that international organizations were "perpetuating colonialist power relations under the guise of transnational unity."

However, despite many of the challenges, feminists movement started to recognize the significance of more complex and efficient global agenda with the tide of counter-hegemonic movements. The adoption of CEDAW (Convention on the Elimination of All Forms of Discrimination Against Women) by the UN is considered equivalent of the victory in the Kyoto Accord on global warming. In addition, the development of a new organization in places such as India, South Africa, Turkey, and other countries in Southeast Asia, Africa and Latin America, called the Self-Employed Women's Association (SEWA) has become an intricate part of many cultures and governments.Due to the fact that this organization incorporates informal sector employment, consisting of the least privileged women of the global South, SEWA is considered the leading transnational organization to adopt "feminism without borders" agenda.

Environmental Movement

Global environment movements are usually considered the most successful of counter-hegemonic social movements.From environment movement's success, we see many advantageous correlations with the other two movements: labor movements and women's movements. Firstly, Just like the other two movements, political clout for environmental movements depend on the diffusion of universal ideology such as "saving the planet" as of "human rights" and "democracy" for women's movement and labor movement respectively. Secondly, the possibility of using governance structures empowered by hegemonic globalization also applies to the case of environment movement. UN system had been proved extremely valuable and effective in supporting and empowering transnational environmental movement. UN helps to organize international conferences, and to solidify transnational networks. From environment movement, we see counter-hegemonic movements, once again, leveraging the ideas and organizational structures implemented by hegemonic globalization.

However, the obstacles for environment movement still remains. The formidable gap separating the South's "environmentalism of the poor" and the "conservationist" of traditional Northern environmental groups still restrict many possible transnational environmental activities. In addition, building a global organization that can effectively integrate international interest of environment rather than focusing on nations' self-interest still remain as a challenge as well.

Narmada Valley Project

The Narmada Valley Project includes the Sardar Sarovar Dam, one of the most controversial projects in India. The communities of India protested against destroying prime agricultural land, large tracks of forests, rich horticulture, and hilly as well as densely populated habitats through lop-sided development, displacement and disparity growing with the presently imposed growth-centric paradigm of development for dominating corporate.

Global Citizens Movement

In most discussions, the global citizens movement is a socio-political process rather than a political organization or party structure. The term is often used synonymously with the anti-globalization movement or the global justice movement.

"Global citizens movement" has been used by activists to refer to a number of organized and overlapping citizens groups who seek to influence public policy often with the hope of establishing global solidarity on an issue. Such efforts include advocacy on ecological sustainability, corporate responsibility, social justice, and similar progressive issues.

In theoretical discussions of social movements, global citizens movement refers to a complex and unprecedented phenomena made possible by the unique subjective and objective conditions of the planetary phase of civilization. The term is used to distinguish the latent potential for a profound shift in values among an aware and engaged citizenry from existing transnational citizens movements which tend to focus on specific issues (such as the anti-war movement or the labor movement).

Background

The concept of global citizenship first emerged among the Greek Cynics in the 4th Century BCE, who coined the term "cosmopolitan" – meaning *citizen of the world*. The Stoics later elaborated on the concept. The contemporary concept of cosmopolitanism, which proposes that all individuals belong to a single moral community, has gained a new salience as scholars examine the ethical requirements of the planetary phase of civilization.

The idea that today's objective and subjective conditions have increased the latency for an emergent global civic identity has been argued by the authors of the Global Scenario Group's final report *Great Transition: the Promise and Lure of the Times Ahead*. Similar arguments for the existence of a latent pool of tens of millions of people ready to identify around new values of earth consciousness have been put forth by such authors as Paul Raskin, Paul H. Ray, and David Korten. Organizations, such as Oxfam International believe that a global citizens movement rooted in social and economic justice is emerging and is necessary for ending global poverty.

Goals

In the last chapter of his book *Red Sky at Morning*, Gus Speth describes the potential for a new type of social movement composed of "we the people, as citizens" rooted in the principles of the Earth Charter to lead the transition in consciousness and values necessary for the emergence of a new planetary civilization.

Orion Kriegman, author of *Dawn of the Cosmopolitan: The Hope of a Global Citizens Movement*, states, "Transnational corporations, governments, and non-governmental organizations (NGOs) remain powerful global actors, but all of these would be deeply influenced by a coherent, worldwide association of millions of people who call for priority to be placed on new values of quality of life, human solidarity, and environmental sustainability."

Kriegman distinguishes this "coherent, worldwide association of millions" from the existing fragmented social movements active in the World Social Forum. These movements tend to be issue-specific – focused on labor, environment, human rights, feminist issues, indigenous struggles, poverty, AIDS, and numerous other interrelated but "siloed" efforts. Coherence among these movements would require a reframing of their work under the rubric of the struggle for a socially just and ecologically sustainable global society and the establishment of an institutional structure to defend the rights of humanity, future generations, and the biosphere.

Critiques

The major critique of the notion of a global citizens movement centers on the potential for the emergence of solidarity on issues at the global level. Nationalism, racism, and the dominance of the Westphalian state system are considered antithetical to the adoption of a global civic identity. However, some scholars point out that the historical emergence of nationalism must have felt just as improbable in a time of warring city-states, and yet in retrospect it appears inevitable.

A more radical critique stems from the arguments put forth by Michael Hardt and Antonio Negri in their book *Multitude* and enshrines Michel Foucault's notion of a "plurality of resistance" as the only legitimate path forward. This argument asserts that an organized movement among the vast multitude is both undesirable and impossible. Instead of leadership and organizational structures, Hardt and Negri put faith in the emergence of spontaneous coherence due to increasing self-organized networks among various autonomous resistance movements. They critique the notion that there could be legitimate leaders, democratically chosen through a formal network of grassroots structures, acting on behalf of a big-tent pluralistic association of global citizens to directly confront the entrenched power of transnational corporations and state governments. However, it remains unclear how a network of autonomous movements would differ in practice from the vision of an authentic global citizens movement.

References

- Christian-Smith, Juliet; Peter H. Gleick; Heather Cooley; et al. (2012). A twenty-first century US water policy. Oxford: Oxford University Press. ISBN 9780199859443

- Mohai, Paul; Pellow, David; Roberts, J. Timmons (2009). "Environmental Justice". Annual Review of Environment and Resources. 34 (1): 405–430. doi:10.1146/annurev-environ-082508-094348

- Space for Movement: Reflections from Bolivia on climate justice, social movements and the state PDF, edited by Building Bridges collective, July 2010, ISBN 978 0 85316 294 0

- Pleyers, Geoffrey (March 2009). "WSF 2009: A generation's challenge". OpenSpaceForum. Retrieved 2009-04-09. Pleyers, Geoffrey (December 2010). "Alter-Globalization". Polity Press

- Scerri, Andy (2013). "The World Social Forum : Another World Might Be Possible". Social Movement Studies: Journal of Social, Cultural and Political Protest. 12 (1): 111–120. doi:10.1080/147 42837.2012.711522

- Giroux, Henry A. (2006). "Reading Hurricane Katrina: Race, Class, and the Biopolitics of Disposability". College Literature. 33 (3): 171–196. doi:10.1353/lit.2006.0037

- Perkins, John. 2003. Confessions of an Economic Hit Man: The Shocking Story of How America Really Took Over the World. Ebury Press. ISBN 978-0-09-190910-9

- Masozera, Michel (2007). "Distribution of impacts of natural disasters across income groups: A case study of New Orleans". Ecological Economics. 63 (2-3): 299–306. doi:10.1016/j.ecolecon.2006.06.013

- Mayo, Marjorie. Global Citizens: Social Movements and the Challenge of Globalization. New York: Palgrave Macmillan, 2005. ISBN 978-1-84277-138-9

- Bakari, Mohamed El-Kamel. "Globalization and Sustainable Development: False Twins?". New Global Studies. 7 (3): 23–56. ISSN 1940-0004. doi:10.1515/ngs-2013-021

Permissions

Index

Lightning Source UK Ltd.
Milton Keynes UK
UKHW05n0722210518
322900UK00003B/46/P